WITH KITCHENER TO KHARTUM

WITH

KITCHENER TO KHARTUM

BY

G. W. STEEVENS

AUTHOR OF
'EGYPT IN 1898,' 'THE LAND OF THE DOLLAR,' 'WITH THE
CONQUERING TURK,' ETC.

WITH MAPS AND PLANS

FOURTH EDITION

WILLIAM BLACKWOOD AND SONS
EDINBURGH AND LONDON
MDCCCXCVIII

THE original intention was to print the concluding chapters of this book from telegraphic reports. In consequence, however, of delays between Omdurman and wire-head, of the great interest attaching to the events of September 2nd and the ensuing days, and of the desirability of illustrating the account of the battle of Omdurman by plans, it has been thought better to delay the publication of this book a week, and produce the final chapters in a fuller form.

EDINBURGH,
27*th September* 1898.

CONTENTS.

I. HALFA TELLS ITS STORY.

II. THE EGYPTIAN ARMY.

III. THE S.M.R.

IV. THE CORRESPONDENT'S PROGRESS.

V. I MARCH TO BERBER.

VI. THE SIRDAR.

VII. ARMS AND MEN.

VIII. IN THE BRITISH CAMP.

IX. FORT ATBARA.

X. THE MARCH OUT.

XI. THE CONCENTRATION.

XII. AT KENUR.

XIII. ON THE ATBARA.

XIX. THE TRIUMPH.

XX. EGYPT OUT OF SEASON.

XXI. GOING UP.

XXII. THE FIRST STEPS FORWARD.

XXIII. IN SUMMER QUARTERS.

XXIV. DEPARTURES AND ARRIVALS.

XXV. THE PATHOLOGY OF THIRST.

XXVI. BY ROAD, RIVER, AND RAIL.

XXVII. THE LAST OF FORT ATBARA.

XXVIII. THE DESERT MARCH TO OMDURMAN.

XXIX. METEMMEH.

XXX. A CORRESPONDENT'S DIARY.

XXXI. THE RECONNAISSANCES.

XXXII. THE BATTLE OF OMDURMAN.

XXXIII. ANALYSIS AND CRITICISM.

XXXIV. OMDURMAN.

XXXV. THE FUNERAL OF GORDON.

XXXVI. AFTER THE CONQUEST.

LIST OF MAPS.

THE CHIEF EVENTS IN THE ATBARA AND
OMDURMAN CAMPAIGNS.

Sirdar asks for reinforcements of British troops	Dec. 31,	1897
British brigade starts for front from Abu Dis	Feb. 26,	1898
„ „ reaches Dibeika, beyond Berber	March 3,	„
Sirdar leaves Berber	„ 15,	„
Concentration at Kenur	„ 16,	„
Army moves up the Atbara	„ 20,	„
First contact with Dervish cavalry . .	„ 21,	„
Shendi raided and destroyed	„ 27,	„
General Hunter reconnoitres Mahmud's zariba	„ 30,	„
Second reconnaissance : cavalry action before Mahmud's zariba	April 4,	„
Battle of the Atbara	„ 8,	„
Sirdar's triumphal entry into Berber . .	„ 11,	„
Railhead reaches Abeidieh : construction of new gunboats begun	„ 18,	„
Railhead reaches Fort Atbara . . .	June (middle)	„
Lewis's Brigade leaves Atbara for south .	July (early)	„
Second British brigade arrives at Atbara .	Aug. 3-17,	„
Sirdar leaves Atbara for front . . .	„ 13,	„
Last troops leave Atbara	„ 18,	„
Final concentration at Gebel Royan . .	„ 28,	„
March from Gebel Royan to Wady Abid (eight miles)	„ 29,	„
March from Wady Abid to Sayal (ten miles)	„ 30,	„
„ Sayal to Wady Suetne (eight miles)	„ 31,	„
Kerreri reconnoitred and shelled . . .	„ 31,	„
March from Wady Suetne to Agaiga (six miles); Omdurman reconnoitred and forts silenced	Sept. 1,	„
Battle and capture of Omdurman . . .	„ 2,	„
Funeral of Gordon	„ 4,	„
Sirdar starts for Fashoda	„ 9,	„
Battle of Gedaref	„ 22,	„
Sirdar returns from Fashoda	„ 24,	„

GENERAL MAP—EGYPT TO UGANDA

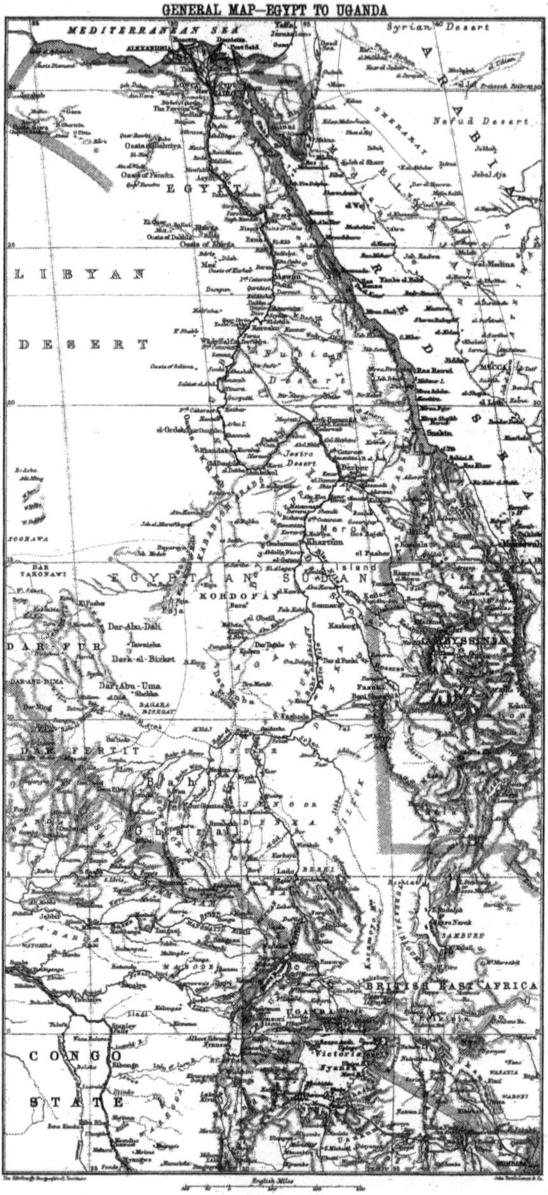

WITH KITCHENER TO KHARTUM.

I.

HALFA TELLS ITS STORY.

To walk round Wady Halfa is to read the whole romance of the Sudan. This is the look-out whence Egypt has strained her vision up-Nile to the vast, silent, torrid, murderous desert land, which has been in turn her neighbour, her victim, all but her undoing, and is now to be her triumph again. On us English, too, the Sudan has played its fatal witchery, and half the tale of Halfa is our own as well as Egypt's. On its buildings and up and down its sandy, windy streets we may trace all the stages of the first conquest, the loss, the bitter failures to recover, the slow recommencement, the presage of final victory.

You can get the whole tale into a walk of ten minutes. First look at that big white building: it is

A

the Egyptian military hospital, and one of the largest, solidest structures of Halfa. In shape and style, you will notice, it is not unlike a railway-station—and that is just what it was meant to be. That was the northern terminus of Ismail Pasha's great railway to Khartum, which was to have run up-river to Dongola and Debbeh, and thence across the Bayuda, by Jakdul and Abu Klea to Metemmeh. The scheme fell short, like all Ismail's grandiose ambitions; Gordon stopped it, and paid for his unforesight with his life. The railway never reached the Third Cataract. The upper part of it was torn to pieces by the Dervishes, who chopped the sleepers into firewood, and twisted the telegraph-wires to spear-heads; the part nearer Halfa lay half-derelict for many years, till it was aroused at length to play its part in the later act of the tragedy of the Sudan.

Now, twenty yards along the line—in this central part of Halfa every street is also a railway—you see a battered, broken-winded engine. It was here in 1884. That is one of the properties of the second act —the nerveless efforts to hold the Sudan when the Mahdi began to rip it loose. For in the year 1881, before we came to Egypt at all, there had arisen a religious teacher, a native of Dongola, named Mohammed Ahmed. The Sudan is the home of fanaticism: it has always been called "the Land of the Dervishes," and no rising saint was more ascetic than the young Dongolawi. He was a disciple of a holy man named

Mohammed Sherif, and one day the master gave a feast at which there was dancing and singing. Such frivolity, said Mohammed Ahmed, was displeasing to Allah; whereat the Sherif was angry, cursed him, and cast him out. The disciple sprinkled ashes on his head, put a yoke on his neck, and fell at his master's feet, imploring forgiveness. Again Mohammed Sherif cursed him and cast him out.

Angered now himself, Mohammed Ahmed joined a new teacher and became a straiter ascetic than ever. The fame of his sanctity spread, and adherents flocked to him. He saw that the people of the Sudan, smarting under extortion and oppression, could but too easily be roused against the Egyptian Government: he risked all, and proclaimed himself El Mahdi el Muntazer, the Expected Guide, the Mussulman Messiah. The Governor - General at Khartum sent two companies to arrest him: the Mahdi's followers fell on them unawares and destroyed them. More troops were sent; the Mahdists destroyed them: next came a small army, and again the Mahdists destroyed it. The barbarous tribesmen flocked to the Mahdi's standard, and in September 1882 he laid siege to El Obeid, the chief city of Kordofan. His assault was beaten back with great slaughter, but after five months' siege the town surrendered; sack and massacre taught doubters what they had to expect.

The Sudan doubted no longer: of a truth this was the Mahdi. Hicks Pasha's army came down from the

North only to swell the Mahdi's triumph to immensity.
Unorganised, unwieldy, afraid, the Egyptians crawled
on towards El Obeid, harassed by an enemy they
never saw. They saw them at last on November 4,
1883, at Shekan : the fight lasted a minute, and the
massacre spared only hundreds out of ten thousand.
The rest you know — Gordon's mission, the loss of
Berber, the siege of Khartum, the massacre of Baker's
levies at El Teb, Graham's expedition to Suakim, and
the hard-fought fights of the second Teb and Tamai,
Wolseley's expedition up the Nile, with Abu Klea and
the Gubar and Kirbekan, the second Suakim campaign and M'Neill's zariba. Everybody knows these
stories, so gallant, so futile. I remember thirteen
and fourteen years ago being enormously proud and
joyful about Tamai and Abu Klea. I was very young.
Read over the tale again now—the faltering and the
folly and the failure—and you will feel that if Egypt
has Baker's Teb and Hicks's ruin to wipe out, England was not so very far from suffering precisely the
same humiliations. And in the end we failed, with
what loss we still remember, and gave the Sudan
away. The second act is not a merry one.

The third was less tragic, but it was perhaps even
harder to play. We pass by a mud-walled quadrangle, which was once the artillery barracks ; through
the gateway you look across sand to the mud ram-
parts of Halfa. That is the stamp of the days of
reorganisation, of retrenchment, of difficulties and

discouragements, and unconquerable, undisappointed work. Those were the days when the Egyptian army was in the making, when Halfa was the frontier fortress. There are old barracks all over it, where the young fighting force of Egypt used to sleep half awake. The brown flanks of those hills beyond the rifle-range, just a couple of miles or so desertwards, have seen Dervishes stealing up in broad day and insolently slashing and stabbing in the main streets of the bazaar. Yet this time was not all unavenged insult: the long years between 1885 and 1896 saw Egypt defended and its assailants smashed to pieces. Little by little Egypt—British Egypt now—gained strength and new resolution.

Four battles mark the stages from weakness and abandonment to confidence and the resolution to reconquer. At Ginnis, on the last day but one of 1885, came the first Anglo - Egyptian strategical victory. The Mahdists had been tactically beaten before—well beaten; but the result had always been that we fell back and they came on. After Ginnis, fought by the British army of occupation, aided by a small number of the new Egyptian army, we stood firm, and the Dervishes were washed back. There were men of the Cameron Highlanders on the Atbara, who had fought in that battle: it was not perhaps a very great one, but it was the first time the enemy had been brought to a standstill. He retired behind the Third Cataract.

Then followed three years of raid and counter-raid. Chermside cut up their advance-guard at Sarras; they captured the fort of Khor Musa, and Machell Bey of the 13th Sudanese drove them out within twelve hours. On the Suakim side the present Sirdar made head against Osman Digna with what irregulars and friendlies he could get together. Then in 1888 Osman waxed insolent and threw up trenches against Suakim. It became a regular siege, and Dervish shells fell into the town. But on December 20 Sir Francis Grenfell, the Sirdar, came down and attacked the trenches at the battle of Gemaizeh, and Osman fell back shattered: never again did he come so near his soul's ambition.

Meanwhile Wad-en-Nejumi — the great Emir, the conqueror of Hicks and the captor of Khartum—had hung on the southern frontier, gathering strength for his attack on Egypt. He came in 1889, skirting Halfa in the western desert, striking for a point in Egypt proper above Assuan. His Emirs got out of hand and tried to get to the Nile; in a hard day's tussle at Argin, Colonel Wodehouse and the Halfa garrison threw him back into the desert again. Nejumi pushed on southward, certain of death, certain of Paradise. At Toski Grenfell brought him to battle with the flower of the Egyptian army. At the end of the day Nejumi was dead and his army was beginning to die of thirst in the desert. Egypt has never been attacked since.

Finally, in 1891 Colonel Holled - Smith marched against Osman Digna's base outside Suakim, the oasis of Tokat. The Dervishes sprang upon him at Afafit, but the days of surprise and panic were over. They were rolled back and shattered to pieces; their base was occupied; and Suakim as well as Halfa had peace. Now all ground was finally maintained, and all was ripe for attack again. England heard little of this third act; but for all that, unadvertised, hard-working, it was the turning-point of the whole drama.

And now we have come to the locomotive-sheds and the fitting-shops, the boiler-houses and the store-rooms; we are back in the present again, and the Halfa of to-day is the Egypt of to-day. Halfa has left off being a fortress and a garrison; to-day it is all workshop and railway terminus.   To-day it makes war not with bayonets, but with rivets and spindle-glands. Railways run along every dusty street, and trains and trucks clank up and down till Halfa looks for all the world like Chicago in a turban.   In chains, too, for to Halfa come all the worst villains of Egypt. You must know that, till the other day, no Egyptian could be hanged for murder except on the evidence of eyewitnesses—just the people whom most murderers try to avoid.   So the rails and sleepers are slung ashore to the jingle of ankle - chains; and after a day in Halfa it startles you in no way to hear that the black foreman of the engine - shop did his five murders, and that, nevertheless, he is a most intelli-

gent, industrious, and harmless creature. On the contrary, you find it admirable that Egypt's ruffians are
doing Egypt's work.

Halfa clangs from morning till night with rails
lassoed and drawn up a sloping pair of their fellows
by many convicts on to trucks; it thuds with sleepers
and boxes of bully-beef dumped on to the shore. As
you come home from dinner you stumble over strange
rails, and sudden engine-lamps flash in your face, and
warning whistles scream in your ears. As you lie
at night you hear the plug-plug of the goods engine,
nearer and nearer, till it sounds as if it must be
walking in at your tent door. From the shops of
Halfa the untamed Sudan is being tamed at last. It
is the new system, the modern system — mind and
mechanics beating muscle and shovel-head spear. It
takes up and digests all the past: the bits of Ismail's
railway came into the Dongola line; the engine of
Wolseley's time has been rebuilt, and is running
again; the artillery barracks are a store for all things
pertaining to engines. They came together for the
fourth act—the annihilating surprise of Ferkeh, the
masterly passage of Hafir, the occupation of Dongola
and Merawi, the swift march and sharp storm of Abu
Hamed, the swoop on Berber. They were all coming
together now for the victorious end, ready to enter
for the fifth act and the final curtain on Khartum.

But that is not all Halfa, and it is not all the
Sudan. Looking at it hence from its threshold, the

Sudan seems like a strong and swift wild beast, which many hunters have pursued, none subdued. The Sudan is a man-eater — red-gorged, but still insatiable. Turn your pony's head and canter out a mile; we are at the cemetery. No need to dismount, or even to read the names—see merely how full it is. Each white cross is an Englishman devoured by the Sudan. Go and hear the old inhabitants talk—the men who have contrived to live year in, year out, in the Sudan, in splitting sun and red-hot sand. You will notice it best with the men who are less trained to take a pull on their sentiment than are British officers—with the engineer corporals and the foreman mechanics, and all the other plain, efficient Englishmen who are at work on Halfa. Their talk is half of the chances of action, and the other half of their friends that have died.

" Poor Bill, 'e died in the desert surveying to Habu 'Amed. Yes, 'e's 'ere in the cemetery. No; there wasn't any white man there at the time."

" Ah, yes; he was a good fellow, and so was poor Captain Blank; a real nice man, he was now; no better in all the Egyptian army, sir, and I tell you that's saying a good deal, that is. Fought, too, against it; he was engaged to a girl at home, you know, sir, and he wouldn't give up. I nursed him till the doctor come, and then till the end. Didn't you see him when you was out at the cemetery; he's next to poor Dash ? "

"Ah, yes," says the third; "don't you remember that night out at Murat—poor Blank, and poor Dash, and poor Tertius, and you, and me. Five we were, and now there's only us two left. Dear, yes; and I slept in Tertius's bed the night before he took it; he was gone and buried forty-eight—no, thirty-six, it was—thirty-six hours later. Ah, yes; he was a good fellow, too. The way those niggers cried!"

Yes; it is a murderous devil, the Sudan, and we have watered it with more of our blood than it will ever yield to pay for. The man-eater is very grim, and he is not sated yet. Only this time he was to be conquered at last.

II.

THE EGYPTIAN ARMY.

THE Anglo-Egyptian army is not quite sixteen years old. The old Turco-Egyptian army was knocked to pieces by Lord Wolseley at Tel-el-Kebir, and the Mahdi ground the fragments to powder. Out of the nothing which remained sixteen years of British leadership have sufficed to build up an army capable of fighting foot for foot with the victors of Tel-el-Kebir, and accustomed to see the backs of the conquerors of Hicks and Baker and Gordon.

Sixteen years of active service have seen a great increase on the eight battalions which were Sir Evelyn Wood's original command. To-day the Egyptian army numbers nineteen battalions of infantry, ten squadrons of cavalry, one horse and four field batteries, and Maxims, a camel corps of eight companies, and the usual non-combatant services. Lord Dufferin limited the original army to 6000 men, with 25 white officers; to-day it counts three times that number with over 140.

The army is of course raised by conscription. But probably the conscription sits less heavily on Egypt than on any country in the world. Out of ten millions it takes—counting the railway battalions—under 20,000 men,—that is to say, one out of every 500 of population; whereas Germany takes 1 in 89, and France 1 in 66. That is only on the peace-footing, moreover; Egypt has been at war ever since the birth of the new army; no conscriptive nation ever carried war so lightly. On the other hand, the Egyptian soldier is called on to serve six years with the colours and nine in the reserve or the police. The small proportion of men taken enables the War Office to pick and choose; so that in point of physique also the Egyptian army could probably give weight to any in the world. And not only is it the smallest of conscriptive armies—it is also the best paid. The fellah receives a piastre (2½d.) a-day—a magnificent salary, equal to what he would usually be making in full work in his native village.

Even these figures do not do justice to the easy conditions on which Egypt supports her army. For of the eighteen battalions of infantry, six—9th to 14th—are Sudanese blacks. The material of these is not drawn from Egypt proper, nor, properly speaking, by conscription. The black is liable to be enlisted wherever he is found, as such, in virtue of his race; and he is enlisted for life. Such a law would be a terrible tyranny for the fellah: in the estimation of the black

it only gives comfort and security in the natural
vocation of every man worth calling such—war. Many
of the black soldiers have fought against us in the
past, with the same energy and enjoyment as they
now exhibit in our service. After each victory the
more desirable of the prisoners and deserters are
enlisted, to their great content, in one black battalion
or another. Every morning I had seen them on the
range at Halfa—the British sergeant-instructor teach-
ing the ex-Dervishes to shoot. When the recruit
made a bull—which he did surprisingly often—the
white sergeant, standing behind him with a paper,
cried, " *Quaiss kitir* "—" Very good." When he made
a fool of himself, the black sergeant trod on him as he
lay flat on his belly: he accepted praise and reproof
with equal satisfaction, as part of his new game of
disciplined war. The black is a perennial schoolboy,
without the schooling.

The black soldier is not adapted to garrison life.
They brought a battalion down to Cairo once; but the
soldiers insisted on driving about all day in carriages,
and then beat the driver when he asked for his fare.
Ever since then the Sudanese battalions have been
kept on the frontier—either up the Nile or on the
Suakim side, wherever there has been fighting to do.
Having neither knowledge of civilised enjoyments
nor desire for them, they are very happy. Their pay
is, properly, higher than that of the fellahin—14s. a-
month to begin with and 3¾d. a-day allowance for the

wife and family of such as are allowed to marry. The allowance is given generously, for woman is to the black soldier a necessary of life. On a campaign he must, of course, leave his wife and children behind: there is a large village of them just above Assuan. But since their time, I am afraid, as the frontier has ever advanced up - river, the inconstant warrior has formed fresh ties; and now at Halfa, at Dongola, at Berber, the path of victory is milestoned with expectant wives and children.

It is not so abandoned as it sounds, for the Sudanese are born of polygamy, and it would be unreasonable to expect them not to live in it. Here is a typical case. One day a particularly smart soldier came and desired to speak with his commanding officer.

"I wish to marry, O thou Bey," he said.

"But aren't you married?"

"Yes; but my wife is old and has no child, and I desire a child. I wish therefore to marry the sister of Sergeant Mohammed Ali, and he also is willing."

"Then you want to send away your present wife?"

"O no, Excellency. My wife cooks very well, and I want her to cook my rations. She also is willing."

So, everybody being willing, the second marriage took place. Mohammed Ali's sister duly bore a son, and the first wife cooked for the whole family, and they all lived happy ever afterwards.

Each infantry battalion, black and Egyptian alike, is divided into six companies, which parade between 100 and 120 strong; a battalion thus counts roughly, with band and bearer parties, from 650 to 750 rifles. The normal strength of a battalion is 759. The uniform is much the same for all arms — brown jersey, sand-coloured trousers, and dark-blue putties. Over the tarbush the Egyptians have a cover which hangs down behind over the nape of the neck: the blacks need no such protection from their native sun, and do with plaited-straw round the tarbush, bearing a badge whose colour varies with the various battalions. The infantry rifle is the Martini.

The cavalry are all Egyptians, recruited mostly from the Fayum oasis: a black can never be made to understand that a horse needs to be groomed and fed. The horses are stout, hardy beasts of 13 hands or so: they get through an amazing amount of work, and so do the men, though they are a little heavy in the saddle. The strength of a squadron is about 100; the front rank, as in all civilised armies, carry lance as well as sabre and Martini carbine. Seven of the squadron leaders are Englishmen.

Two batteries of field-artillery are armed with new Maxim-Nordenfeldt quick-firing 9-pounders, or 18-pounders with a double shell—handy little creatures which a couple of mules draw easily. The horse-battery has 12-pounder Krupps, the rest 9-pounders. Each battery has a white commander: all the men

are Egyptians, and their physical strength and teach-
ableness make them almost ideal gunners.

The camel corps is some 800 strong—half black,
half fellah. They use the mounted-infantry saddle,
sitting astride, and carry Martini and bayonet. There
are five white officers.

Of the fellah battalions some are officered by
Englishmen, some not. The former are 1st to 4th
and 15th to 18th; 5th to 8th are officered entirely
by natives. Until this campaign the normal number
of white officers has been three to an Egyptian and
four to a Sudanese battalion: the latter require more
holding, and also usually see more fighting, than the
former. Most of them were one or even two short.
But for this campaign—the final campaign, the climax
for which the Anglo-Egyptian army has existed and
drudged sixteen years—the number of British officers
had been raised to four in some battalions for the
fellahin and five for the blacks. There has been com-
plaining, both in Egypt and at home, that the proportion of British to Egyptian officers seems to grow
greater, whereas in theory it ought to grow less;
but the objection is political rather than military.
Many good judges would like to see a few black battalions officered right through by white men, like our
West India Regiment. There is no better regimental
officer than the Englishman; there is no better natural
fighter than the Sudanese: there would hardly be a
likelier force in the world.

The native officers are largely of Turkish, Circassian, or Albanian race, with the qualities and defects of their blood; their standard of professional attainment and duty is higher than that of the Turkish army, their courage in action no lower. Native Egyptians have furnished the army with one or two conspicuously useful officers. There is also a certain proportion of black captains and subalterns among the Sudanese: they are keen, work well with the British, and, of course, are utterly fearless; but, as a rule, lack of education keeps them out of the higher grades.

Finally, we must not forget Sergeant Whatsisname, as with grateful appreciation of fame at Mr Kipling's hands he is proud to call himself. Each battalion has as instructor a British non-commissioned officer; he drills it, teaches it to shoot, makes soldiers of it. Perhaps there is no body of men in the world who do more unalloyed and unlimited credit to their country than the colour-sergeants and sergeants with the Egyptian army. In many ways their position is a very difficult one. Technically they are subordinate to all native officers down to the latest-joined sub-lieutenant. The slacker sort of native officer resents the presence of these keenly military subordinates, and does his best to make them uncomfortable. But the white sergeant knows how not to see unpleasantness till it is absolutely unavoidable; then he knows how to go quietly to his colonel and assert his posi-

B

tion without publicly humiliating his superior. When
you hear that the sergeant - instructors are highly
endowed with tact, you will guess that in the virtues
that come more naturally to the British sergeant they
shine exceedingly. Their passionate devotion to duty
rises to a daily heroism. Living year in, year out, in
a climate very hard upon Europeans, they are naturally unable to palliate it with the comparative luxuries
of the officer; though it must be said that the con-
sideration of the officer for his non - commissioned
comrade is one of the kindliest of all the many kindly
touches with which the British-Egyptian softens pri-
vation and war. But the white officer rides and the
white sergeant marches. "Where a nigger can go, I
can go," he says, and tramps on through the sun.
Early in the year one of them marched with the 4th
every step of the road from Suakim—the only white
man who ever did it. In action the white sergeant
has no particular place or duties, so he charges ahead
of the first line. At Halfa, training the recruits, he
has no officer set over him, and can do pretty well
what he likes; so he stands five hours in the sun
before breakfast with his men on the range. He
must needs be a keen soldier or he would not have
volunteered for his post, and a good one, or he would
not have got it. But on the top of this he is also
essentially a fine man. Stiffened by marches and
fights and cholera camps, broadened by contact with
things new and strange, polished by a closer associa-

tion with his officers than the service allows at home, elevated by responsibility cheerfully undertaken and honourably sustained, — he is a mirror of soldierly virtue.

The position of the British officer is as assured as that of the sergeant is ambiguous. No British regimental officer takes lower rank than major (*Bimbashi*); none has any superior native officer in his own corps. The lieutenant-colonel (*Kaimakam*) commanding each battalion is usually a captain or major in the British army, and the *Bimbashis* usually subalterns : so many of both ranks, however, have earned brevets or been promoted, that in talking of officers in the Egyptian army it will be simplest to call a battalion commander Bey, which is the courtesy title by which he is usually addressed, and his British subordinate Bimbashi.

To take a man from the command of a company and put him to command a battalion is a big jump; but with the British officers in Egypt the experiment has richly justified itself. The Egyptian army is an army of young men. The Sirdar is forty-eight years old ; General Hunter was a major-general before he was forty. The whole army has only one combatant officer over fifty. Through the Dongola campaign majors commanded brigades and captains battalions ; at Abu Hamed, last year, a subaltern of twenty-eight led his regiment in action. With men either rash or timid such sudden promotion might be dangerous ;

but the officers of the Egyptian army are at the
same time unafraid of responsibility and equal to it.
Their professional success has been very great—some
whisper, too great.   "After Tel-el-Kebir," said a
captain in the British brigade, "one of our officers
came to me and talked of joining the Egyptian army.
'For God's sake, don't,' I said; 'don't: you'll spend
your life thrashing fellahin into action with a stick.'
Now, here am I commanding a company, and a man
who was under me in the Kandahar show is commanding a brigade."   Certainly the Egyptian officers
may have passed over men as good as they; but their
luck has lain solely in getting the chance to show their
merit.

For after all the fact remains, that while the British
campaigns in the Sudan are a long story of failure
brightened only by stout fighting, the Egyptian
campaigns have been a consistent record of success.
With inferior material, at a tithe of the expense, they
have worn their enemy down by sheer patience and
pluck and knowledge of their business.   In the old days
campaigns were given up for want of transport; now
rations are as certain in Khartum as in Cairo.   In the
old days we used to be surprised and to fight in square;
now we surprise the enemy and attack in line.   In
quite plain language, what Gordon and Wolseley failed
to do the Sirdar has done.   The credit is not all his:
part must go to Sir Evelyn Wood and Sir Francis
Grenfell, his predecessors, and to the whole body of

officers in due proportion. They have paid for their promotion with years on the frontier—years of sweat and sandstorm by day, of shivering and alarms by night, of banishment always; above all, they have richly earned it by success. Now that the long struggle is crowned with victory, we may look back on those fourteen indomitable years as one of the highest achievements of our race.

III.

THE S.M.R.

HALFA is nearly four hundred miles from the Atbara; yet it was the decisive point of the campaign. For in Halfa was being forged the deadliest weapon that Britain has ever used against Mahdism — the Sudan Military Railway. In the existence of the railway lay all the difference between the extempore, amateur scrambles of Wolseley's campaign and the machine-like precision of Kitchener's. When civilisation fights with barbarism it must fight with civilised weapons; for with his own arts on his own ground the barbarian is almost certain to be the better man. To go into the Sudan without complete transport and certain communications is as near madness as to go with spears and shields. Time has been on the Sirdar's side, whereas it was dead against Lord Wolseley; and of that, as of every point in his game, the Sirdar has known how to ensure the full advantage. There was fine marching and fine fighting in the campaign of the Atbara: the campaign would have

failed without them; but without the railway there
could never have been any campaign at all. The
battle of the Atbara was won in the workshops of
Wady Halfa.

Everybody knew that a railway from Halfa across the
desert to Abu Hamed was an impossibility—until the
Sirdar turned it into a fact. It was characteristic of
the Sirdar's daring—daring based on complete knowledge and just confidence in himself and his instru-
ments; but to the uninformed it seems mad reckless-
ness—that he actually launched his rails and sleepers
into the waterless desert, while the other end of the line
was still held by the enemy. Water was bored for, and,
at the third attempt, found, which lightened the task;
but the engineers are convinced that, water or no water,
the Sirdar's ingenuity and determination would have
carried the enterprise through. Long before the line
was due to arrive Abu Hamed had fallen: before the
end of 1897 the line touched the Nile again at that
point, 234 miles from Halfa, and the journey to Berber took a day instead of weeks.

There was no pause at Abu Hamed; work was begun
immediately on the 149-mile stretch to the Atbara.
At the beginning of the year, when the rumours of
Mahmud's advance began to harden into credibility
and the British regiments were started up the river,
rail-head was some twenty miles south of Abu
Hamed. The object, of course, was to push it on
south of the series of rapids ending at Geneineteh,

some twenty-odd miles short of Berber, which are
called the Fifth Cataract. On the falling river camel
portage had to be used round the broken water, which
was a serious difficulty in the way of the transport.
A second object in hurrying on the work was to get
the sections of the three new gunboats to the same
point south of the cataract, where they could be put
together ready for the final advance.

It was a heavy strain, for the railway had not only
to carry up supplies and stores : it had also to carry
the materials for its own extension. There is no
wood for sleepers between Abu Hamed and the
Atbara, much less any possibility of providing rails.
So that all day long you heard the wailing lilt, without which no Arab can work in time ; all day at
intervals the long material train pulled out from the
beach-siding piled up with rails and sleepers, paused
awhile at the bank of sand which is the platform of
the northern terminus, and in due time puffed off
southward till it was lost among the desert sand-
hills.

It was a heavy handicap that an infant railway
should be asked for double work, but that was only
the beginning of the difficulty. The S.M.R., like every
thing else in Egypt, must be worked on the cheap.
There is no trouble about the labour—the Railway
Battalions supply that. The Railway Battalions are
raised by conscription, only instead of fighting with
Martini and bayonet the conscripts fight with shovel

and pick. I have heard it called the *Corvée* in another form: so, if you like, it is. But it is no more
Corvée than the work of sappers in any European
army. The fellah has to shovel for his country instead of fighting for it, and he would much rather.
It is war service which happens to retain a permanent
value when war is over; so much the better for
everybody.

But if navvy labour is abundant and cheap and
efficient, everything else is scarce and cheap and
nasty. English firemen and drivers are hard to get,
and Italian mechanics are largely employed—so much
so, that the Director of Railways has found it worth
while to spare a café for them out of his cramped
elbow-room. As for native mechanics, there are
branches of work in which they are hopeless. As
fitters they are a direct temptation to suicide, for the
Arab mind can never be brought to see that a tenth
of an inch more or less can possibly matter to anybody. "*Malesh*," he says, "it doesn't matter; shove
it in." And then the engine breaks down.

As for engines and rolling-stock the S.M.R. must
make the best of what it can get. Half-a-dozen new
engines of English breed there were when I got to
Halfa—fine, glossy, upstanding, clean-limbed, powerful creatures; and it was a joy to watch the marvelling
black sentry looking up to one of them in adoration
and then warily round lest anybody should seek to
steal it. There were others ordered, but—miracle of

national lunacy!—the engineering strike intervened, and the orders had to go to Baldwin's of Philadelphia. For the rest the staff had to mend up anything they found about. Old engines from Ismail's abortive railway, old engines from Natal, from the Cape, broken and derelict, had to be patched up with any kind of possible fittings retrieved and adapted from the scrapheap. Odd parts were picked up in the sand and fitted into their places again: if they were useless they were promptly turned into something else and made useful. There are a couple of Ismail's boilers in use now which were found lying miles away in the desert and rolled in by lever and hand. In the engine-shed you see rusty embryos of engines that are being tinkered together with bits of rubbish collected from everywhere. And still they move.

Who moves them? It is part of the Sirdar's luck —that luck which goes with genius—that he always gets the best conceivable subordinates. Conceive a blend of French audacity of imagination, American ingenuity, and British doggedness in execution, and you will have the ideal qualities for such a work. The Director of Railways, Bimbashi Girouard, is a Canadian, presumably of French derivation. In early life he built a section of the Canadian Pacific. He came out to Egypt for the Dongola campaign—one of three subalterns specially chosen from the Railway Department of the Royal Engineers. The Sudan killed the other two out of hand, but Bimbashi

Girouard goes on building and running his railways.
The Dongola line runs as far as Kerma, above the
Third Cataract. The Desert Line must wait at the
Atbara for a bridge before it can be extended to Khartum. But already here is something over five hundred
miles of rail laid in a savage desert—a record to make
the reputation of any engineer in the world, standing
to the credit of a subaltern of sappers. The Egyptian
army is a triumph of youth on every side, but in none
is it more signal than in the case of the Director of
Railways. He never loses his head nor forgets his
own mind : he is credited with being the one man in
the Egyptian army who is unaffectedly unafraid of
the Sirdar.

Having finished the S.M.R. to the Atbara, Bimbashi
Girouard accepted the post of Director-General of all
the Egyptian railways. There will be plenty of scope
for him in the post, and it will not be wasted. But
just reflect again on this crowning wonder of British
Egypt — a subaltern with all but Cabinet rank and
£2000 a-year !

When the time came to go up by the desert line an
engine, two trucks, and a fatigue-party called at the
door for our baggage : that is the advantage of a rail-
way-traffic managed by subalterns. We had the luck
to get berths in the big saloon. It is built on the Indian
plan—four beds in one compartment, eight in the other,
plenty of room on the floor, and shutters everywhere
to keep out the sand. The train looked as if the other

end of it must be at Abu Hamed already—a vista of
rails, sleepers, boxes, camels, and soldiers, and two
turkeys, the property of a voluptuous Brigadier, bub-
bling with indignation through the darkness. However she ran out smoothly enough towards midnight.
We slept peacefully, four of us — the other made
night hideous with kicks, and exhortations to vision-
ary soldiers to fire low—and in the morning woke up
rather less than a hundred miles on our way. But
then the first hundred miles is all up-hill, though the
gradient is nowhere difficult. The train ran beautifully, for while the surface sand is very easy to work
it has a firm bottom, and the rails do not settle. All
day we rumbled on prosperously, with no mischance
more serious than a broken rail, and we crawled safely
over that.

Half the day we read and half the day we played
cards, and when it grew dark we sang, for all the world
like Thomas Atkins. Every now and then we varied the
monotony with a meal; the train stopped frequently,
and even when it did not the pace was slow enough
for an agile butler to serve lunch by jumping off his
truck and climbing on to the saloon foot-board. The
scenery, it must be owned, was monotonous, and yet
not without haunting beauty. Mile on mile, hour on
hour, we glided through sheer desert. Yellow sand to
right and left—now stretching away endlessly, now
a valley between small broken hills. Sometimes the
hills sloped away from us, then they closed in again.

Now they were diaphanous blue on the horizon,
now soft purple as we ran under their flanks. But
always they were steeped through and through with
sun — hazy, immobile, silent. It looked like a part
of the world quite new, with none of the bloom
rubbed off. It seemed almost profanity that I should
be intruding on the sanctity of the prime.

But I was not the first intruder. Straight, firm,
and purposeful ran the rails. Now they split into a
double line: here was another train waiting—a string
of empty trucks—and also a tent, a little hut made of
sleeper baulks, a tank, points, and a board with the
inscription " No. 5." This was a station—a wayside
station. But No. 6 is a Swindon of the desert.
Every train stops there half-an-hour or more to fill
up with water, for there is a great trifoliate well
there. Also the train changes drivers. And here, a
hundred miles into the heart of the Nubian desert,
two years ago a sanctuary of inviolate silence, where
no blade of green ever sprang, where, possibly, no
foot trod since the birth of the world, here is a little
colony of British engine-drivers. They have a little
rest-house shanty of board and galvanised iron; there
are pictures from the illustrated papers on the walls,
and a pup at the door. There they swelter and
smoke and spit and look out at the winking rails and
the red-hot sand, and wait till their turn comes to
take the train. They don't love the life—who would?
—but they stick to it like Britons, and take the trains

out and home.   They, too, are not the meanest of the
conquerors of the Sudan.

Towards dusk mimosa bushes, dotted park-wise over
the sand, began to rise up on both sides of us, then
palms; soon we were in a thickish scrub.   The air
cooled and moistened from death to life: we were
back again on the Nile, at Abu Hamed.   Thereafter
we slept peacefully again, and awoke in the midst
of a large camp of white tents.   They unhooked the
saloon, but the train crawled on, disgorging rails and
sleepers, till it came to a place where a swarm of
fellahin was shovelling up sand round the last metals.
The naked embankment ran straight and purposeful
as ever, so far as you could see.   Small in the distance was a white man with a spirit-level.

IV

THE CORRESPONDENT'S PROGRESS.

I SAT on a box of tinned beef, whisky, and other
delicacies, dumped down on a slope of loose sand.
Round me lay another similar case, a tent, bed, and
bath, all collapsible and duly collapsed into a brown
canvas jacket, two brown canvas bags containing
saddlery, towels, and table-linen, a chair and a table
lashed together, a wash - hand basin with shaving
tackle concealed inside its green canvas cover, a
brown bag with some clothes in it, a shining tin
canteen, a cracking lunch-basket, a driving-coat, and
a hunting-crop. On one side of me rose the embankment of the main line to Berber; fifty yards
on it ended suddenly in the sand, and a swarm of
Arabs were shovelling up more of it for their lives.
On the other side of me, detached, empty, quite alone,
stood the saloon which brought me from Halfa. It
was going back again to-night, and then I should
be quite loose and outcast in the smiling Sudan.

I sat and meditated on the full significance of the

simple military phrase, " line of communications." It
is the great discovery of the Sirdar that he has recognised that in the Sudan the communications are
the essence and heart of the whole problem. And
now I recognised it too.

It was a long, long story already. I was now just
at the threshold of what was regarded officially as the
difficult part of the 1150 odd miles between Cairo and
the front; I was still seventy miles or so from Berber
—and my problem, instead of just beginning, appeared
just on the point of an abrupt and humiliating finish.
The original question was how I was to get myself
and my belongings to the front; the threatened solu-
tion was that I should get there, if at all, on my feet,
and that my belongings would serve to blaze the track
for anybody desperate enough to follow.

I am not an old campaigner. The old campaigner,
as you know, starts out with the clothes he stands
up in and a tin-opener. The young campaigner pro-
vides the change of linen and tins for the old campaigner to open. So in Cairo I bought everything
I could think of as likely to palliate a summer in
the Sudan. I wore out my patience and my legs a
whole week in drapers' shops, and saddlers' shops, and
apothecaries' shops, and tobacconists' shops, and tin-
and-bottle shops, and general shops. I bought two
horses and two nigger boys—one to look after the
horses and one to look after me. One of them I
bought through Cook, as one takes a railway-ticket;

the other suddenly dashed at me in the street with a bundle of testimonials unanimously stating that he could cook more or less, and clean things if he were shown how. Both wore tarbushes and striped nightgowns, and nothing else visible, which was natural; though afterwards they emerged in all kinds of gorgeousness. What was inconvenient was that they neither of them understood any language I could talk, that they both had the same name, and that I could not for the life of me remember what it was. However, one was black with red eyes, and the other yellow with white; and it was something to know them apart. The black-and-red one originally alleged that he could talk English. It was true that he could understand a dozen words of that lingo if pronounced sloppily enough and put ungrammatically together. But when it came to his turn he could say "Yes, sir," and then followed it up with an inarticulate burble more like the sound of a distant railway train than any known form of human speech.

Anyhow, I started. I started with the properties above named and six packages besides. Some went with me on the tourist boat; others went by rail or post boat, or Government barge, to await me; others stayed behind to follow me. I got to Assuan, and there a new trial awaited me. I had no camels, and it would be absurd to go to the Sudan without camels. Now I knew nothing at all of the points of a camel, nor of its market price, nor what it eats, nor could I

ride it.   However, camels had to be bought, and I
borrowed an interpreter, and went out to the Bisharin
village outside Assuan and bought some.   The interpreter said he knew all about camels, and that
they were worth £27 a pair.

First, though, they had to be tried.   The Bisharin
were all standing about grouped round little heaps of
dry, cracked mud, which it took a moment's consider-
ation to recognise as their houses.   Their costume
consisted mainly of their hair—in little tight plaits
tumbling every way over their heads ; they have it
done thus in infancy, and never take it out of curl :
it looks like the inside hair of a horse's tail, where
the brush can't get at it.   They all talked at the
same time, and gesticulated furiously.

The first Bishari was a wizened old man, with
a wisp or two of grey beard, a black shawl, and
a large expanse of chest, back, arm, and leg, of
a delicate plum-colour.   With horrible noises he
pulled his camel down on to its knees.   The camel
made still more horrible noises ; it growled, and
screeched, and snarled, and brayed, and gurgled out
big pink bladders from its inside.   Then the old man
tied a pad of sackcloth on to the beast's hump by way
of saddle, seized the halter, and leaped on sideways ;
the camel unfolded its legs joint by joint and leaped
forward.   The old man whacked with a will, the
camel bounded up and down, the old man bounced
in his saddle like an india-rubber ball, his shawl

flapped out like wings, till all his body was native plum-colour. Then, suddenly, the camel gathered itself together and soared aloft—and the next thing was the old man flying up to heaven, slowly turning over, and slowly, then quickly, thudding to earth. Everybody roared with laughter, including the victim; red was flowing fast over the plum-colour arm, but he didn't notice it. I bought that camel on the spot—to carry five hundredweight of baggage, not me.

There was one other cropper before the trials were over, and two of the camels cantered and galloped round the mud warren in a way that made me tremble. However, I trusted to luck against the time when I might have to ride any of them, and bought with a light heart. I also bought two camel-men—a black, apparently answering to the name of Jujube, and a yellow, who asserted he was my groom's brother. The latter produced, with great pride, a written testimonial: it was from a British officer, to the effect that he had discharged the bearer, and would the Director of Transport kindly send him home. But I chanced that too; and now, with the exception of the few necessaries that were following me—and presumably are still—I was ready to march on Khartum.

And now came in the question of the lines of communication. I went to the commandant of Assuan; could he kindly send up my horses by steamer? Yes, certainly, when there was a steamer to send them by.

But steamers were few and much in request for railway stores and supplies. It was a question of waiting till there should appear military horses to go up river. Mine must go and stand in the camp meanwhile. Hurrah! said I; never mind about a few days: that was one load off my mind. So I hauled the horses out of the stable, and gave the syce some money, and a letter to say who he was, and peacefully left him to shift.

Camels, being straggling and unportable beasts, could not go by boat; so I gave their attendants also money, and told them to walk to Halfa. Then I went to Halfa myself, and waited.

At Halfa, knowing its name so well, I had expected to find a hotel. So there was one—the "Hotel des Voyageurs"—staring the landing-stage in the face. But it was a Greek hostelry, very small, a mile from the military post of Halfa, and at this stage I had a mind above Greek hotels. So I went to Walker & Co., the universal provider of Halfa. There was no immediate accommodation for correspondents. So I pitched my tent a little disconsolately in the compound, and sat down to wait until there was. Presently there was a room, and in that I sat down to wait for the camels. One day their attendant grinned in, and shook hands with me; the camels were accommodated with a bunk apiece in the garden, and I sat down again to wait for the horses. I waited many days and then wired; the commandant wired

back, "Your horses cannot go by steamer at present."
When was "at present" going to end? So next I
wired to Cook's agent to send them by road; he
replied that they had started four days before. So
far, so good. I sat down to wait some more.

Only two days before they might be expected, on
March 1, came the news that the British brigade
had gone up to Berber, and that correspondents might
go too.

Hurrah again! Only when, how? O, you can
go to-morrow in the saloon, of course, to rail-head.
And beyond? Well, beyond you must take your
chance. Can camels go by train? It was hardly
likely. Horses? Not at present—and—well—you
had better go very light.

Clearly everything that was mine must take its
chance too. I started the camels to walk across the
desert—two hundred and thirty-four miles from Nile
to Nile again—and told them to be quick about it.
Of course they could never have done it, but that
the traffic-manager kindly gave them authority to
drink some of the engines' water on the way. I left
orders to the horses to do the same; left all my
heaviest goods lying about on the bank of the Nile;
definitely gave up all hope of the things that were
supposed to be coming up after me; started, and
arrived in the early morning of March 3.

Now came the time to take my chance. And here,
sure enough, comes a chocolate Arab, with the in-

formation that he has any number of camels to let.
The chance has turned out a good one, after all. But
then comes along a fair Englishman, on a shaggy grey
pony; I was told he was the Director of Transport.
That's all right; I'll ask his advice. Only, before I
could speak, he suavely drew the attention of correspondents to the rule that any Arab hiring camels
already hired by the army was liable to two years
imprisonment. The news was not encouraging; and
of course the Arabs swore that the army had not
hired the best camels at all. I believed it at the
time, but came to know the Arab better afterwards.
Anyhow here I sat, amid the dregs of my vanishing
household, seventy miles from Berber—no rail, no
steamer, no horse, no camel. Only donkeys, not to be
thought of—and, by George, legs! I never thought
of them, but I've got 'em, and why not use 'em.
I'll walk.

V.

I MARCH TO BERBER.

THE donkeys had been hired, at war prices, about ten in the morning, delivery promised within an hour. At three in the afternoon two of us sweated over from the rail-head to the village, to try and hurry them up. Fifteen had been ordered; five were nearly ready. The sheikh swore by Allah that all should be ready within an hour. At five we went over again. There were only four by now; the sheikh swore by Allah that the others should be ready within an hour.

On that we began to threaten violence; whereupon round a mud-wall corner trotted eighteen donkeys, followed by eight black men and a boy. Twenty-two! It was late, but it was better than could be expected of any Arab. We kept them sedulously in our eye till we had them alongside the mountainous confusion of three correspondents' light baggage. Arrived at the scene of action, they sat down with one consent and looked at it.

The only way to hurry an Arab is to kill him, after which he is useless as a donkey-driver; so we sat down too, and had some tea, and looked at them. Presently they made it known that they had no rope. A rope was produced and cut into lengths; each took one, and sat and looked at it. Finally arose an old, old man, attired in a rag round his head and a pair of drawers: with the eye of experience he selected the two lightest articles, and slowly tied them together. Example works wonders. There was almost a rush to secure the next smallest load, and in ten minutes everything was tied together and slung across the little pack-saddles, except one load. This they looked at for a good long time, reluctant to get a piece of work finished; at last they felt justified· in loading this on also.

We were ready: we were actually about to start. Gratitude and wonder filled my soul.

Three men, nine Arabs, nine more to see them off, twenty-two donkeys—and, Heaven forgive me, I had almost forgotten the horse. That is to say, his owner applied to him an Arab word which I understood to mean horse—plural before he was produced, singular when it was no longer possible to allege that there was more than one of him. Experts opined that he might in the remote past have been a dervish horse— a variation from the original type, produced by never feeding the animal. His teeth, what remained of them, gave no clear evidence of his age, but on a

general view of him I should say he was rising ninety.
Early in the century he was probably chestnut, but
now he was partly a silver chestnut and partly presented no impression of colour at all: he was just
faded. He wore a pessimistic expression, a coat about
an inch and a quarter long, an open saddle sore, and
no flesh of any kind in any corner. We offered him
fodder—something like poor pea-halm and something
like string, only less nutritious. He looked at it
wearily, smelt it, and turned in perplexity to his
master as if asking instructions. He had forgotten
what food was for.

The young moon was climbing up the sky when
we set off. With chattering and yells the donkeys
and Arabs streamed out on to the desert track. The
first load came undone in the first five minutes, and
every one had to be readjusted in the first hour. The
Arab, you see, has only been working with donkeys
for ten thousand years or so, and you can't expect
him to have learned much about it yet. But we kept
them going. I was rearguard officer, with five Arabic
words, expressing "Get on" in various degrees of
emphasis, and a hunting-crop.

We only marched three hours to camp that night,
but by the time we off-loaded in a ring of palms, with
the Nile swishing below and the wind swishing overhead, we had earned our dinner and some sleep: had
we not induced Arabs to start? And now came in
one of the conveniences—so far the only one—of

travelling in the Sudan. "Three angarebs," said the
correspondent of experience; and back came the servants presently with three of the stout wooden frames
lashed across with thongs that form the Sudan bed:
you can get them anywhere there is a village—as
a rule, to be sure, there is none—and they are luxuri-
ous beyond springs and feathers.

At half-past one I opened my eyes and saw the
moon stooping down to meet the fringe of palm leaves.
The man of experience sat up on his angareb and cried
Awake." They did awake: three hours' sleep is not
long enough to make you sleepy. We loaded up by
the last moonlight, and took the road again. For
nearly three hours the rustling on our right and the
line of palms showed that we kept to the Nile bank;
then at five we halted to water the donkeys—they eat
when they can and what they can—and started for a
long spell across the desert. Grey dawn showed us a
gentle swell of stony sand, hard under foot; freshness
came with it to man and beast, and we struck forward
briskly.

When the sun came up on us, I saw the caravan
for the first time plainly; and I was very glad we
were not likely to meet anybody I knew. My kit
looked respectable enough in the train, and in Berber
it went some way to the respectable furnishing of a
house. But as piled by Sudanese Arabs on to donkeys
it was disreputable, dishevelled, a humiliation beyond
blushes. The canteen, the chair and table that had

looked so neat and workmanlike, on the donkey became the pots and sticks of a gipsy encampment. My
tent was a slipshod monstrosity, my dressing - case
blatantly secondhand, my washing basin was posi-
tively indecent. To make things worse, they had
trimmed my baggage up with garbage of their own
—dirty bags of dates and cast - off clothing. They
mostly insisted on riding the smallest and heaviest-
laden donkeys themselves, jumping at a bound on
to the jogging load of baggage with four legs patter-
ing underneath, and had to be flogged off again. And
to finish my shame, here was I trudging behind,
cracking and flicking at donkeys and half-naked black
men, like a combination of gipsy, horse - coper, and
slave-driver.

But we travelled. Some of the donkeys were
hardly bigger than collies, and their drivers did all
that laziness and ineptitude could suggest to keep
them back; but we travelled. It came to my turn
of the horse about half-past six or so: certainly he
was not a beast to make comparisons on, but the
donkeys left him behind unless you made him trot,
which was obviously cruel. I should say they kept
up four miles an hour with a little driving.

We gave ourselves an hour at eight for breakfast,
and the end of the march was in soft sand under a
cruel sun. It was not till nearly one that the camel
thorn—all stalk and prickles, no leaves—gave way
to palms again, and again we looked down on the

Nile.   A single palm gives almost as much shade
as an umbrella with the silk off, but we found four
together, and a breeze from the river, and a drink—
O that first drink in a Sudan camp!—and lunch and
a sleep, and a tub and tea, and we reflected on our
ten hours' march and were happy.   At five we
joggled off again.

We lost the place we had intended to camp at, and
the desert began to get rugged and to produce itself
ever so far both ways, like the parallel lines in Euclid,
and we never got any farther forward on it.   It got
to be a kind of treadmill—we going on and the desert
going back under us.   But at last we did get to a
place—didn't know its name, nor cared—and went to
sleep a little more.   And in the pale morning by
happy luck we found two camels, and two of us
trotted joyously forward past swimming mirages and
an endless string of ruined mud villages into mud
Berber.   The donkeys were not much behind either:
they did about seventy miles in forty-two hours.   But
I am afraid it must have been the death of the horse,
and I am sorry.   It seems a cruelty to kill him just as
he was beginning to be immortal.

VI.

THE SIRDAR.

MAJOR-GENERAL SIR HORATIO HERBERT KITCHENER is forty-eight years old by the book; but that is irrelevant. He stands several inches over six feet, straight as a lance, and looks out imperiously above most men's heads; his motions are deliberate and strong; slender but firmly knit, he seems built for tireless, steel-wire endurance rather than for power or agility: that also is irrelevant. Steady passionless eyes shaded by decisive brows, brick - red rather full cheeks, a long moustache beneath which you divine an immovable mouth; his face is harsh, and neither appeals for affection nor stirs dislike. All this is irrelevant too: neither age, nor figure, nor face, nor any accident of person, has any bearing on the essential Sirdar. You could imagine the character just the same as if all the externals were different. He has no age but the prime of life, no body but one to carry his mind, no face but one to keep his brain behind. The brain and the will are the essence and the whole of the man—a brain and a will so perfect in their workings that, in the face of extremest difficulty, they never seem to know what struggle is. You cannot imagine the Sirdar otherwise than as seeing the right thing to do and doing it. His precision is so inhumanly unerring, he is more like a machine than a man. You feel that he ought to be patented and shown with pride at the Paris International Exhibition. British Empire: Exhibit No. I., *hors concours*, the Sudan Machine.

It was aptly said of him by one who had closely watched him in his office, and in the field, and at mess, that he is the sort of feller that ought to be made manager of the Army and Navy Stores. The aphorist's tastes lay perhaps in the direction of those more genial virtues which the Sirdar does not possess, yet the judgment summed him up perfectly. He would be a splendid manager of the Army and Navy Stores. There are some who nurse a desperate hope that he may some day be appointed to sweep out the War Office. He would be a splendid manager of the War Office. He would be a splendid manager of anything.

But it so happens that he has turned himself to the management of war in the Sudan, and he is the complete and the only master of that art. Beginning life in the Royal Engineers—a soil reputed more favourable to machinery than to human nature—he early turned to the study of the Levant. He was one of Beaconsfield's military vice-consuls in Asia Minor; he

was subsequently director of the Palestine Explora-
tion Fund. At the beginning of the Sudan troubles
he appeared. He was one of the original twenty-five
officers who set to work on the new Egyptian army.
And in Egypt and the Sudan he has been ever since—
on the staff generally, in the field constantly, alone
with natives often, mastering the problem of the
Sudan always. The ripe harvest of fifteen years is
that he knows everything that is to be learned of his
subject. He has seen and profited by the errors of
others as by their successes. He has inherited the
wisdom and the achievements of his predecessors. He
came at the right hour, and he was the right man.

Captain R.E., he began in the Egyptian army as
second-in-command of a regiment of cavalry. In
Wolseley's campaign he was Intelligence Officer. During the summer of 1884 he was at Korosko, negoti-
ating with the Ababdeh sheiks in view of an advance
across the desert to Abu Hamed; and note how
characteristically he has now bettered the then
abandoned project by going that way to Berber and
Khartum himself—only with a railway! The idea of
the advance across the desert he took over from Lord
Wolseley, and indeed from immemorial Arab caravans;
and then, for his own stroke of insight and resolution amounting to genius, he turned a raid into an
irresistible certain conquest, by superseding camels
with the railway. Others had thought of the desert
route: the Sirdar, correcting Korosko to Halfa, used

it. Others had projected desert railways: the Sirdar
made one. That, summarised in one instance, is the
working of the Sudan machine.

As Intelligence Officer Kitchener accompanied Sir
Herbert Stewart's desert column, and you may be
sure that the utter breakdown of transport which
must in any case have marred that heroic folly was
not unnoticed by him. Afterwards, through the long
decade of little fights that made the Egyptian army,
Kitchener was fully employed. In 1887 and 1888 he
commanded at Suakim, and it is remarkable that his
most important enterprise was half a failure. He
attacked Osman Digna at Handub, when most of the
Emir's men were away raiding; and although he
succeeded in releasing a number of captives, he
thought it well to retire, himself wounded in the
face by a bullet, without any decisive success. The
withdrawal was in no way discreditable, for his force
was a jumble of irregulars and levies without discipline. But it is not perhaps fanciful to believe that
the Sirdar, who has never given battle without making certain of an annihilating victory, has not forgotten his experience of haphazard Bashi-Bazouking
at Handub.

He had his revenge before the end of 1888, when
he led a brigade of Sudanese over Osman's trenches at
Gemaizeh. Next year at Toski he again commanded
a brigade. In 1890 he succeeded Sir Francis Grenfell as Sirdar. That he meant to be Sirdar in fact as

well as name he showed in 1894. The young Khedive travelled south to the frontier, and took the occasion to insult every British officer he came across. Kitchener promptly gave battle : he resigned, a crisis came, and the Khedive was obliged to do public penance by issuing a General Order in praise of the discipline of the army and of its British officers. Two years later he began the reconquest of the Sudan. Without a single throw-back the work has gone forward since—but not without intervals. The Sirdar is never in a hurry. With immovable self-control he holds back from each step till the ground is consolidated under the last. The real fighting power of the Sudan lies in the country itself—in its barrenness which refuses food, and its vastness which paralyses transport. The Sudan machine obviates barrenness and vastness : the bayonet action stands still until the railway action has piled the camp with supplies or the steamer action can run with a full Nile. Fighting men may chafe and go down with typhoid and cholera : they are in the iron grip of the machine, and they must wait the turn of its wheels. Dervishes wait and wonder, passing from apprehension to security. The Turks are not coming; the Turks are afraid. Then suddenly at daybreak one morning they see the Sirdar advancing upon them from all sides together, and by noon they are dead. Patient and swift, certain and relentless, the Sudan machine rolls conquering southward.

In the meantime, during all the years of preparation
and achievement, the man has disappeared. The man
Herbert Kitchener owns the affection of private
friends in England and of old comrades of fifteen
years' standing; for the rest of the world there is
no man Herbert Kitchener, but only the Sirdar,
neither asking affection nor giving it. His officers and
men are wheels in the machine: he feeds them enough
to make them efficient, and works them as mercilessly
as he works himself. He will have no married officers in his army — marriage interferes with work.
Any officer who breaks down from the climate goes
on sick leave once: next time he goes, and the Egyptian army bears him on its strength no more. Asked
once why he did not let his officers come down to
Cairo during the season he replied, "If it were to
go home, where they would get fit and I could get
more work out of them, I would. But why should I
let them down to Cairo?" It is unamiable, but it
is war, and it has a severe magnificence. And if you
suppose, therefore, that the Sirdar is unpopular, he is
not. No general is unpopular who always beats the
enemy. When the columns move out of camp in the
evening to march all night through the dark, they
know not whither, and fight at dawn with an enemy
they have never seen, every man goes forth with a
tranquil mind. He may personally come back and
he may not; but about the general result there is not
a doubt. You bet your boots the Sirdar knows: he

wouldn't fight if he weren't going to win. Other
generals have been better loved; none was ever better
trusted.

For of one human weakness the Sirdar is believed not to have purged himself — ambition. He
is on his promotion, a man who cannot afford to
make a mistake. Homilies against ambition may be
left to those who have failed in their own: the
Sirdar's, if apparently purely personal, is legitimate
and even lofty. He has attained eminent distinction
at an exceptionally early age: he has commanded victorious armies at an age when most men are hoping
to command regiments. Even now a junior Major-
General, he has been intrusted with an army of six
brigades, a command such as few of his seniors have
ever led in the field. Finally, he has been charged
with a mission such as almost every one of them
would have greedily accepted,—the crowning triumph
of half a generation's war. Naturally he has awak-
ened jealousies, and he has bought permission to take
each step on the way only by brilliant success in the
last. If in this case he be not so stiffly unbending to
the high as he is to the low, who shall blame him?
He has climbed too high not to take every precaution
against a fall.

But he will not fall, just yet at any rate. So far
as Egypt is concerned he is the man of destiny—the
man who has been preparing himself sixteen years for
one great purpose. For Anglo - Egypt he is the

Mahdi, the expected; the man who has sifted experience and corrected error; who has worked at small
things and waited for great; marble to sit still and fire
to smite; steadfast, cold, and inflexible; the man who
has cut out his human heart and made himself a
machine to retake Khartum.

VII.

ARMS AND MEN.

THE campaign of 1897, which opened with General
Hunter's advance from Merawi on Abu Hamed,
ended with the occupation of the Nile valley as far
as Ed Damer, seven miles beyond the junction of that
river and the Atbara. At the beginning of March,
when I reached the front, the advanced post had
been withdrawn from Ed Damer, which had been
destroyed, and established at Fort Atbara in the
northern angle of the two rivers. Between that
point and Berber, twenty - three miles north, was
stationed the army with which it was proposed to
meet the threatened attack of Osman Digna and
Mahmud.

It was not possible to use the whole force at the
Sirdar's disposition for that purpose. The Anglo-
Egyptian strategical position was roughly a semi-
circle, with Omdurman and Khartum for a centre, so
that the Khalifa held the advantage of the interior.
The westward horn of the semicircle was the

garrisons of Dongola, Korti, and Merawi; the east-
ward that of Kassala. In advance of the regular
garrisons, friendly Arabs held a fan - shaped series
of intelligence posts in the Bayuda desert, and at
Adarama, Gos Redjeb and El Fasher on the upper
reaches of the Atbara. The Dervishes maintained
one desert post at Gebra to the north-west of Omdurman, and one to the north-east at Abu Delek. But
hemmed in as they were, they had the manifest
advantage that they could always strike at the newly
recovered province of Dongola by the various routes
across the Bayuda desert. So that Korti and Merawi
had to be garrisoned, as well as Kassala.

The garrisons, though they never so much as saw
the enemy, played, nevertheless, an indispensable part
in the Atbara campaign. The infantry of the force
immediately under the Sirdar's eye was divided into
four brigades—three Egyptian, one British. The division of the Egyptian army, counting three brigades,
was under the command of Major-General Archibald
Hunter.

If the Sirdar is the brain of the Egyptian army,
General Hunter is its sword-arm. First and above
everything, he is a fighter. For fourteen years he
has been in the front of all the fighting on the
Southern border. He was Intelligence Officer during the anxious days before Ginnis, when the
Camerons and 9th Sudanese were beset by triumphant dervishes in Kosheh fort, and reinforce-

ments were far to the northward. Going out on a
sortie one day, he lingered behind the retiring force
to pick off dervishes with a rifle he was wont to
carry on such occasions: there he received a wound
in the shoulder, which he is not quit of to-day.
When Nejumi came down in '89, Hunter was in
the front of everything: he fought all day at the
head of the blacks at Argin, and commanded a
brigade of them at Toski. Here he was again
wounded — a spear-thrust in the arm while he was
charging the thickest of the Dervishes at the head
of the 13th. Thereafter he was Governor of the
frontier at Halfa, Governor of the frontier at Dongola, Governor of the frontier at Berber—always on
the frontier. When there was fighting he always led
the way to it with his blacks, whom he loves like
children, and who love him like a father. Fourteen
years of bugle and bullet by night and day, in summer and winter, fighting Dervishes, Dervishes year in
and year out—till fighting Dervishes has come to be
a holy mission, pursued with a burning zeal akin to
fanaticism. Hunter Pasha is the crusader of the
nineteenth century.

In all he is and does he is the true knight-errant
—a paladin drifted into his wrong century. He is
one of those happy men whom nature has made all
in one piece—consistent, simple, unvarying; everything he does is just like him. He is short and thick-
set; but that, instead of making him unromantic, only

draws your eye to his long sword. From the feather in his helmet to the spurs on his heels, he is all energy and dancing triumph; every movement is vivacious, and he walks with his keen conquering hazel eye looking out and upward, like an eagle's. Sometimes you will see on his face a look of strain and tension, which tells of the wound he always carries with him. Then you will see him lolling under a palm-tree, while his staff are sitting on chairs; light-brown hair rumpled over his bare head, like a happy schoolboy. When I first saw him thus, being blind, I conceived him a subaltern, and offered opinions with indecorous freedom: he left the error to rebuke itself.

Reconnoitring almost alone up to the muzzles of the enemy's rifles, charging bare-headed and leading on his blacks, going without his rest to watch over the comfort of the wounded, he is always the same— always the same impossible hero of a book of chivalry. He is renowned as a brave man even among British officers: you know what that means. But he is much more than a tilting knight-errant; he is one of the finest leaders of troops in the army. Report has it that the Sirdar, knowing his worth, leaves the handling of the actual fighting largely to Hunter, and he never fails to plan and execute a masterly victory. A sound and brilliant general, you would say his one fault was his reckless daring; but that, too, in an army of semi-savages, is a necessary quality of generalship. Furthermore, they say he is

as good in an office as he is in action. Above all,
he can stir and captivate and lead men. "General
Archie" is the wonder and the darling of all the
Egyptian army. And when the time comes that
we want a new national hero, it may be he will be
the wonder and the darling of all the Empire also.

The First Brigade of Hunter's division was still
quartered in Berber. It consisted of the 9th Sudanese
under Walter Bey, 10th Sudanese (Nason Bey), 11th
Sudanese (Jackson Bey), and 2nd Egyptian (Pink
Bey). The brigadier was Lieutenant-Colonel Hector
Archibald Macdonald, one of the soundest soldiers in
the Egyptian or British armies. He had seen more
and more varied service than any man in the force.
Promoted from the ranks after repeated and con-
spicuous acts of gallantry in the Afghan war, he was
taken prisoner at Majuba Hill. He joined the Egyptian army in 1887, and commanded the 11th Sudanese
at Gemaizeh, Toski, and Afafit. At Gemaizeh the
11th, ever anxious to be at the enemy, broke its
formation; and it is said that Macdonald Bey, after
exhausting Arabic and Hindustani, turned in despair
to abusing them in broad Scots. Finally, he rode up
and down in front of their rifles, and at last got them
steady under a heavy fire from men who would far
rather have killed themselves than him. In the campaigns of '96 and '97 he was intrusted with a brigade;
he showed a rare gift for the handling of troops, and
wherever the fighting was hardest there was his

brigade to be found. In person, "old Mac"—he is under fifty, but anything above forty is elderly in the Egyptian army—is of middle height, but very broad,— so sturdily built that you might imagine him to be armour-plated under his clothes. He walks and rides with a resolute solidity bespeaking more strength than agility. He has been known to have fever, but never to be unfit for duty.

The Second Brigade also consisted of three Sudanese battalions and one Egyptian — the 12th, 13th, and 14th Sudanese (Townshend, Collinson, and Shekleton Beys), and the 8th Egyptian under Kiloussi Bey, a soldierly old Turk who was through the Russo-Turkish war. Lieutenant-Colonel Maxwell commanded it— an officer who has served in the Egyptian army through all its successes; big, masterful, keen, and reputed an especially able military administrator, he is but just entering middle age, and ought to have a brilliant career before him. This brigade was quartered at Essillem, about half-way between Berber and the Atbara.

At the Atbara was Lieutenant-Colonel Lewis with an all-Egyptian brigade — the 3rd, 4th, and 15th, under Sillem, Sparkes, and Hickman Beys, and the 7th under Fathy Bey, a big, smiling Egyptian of great energy and ability, a standing contradiction of the theory that a native Egyptian can never make a smart officer. The brigadier is one of the most popular officers in this or any other army. Colonel

Lewis's talents and abounding vitality would have
led him to distinction in any career. From the fact
that he is affectionately known as "Taffy," it may be
deduced that he is in whole or part a Welshman—
certainly he is richly dowered with the vivacity, the
energy, and the quickness of uptake of the Celt.
He treats his staff and subordinates like younger
brothers, and discipline never suffers. I have heard
him say that he is always talking, but he is also
always very much worth listening to. Finally, I
once went into a store in Berber and proposed to
buy tinned Brussels sprouts. "But are they fit to
eat?" I asked, in sudden doubt. "Oh yes, sir," cried
the unshaven Greek, with enthusiasm; "Lewis Bey
likes them very much."

Taking the strength of a battalion at 700 rifles,
each infantry brigade would number 2800 men. To
these we must add the cavalry under Lieutenant-
Colonel Broadwood, a rapid, adroit, and daring
leader: long-legged, light, built for a horseman, never
tired, never more than half asleep, never surprised,
never flurried, never slow, he is the ideal of a
cavalry general. The Egyptian trooper is a being
entirely unlike anything else in the world. What
miracles of patience and tact, toil and daring, have
been devoted to him will never be known; for the
men who did it will not tell. The eight squadrons,
with galloping Maxims, were at this time divided
between the three Egyptian camps. So were five

batteries of artillery, the command of which was with Lieutenant-Colonel Long—slow of speech, veiling a passionate tenderness for guns and a deadly knowledge of everything pertaining to them. Finally, there were two companies of camel corps with the Third Brigade. The whole strength of the Egyptian force would thus fall not very far short of 10,000 men, with 46 guns. Operating from Port Atbara were also three gunboats.

One mile north of the Second Brigade, Major-General Gatacre's British were encamped at Debeika. At this time it had only three battalions—the 1st Lincolnshire (10th) under Colonel Verner, 1st Cameron Highlanders (79th) under Colonel Money, and 1st Warwickshire (6th) under Lieutenant-Colonel Quayle-Jones. The 1st Seaforth Highlanders (72nd: Colonel Murray) were under orders, as we heard, to come up and complete the brigade. Besides the infantry, there was a battery of Maxims under Major Hunter-Blair. The brigade was as fine a one as you could well pick out of the army, whether for shooting, average of service, or strength. Two companies of the Warwicks had been sent, to their despair, to Merawi; but even so the strength of the brigade must have been over 2500.

General Gatacre came up with a great reputation, which he seized every occasion to increase. His one overmastering quality is tireless, abounding, almost superhuman energy. From the moment he is first

out of his hut at reveille to the time when he goes
nodding from mess to bed at nine, he seems possessed
by a demon that whips him ever into activity. Of
middle height and lightly built, his body is all steel
wire. As a man he radiates a gentle, serious courtesy.
As a general, if he has a fault it lies on the side of
not leaving enough to his subordinates. Restless
brain and body will ever be at something new—
working out a formation, riding hours across country
looking for a camp, devising means to get through a
zariba, personally superintending the making of a
road, addressing the men after church parade every
Sunday. In the ranks they call him "General
Back-acher," and love him. "He *is* the soldier's
general," I have heard rapturous Tommy exclaim,
when the brigadier has been satisfying himself in
person that nobody wanted for what could be
obtained. Later on in the campaign some thought
he drove his officers and men a little hard. But
whatever he asked of them in labour and discomfort
he was always ready to double and treble for himself.

This, then, was the Sirdar's command—a total of
12,000 to 13,000 men, with 52 guns. The Seaforths
might be expected to add about 1000 more. All
numbers, I should here remark, are based on the
roughest estimates, as, by the Sirdar's wish, they were
never stated publicly. In any case, there was not much
doubt that the force was sufficient to account hand-

somely for anything that was likely to come against
it. Whether the dervishes were even coming at
all was not at this time very certain. It was known
that Mahmud had taken over his force from
Metemmeh, which had hitherto been his headquarters, to join Osman Digna at Shendi on the
eastern bank. That was evidence that the attack,
if it was coming, would fall on us rather than the
Merawi side. Osman's men, it was further reported,
had begun to drift northward in detachments; though
whether this meant business or not it was hard to
say. It seemed difficult to believe that they had let
Berber alone last autumn and winter when it was
weakly garrisoned, only to attack now, when attack
must mean annihilation. But you must remember
the peculiarities of Arab information. The ordinary
Arab spy is as incurious about figures as the Sirdar
himself could desire; "few" and "very few," "many"
and "very many," are his nearest guesses at a total.
It was not at all certain that Mahmud and Osman,
though they probably knew that reinforcements had
come up, had the vaguest idea of the real strength of
the force.

Finally, said those who remembered, this was just
like Toski over again. Whispers and whispers for
months that the horde was coming; disappointment
and disappointment; and then, just when doubt was
becoming security and the attempt madness, a head-

long rush upon inevitable destruction. Such follies
issue from the very nature of the Mahdist polity
—a jealous ill-informed despot safe at Omdurman
and ill-supplied Emirs apprehensive at the front.
Therefore we hoped for the best. What their force
might be, of course we knew hardly better than
they knew ours. It might be 10,000, or 15,000, or
20,000.

If they came they would fight: that was certain.
How they would fight we knew not. It depended
on Mahmud. Osman Digna has become a common-
place of Sudanese warfare—a man who has never
shown himself eminent either for personal courage
or for generalship, yet obviously a man of great
ability, since by evasive cunning and dogged persistence he has given us more trouble than all the
other Emirs together. His own tribe, the Hadendowa,
the most furious warriors of Africa, are long since
reconciled with the Government, and have resumed
their old trade of caravan-leading. That Osman
struggles on might fancifully be traced to his strain
of Turkish blood, contributing a steadfastness of
purpose seldom found in the out-and-out barbarian. He has become a fat old toad now, they
say, and always leaves fights at an early stage for
private prayer; yet he is still as much alive as
when he threw up a position on the Suakim
County Council to join the Expected Mahdi, and

you cannot but half admire the rascal's persistence in his evil ways.

Had Osman been in command, he doubtless knew too much to risk a general engagement. But it seemed that the direction of things lay mainly with Mahmud. And of Mahmud, but for the facts that he was a social favourite in Omdurman, was comparatively young, and had wiped out the Jaalin for the Khalifa, nobody — except probably Colonel Wingate — knew anything at all.

Whatever there was to know, Colonel Wingate surely knew it, for he makes it his business to know everything. He is the type of the learned soldier, in which perhaps our army is not so strong as it is on other sides. If he had not chosen to be Chief of the Intelligence Department of the Egyptian Army, he might have been Professor of Oriental Languages at Oxford. He will learn you any language you like to name in three months. As for that mysterious child of lies, the Arab, Colonel Wingate can converse with him for hours, and at the end know not only how much truth he has told, but exactly what truth he has suppressed. He is the intellectual, as the Sirdar is the practical, compendium of British dealings with the Sudan. With that he is himself the most practical of men, and few realise how largely it is due to the system of native intelligence he has organised, that operations in the Sudan are now certain and unsurprised instead of vague, as they once were. Nothing is hid from Colonel Wingate, whether in Cairo or at the Court of Menelik, or on the shores of Lake Chad. As a press censor he has only one fault. He is so indispensable to the Sirdar that you can seldom get speech of him. His rise in the army has been almost startlingly rapid; yet there is not a man in it but, so far from envying, rejoices in a success earned by rare gifts and unstinted labour, and borne with an inviolable modesty.

VIII.

IN THE BRITISH CAMP.

BEYOND doubt it was a great march. If only there had been a fight immediately at the farther end of it, it would have gone down as one of the great forced-marches of history.

News came to Abu Dis of Mahmud and Osman Digna's advance on a Friday afternoon, February 25; the men were just back from a sixteen - mile, seven-and-a-half-hour route-march in the desert. By eight next morning the last detachment had been conveyed by train to rail-head, which had been moved on past their camp to Surek; by ten at night the brigade was on the march. They marched all night; in the early morning came a telegram bidding them hasten, and they marched on under the Sudan sun into the afternoon. A short halt, and at three on Monday morning they were off again. At ten that night they got into Geneineteh, and were out again by three next morning. Six hours' march, seven hours' halt, eight hours' march again, and they were

close to Berber. And there they learned that the
Dervishes had after all not arrived. A halt of twenty-
four hours outside Berber rather damaged the record;
but that was better than damaging the troops. Not
but that they were quite ready to go on; it was by
the Sirdar that the halt was ordered. They reached
Berber—cheering blacks lining two miles of road, and
massed bands playing the Cameron men, and the
Lincolnshire poacher, and Warwickshire lads, and
especially a good breakfast for everybody — and
marched through to their camp ten miles beyond.

They started out on Saturday night, February 26;
they reached camp on Thursday evening, March 3.
Altogether they made 118 miles within five days—
four, if you leave out the day's halt—or 134 in five
and a half, if you also add the route-march; con-
tinuously they did 98 miles within three days.

That is marching. Furthermore, it was marching
under nearly all conditions that make marching a
weariness. In India troops on the march have a
host of camp-followers to do the hard and disagree-
able work. Of course, you and I could easily walk
twenty-five miles a day for as long as anybody liked
to name. But how would you like to try it with kit
and rifle and a hundred rounds of ammunition? Also,
when you did halt, how would you like to have to
set to work getting wood to make your fire and water
to cook your dinner? How would you like to march
with baggage-camels, so slow that they poach all your

sleep? Especially, how would you like to be a cook
—to come in tired and sweating, hungry and thirsty,
and then stand out in the sun preparing dinner for
your comrades? On the first three days' march some
of the cooks got no more than four hours' sleep, and
had to be relieved lest they dropped at their posts;
few of the officers got more. Plenty of men went to
sleep while marching; others dropped with weariness
and vigil, like a boxer knocked stupid in a fight. One
subaltern, being with baggage in the rear-guard, fell
off his camel without noticing it, and went on peacefully slumbering in the sand. He woke up some time
in the dead of night, and of course had not the vaguest
idea where the army had gone to or in which direction he ought to follow it. He had hung his helmet
and belts on the camel, which of course had gone on
composedly, only glad to get rid of him. He was
picked up by a man who was looking for somebody
else.

A gunner in the Maxim battery had a worse time.
He too dropped asleep, and woke up to find himself
alone. He found himself near the river, and went
on to overtake the force. Only unluckily—so magnificently unreasoning can the British soldier sometimes be — he followed down the stream instead of
up. On top of that, he conceived an idea that he
was in the enemy's country, with prowling dervishes
ambushed behind every mimosa bush. So that while
search parties quested for him by day, he carefully

hid himself, and at night pushed on again towards Cairo. It was several days before he was
picked up.

All these are inevitable accompaniments of a forced
march; what might have been avoided, and should
have been, was the scandal that the men's boots gave
out. True, the brigade had done a lot of marching
since it came up-country, some of it—not much—
over rock and loose sand. True, also, that the Sudan
climate, destructive of all things, is particularly destructive of all things stitched. But the brigade had
only been up-river about a month, after all, and no
military boot ought to wear out in a month. We
have been campaigning in the Sudan, off and on, for
over fourteen years; we might have discovered the
little peculiarities of its climate by now. The Egyptian
army uses a riveted boot; the boots our British boys
were expected to march in had not even a toe-cap.
So that when the three battalions and a battery
arrived in Berber hundreds of men were all but barefoot: the soles peeled off, and instead of a solid double
sole, revealed a layer of shoddy packing sandwiched
between two thin slices of leather. Not one man fell
out sick; those who dropped asleep went on as soon
as they came to, and overtook their regiments. But
every available camel was burdened with a man who
lacked nothing of strength or courage to march on—
only boots. General Gatacre had half-a-dozen chargers;
every one was carrying a bare-footed soldier, while

the general trudged with his men. All the mounted officers did the same.

It is always the same story—knavery and slackness clogging and strangling the best efforts of the British soldier. To save some contractor a few pence on a boot, or to save some War Office clerk a few hours of the work he is paid for not doing, you stand to lose a good rifle and bayonet in a decisive battle, and to break a good man's heart into the bargain. Is it worth it? But it is always happening; the history of the Army is a string of such disgraces. And each time we arise and bawl, "Somebody ought to be hanged." So says everybody. But nobody ever is hanged.[1]

[1] A certain stir followed the publication of these criticisms in England, penetrating as far as the House of Commons, and even the War Office. The official reply to them was in effect that the boots were very good boots, only that the work done by the brigade over bad ground had tried them too severely. It is a strange sort of answer to say that a military boot is a very good boot, only you mustn't march in it. Having walked myself over most of the same ground as General Gatacre's brigade, I am able to say that, while there is a good deal of rock and loose sand, the greater part of the going is hard sand or gravel. The boots I wore myself I have on at the moment of writing, as sound as ever.

It is possible that the War Office is right, and that for other purposes in other countries the boots supplied were very good boots. But in the Sudan, what with the drought and the fine cutting sand, everything in stitched leather goes to pieces with heart-breaking rapidity. It is to be presumed that our authorities could have discovered this fact: in the Egyptian army it is known perfectly well.

After Mr Powell Williams had more than once implied in the House that there was no foundation for the criticisms in the text,

That these men came so sturdily through the test
stands to everybody's credit, but especially their
brigadier's. From the day he took up his command
General Gatacre set to work to make his men hard.
Amazing stories floated down to Halfa, rebuking us
with the stern simplicity of life at rail-head—no drink,
perpetual marching, sleep every night in your boots.
The general, we heard, had even avowed that he meant
to teach his men to march twenty miles without water-
bottles. He would merely halt them from time to
time and water them—most wisely, since the soldier
either swigs down all his water in the first hour, and
is cooked for the rest of the day, or else, if he thinks
he is in for a short march, pours the confounded thing
out on the sand to lighten it. A most wise thing—
if you can do it. For some of the old inhabitants
of the Sudan shook their heads when they heard such
tales. "He'll get 'em stale," said they; "wait till the
hot weather; in this country you must make yourself
comfortable." They were probably right—they knew;
and for myself, I intended to give comfort the fullest
possible trial. But so far the fact stood that the

Lord Lansdowne, in his speech announcing the proposed transmogri-
fication of the Army Medical Services, gave away the War Office's
case in the following terms: "The Egyptian campaign had brought
to light one weak point which we could not afford to ignore. The
Army boot, although a good boot, was apparently unsuited to resist
the peculiar and insidious action of the desert sand. . . . He
trusted they would be able to invent a boot which even General
Gatacre and the desert sand would not be able to wear out."
—('Daily Mail' Report, May 5.)

British had done their work brilliantly, and that their brigadier trained them to it.

When my camel padded into their camp by moonlight the day's work was done, and they were going to sleep. You came to the camp through a tangle of thick mimosa; a zariba of the same impossible thorns was heaped up all round it; the men were quartered along the river overlooking the foreshore. There was only time to be grateful for supper, and a blanket spread under the lee of a straw-plaited hut. Next thing I knew reveille was sounding, at a quarter past five. Directly on the sound stepped out the general—middle height, build for lightness and toughness together, elastic energy in the set of each limb, and in the keen, grave face a determined purpose to be equal to responsibility. He stayed to drink a cup of cocoa, and then mounted, and was away with his aide-de-camp; General Gatacre's aide-de-camp requires to be a hard man. When breakfast-time came the general was nowhere in camp, nor was he an hour later, nor an hour later still. He had just taken a little twenty-five mile scamper to look out a new site for his camp.

At reveille the camp had suddenly turned from dead to alive. You heard hoarse orders, and the ring of perpetual bugles. The dry air of the Sudan cracks the buglers' lips, as it does everybody else's; to keep them supple they were practising incessantly, so that the brigade is wrapped in bugling best part of the day. To-day it was also wrapped in something else.

It seemed to me that daylight was very long in coming—that lines of khaki figures seemed to pass to and fro in an unlifting mist. But that was only for the first few sleepy moments. As the north wind got up with the sun it soon became very plain what was the matter.

Dust! The camp was on land which had once been cultivated, black cotton land; and black cotton land when the wind blows is neither wholesome nor agreeable. It rose off the ground till the place was like London in a fog. On the horizon it lowered like thunder-clouds; close about you it whirled up like pepper when the lid of the castor comes off. You felt it, breathed it, smelt it, tasted it. It choked eyes and nose and ears, and you ground it between your teeth. After a few hours of it you forgot what being a man was like; you were merely clogging into a lump of Sudan.

It was a bad mistake to pitch on such a spot; and when you came to walk round the camp you saw how ill-equipped were the men to put up with it. Their heavy baggage—officers' and men's alike—had been left at rail-head; over 2500 men had come with 700 camels. The tents had arrived, but they were only just being unloaded from the steamer. The men were huddled under blankets stretched on four sticks; of the officers, some had tents, others sat in tiny elbow-squeezing tukls (huts of straw or rushes), such as the prophet Jonah would not have exchanged for his gourd. There was hardly a shelter in the camp in which a man could stand upright. One or two good tukls had been built—wooden posts with beams lashed across them, and mats or coarse stems of halfa grass plaited between. But, taking the place as a whole, it was impossible to be comfortable, and especially impossible to be clean.

It was nobody's fault in particular, and in this good weather it did not particularly matter. It happened not to have begun stoking up at the time; when it likes it can be mid-summer in March. When it did begin, and especially if it came to a matter of summer quarters, such a camp as Debeika was an invitation to disease and death. You have to learn the Sudan's ways, they say, if you do not want the Sudan to eat you alive. The British brigade had to learn. Sure enough the Sirdar came to inspect it the day after, and on March 11 the brigade shifted camp to the empty and relatively clean village of Darmali, two miles higher up the river.

IX.

FORT ATBARA.

IT needed only half a look at the Egyptian camp to convince you how much the British had to learn. The hospitable dinner-table was quite enough. In accordance with a detestable habit which I intend to correct in future, I arrived late for dinner : it was the fault of the camels, the camel-men, the servants, the guide, my companions, the country, and the weather. None the less kindly was I set down at table and ate of soup and fish, of ragout and fresh mutton and game, and was invited to drink hock, claret, champagne, whisky, gin, lime-juice, ginger-beer, Rosbach, and cognac, or any combination or permutation of the same. I was the guest of men who have been on the Sudan frontier for anything up to fifteen years, during which time they have learned the Sudan's ways and overcome its inhospitality.

As soon as everybody began to show signs of falling asleep at table—which hot days begun at four or five in the morning and worked hard through till half-past

seven soon lead you to consider the most natural
phenomenon in the world—I went to bed under a
roof.   The owner of the tukl was up the river, off
Shendi, on a gunboat.   His house was palatially built
with painted beams from the spoils of a raid on
Metemmeh, and plaited with palm‑leaf and halfa
grass.   Other officers preferred their tents; but the
insides of these were sunk anything from one foot to
four underground, the excavation neatly backed with
dried Nile mud, so that a ten‑foot tent became a lofty
and airy apartment.   The last thing I saw was a vast
upstanding oblong tukl, which looked capable of holding a company.   I was told it was the house of the
mess-servants of one Egyptian battalion.   It was more
palatial than all the edifices in the British camp put
together.

In the morning it was blowing a sand-storm, and
Englishmen's eyes showed bloodshot through blue
spectacles.   It was gritty between the teeth, and to
walk up wind spelt blindness; yet it was clean sand,
and did not form soil in the mouth like the black
dust of Debeika.   In the early morning Fort Atbara
appeared through the driving cloud as through smoked
glass — a long walled camp, with its southern apex
resting on the junction of Nile and Atbara.   To find
so strong a place in the lately won wilderness was
a revelation, not of English energy, which is understood, but of Egyptian industry.   The wall was over
six feet high, firmly built of sun-dried mud; round it

had been a six-foot ditch, only the importunate sand
had already half silted it up again.   On the inside
was a parapet, gun platforms with a couple of carefully clothed Maxims in each, a couple of guard-houses
at the two main gates and a couple of blockhouses
outside.   Across the Atbara was a small fort; at the
angle of the rivers a covered casemate gallery that
would accommodate half a company precluded any
attempt to turn the wall and attack from the fore-
shore.   On the other side of the Nile was a smaller
fort, walled and ditched likewise.   In the inside
straddled a crow's nest—built also with painted beams
from Mahmud's house in Metemmeh—with a view that
reached miles up both rivers.   A couple of miles up
the Atbara you could see dense mimosa thickets; so
much of the bank as could get water has dropped
back almost to virgin forest in the fourteen years of
dervish devilry.   But under the walls of Fort Atbara
was neither mimosa nor Sodom apple nor any kind
of scrub.   Only a forest of stumps showed where the
field of fire had been cleared—over a mile in every
direction.   Upright and regular among the stumps
you could see a row of stakes; each marked a range
of 100 yards up to 500: the Egyptian soldier was
to hold his fire up to that and gain confidence by
seeing his enemy go down.   Best of all, the fort, though
it dominated the country for miles, was itself hardly
visible.   From the ridge of the desert a mile away it
was a few trees, the yardarms of a few sailing barges,

and a shelter trench.   The whole dervish army might
easily have been persuaded to run their heads on it;
but they might have butted in vain against Fort
Atbara till there was not one of them left standing.

The whole of this work had been made by the men
who garrisoned it.   There were none but Fellahin
regiments in Fort Atbara; but the Egyptian soldier
on fatigue duty is the finest soldier in the world.
In a population of ten millions the conscription
only asks for 20,000 men or so, and it can afford to
pick and choose.   In face the fellah soldier is a shade
sullen, not to say blackguardly; in body he would be
a joy to a sculptor.   Shorter than the taller tribes of
blacks, taller than the shorter, he is far better built
all round.   When he strips at bathing-time—for like
all riverine peoples he is more clean than bashful—the
bank is lined with studies for Hercules.   And all the
thews he has he puts into his work.   Work is the
fellah's idea of life, especially work with his native
mud: the fatigue which other soldiers incline to
resent as not part of their proper business he takes to
most kindly of all his soldiering.   Marching, digging,
damming, brick-making, building, tree-felling—you can
never find him unwilling nor leave him exhausted.   He
is the ideal soldier-of-all-work, true son of a country
where human hand-labour has always beaten the
machine.

The troops were housed either in post-and-straw
tukls or in tents; but already a vast mud-brick

SKETCH MAP OF THE NILE AND ATBARA
TO ILLUSTRATE THE OPERATIONS AGAINST MAHMOUD

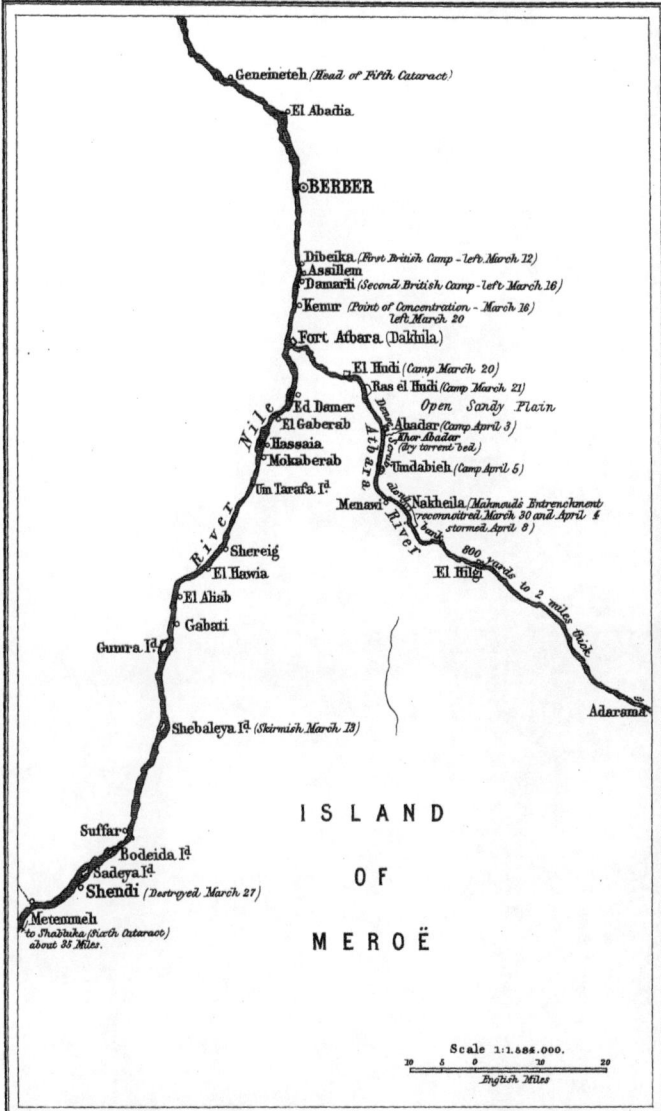

Geneineteh (Head of Fifth Cataract)

El Abadia

BERBER

Dibeika (First British Camp – left March 12)
Assillem
Damarli (Second British Camp – left March 16)
Kenur (Point of Concentration – March 16)
left March 20

Fort Atbara (Dakhila)

El Hudi (Camp March 20)
Ras el Hudi (Camp March 21)

Open Sandy Plain

Ed Damer
El Gaberab
Abadar (Camp April 3)
Khor Abadar
(Dry torrent bed)
Hassaia
Mokaberab
Umdabieh (Camp April 5)

Um Tarafa Id
Menawi
Nakheila (Mahmoud's Entrenchment
reconnoitred March 30 and April 4
stormed April 8)

Nile River

Atbara River

Shereig
El Hawia
El Hilgi   800 yards to 2 miles thick

El Aliab
Gabati

Gumra Id

Adarama

Shebaleya Id (Skirmish March 13)

ISLAND

Suffar
Bodeida Id
Sadeya Id   OF
Shendi (Destroyed March 27)

Metemmeh
to Shabluka (Sixth Cataract)   MEROË
about 35 Miles.

Scale 1:1,584,000.
20 5 0   10   20
English Miles

The Edinburgh Geographical Institute   John Bartholomew & Co.

barrack stretched its skeleton across the camp.
Along the foreshore the mud huts were hospital or
officers' quarters or mess-houses. Already one big
straw tukl was a *café*, where enterprising Greeks had
set up a soda-water machine and instituted a *diner du
jour*. And down on the beach the cluster of slim-
sparred gyassas and the little street of box-and-mat
built Greek shops marked the beginning of a town.
As railway terminus, for this year at present, an
American might almost call it the queen city of the
Sudan. Only for the present it must be a city without native population ; for the inhabitants of this reach
are very few, and subsist on precarious subsidies paid
them for protecting each other against the raids of
the dervish.

Among the craft at the riverside the first you
noticed was the gunboat. White, with tall black
funnel amidships, deck above deck and platform top-
ping platform, it looked more like a building than a
warship. But for all their many storeys these gunboats draw only some two feet of water, while the
loftiness of the gun-platforms enables them to search
the highest bank at the lowest state of Nile. Ahead
on the uppermost deck points the hungry muzzle of
a gun ; there are a couple more amidships, and a
couple of Maxims on a dizzy shaking platform higher
yet.

The war fleet at this time counted three stern-
wheelers—the *Zafir* (Commander Keppel, R.N.), *Fatha*

(Lieutenant Beatty, R.N.), and *Nasa* (Lieutenant Hood,
R.N.) Three more—the *Malik* (King), *Sultan,* and
Sheikh—were down the river, waiting for their sections to be put together against high Nile. Fort
Atbara was the Portsmouth of the Sudan: one of
Captain Keppel's squadron always lay there, taking
a week in its turn to rest and repair anything
needful. The other two would be always up the
river—one cruising off Shendi, and the other patrolling the seventy miles of river between. If necessary the boats could run past Shendi, forty miles
more, to Shabluka, so that they acted as reconnoitring
parties more than a hundred miles from the most
advanced military post.

Naval operations have played a part in Sudan
warfare ever since Gordon's time: was not "the
Admiral" himself on Beresford's *Zafir* through those
famous-infamous days which saw the tantalising
tragedy of Khartum? Here, as elsewhere, the
Sirdar has gathered up the experience of the past
and brought it to full development. Everybody told
him that he would never get the gunboats over the
Fourth Cataract: a general who had been there in
the Wolseley days delivered a lecture demonstrating
unmercifully the mad impossibility of the scheme. A
day or two after the Sirdar sent the boats over. To
be sure one turned turtle in the attempt, and a naval
lieutenant was fished out three-quarters drowned, and

two Egyptians had to be cut out through the bottom
of the boat.   Yet here were three vessels steaming up
and down unperturbed, right under Mahmud's nose.
The value of their services it would be quite impossible to exaggerate : they were worth all the rest of the
Intelligence Department put together.   From their
reports it was known that the dervishes had crossed to
Shendi and were coming down the river.   Moreover,
you may imagine that officers of her Majesty's navy did
not confine their activity to looking on.   A day or two
before this Mahmud had been transferring his war
material in barges from Metemmeh to Shendi.
Knowing the ways of "the devils," as they amiably
call the gunboats, he had entrenched a couple of hundred riflemen to cover the crossing.   But one boat
steamed cheerfully up to the bank and turned on the
Maxims, while the other sunk one nuggar and captured
two.   A fourth lay in quite shallow water under the
very muzzles of the dervish rifles.   But on each boat
are carried about half a company of Egyptian troops
with a white officer.   While the Maxims poppled
away above them, the detachment—it was of the 15th
Egyptians on this occasion—landed and cut out the
nuggar before its owners' eyes.   With men capable of
such things as this about on the river, it was only by
drilling a hole in the bottom of their boats and sinking them during the day that the dervishes could
keep any craft to cross the river in at all.

F

The second day at Fort Atbara I stepped out after lunch, and there were two white sweltering gunboats instead of one. Everybody who had nothing else to do hurried as fast as the heat would let them down to the river. There the first thing they saw was an angareb being laboriously guided ashore by four native soldiers: on it lay a white man. He was a sergeant of marines, shot in the leg while directing the fire of the forward Maxim. "The devils have hit me," they said he cried out, with justly indignant surprise as he felt the bullet, then jumped to the gun and turned it himself on the quarter the shot came from. That was in the early morning; now he was very pale and a little limp, but smiling. Then came down the doctor hastily. "Didn't I say he wasn't to be brought ashore?" he said. "All right, sir," answered the wounded man, still resolutely smiling; "I expect I'm in for hospital anyhow." And away to hospital they bore him, for the boat would be up river again by dawn the next day.

Meantime the detachment of soldiers were stepping ashore with cheerful grins. It was easy to see how valuable was this gunboat work in giving the Egyptians confidence. True, they had lost one man wounded and had a few chips knocked off the stern-wheel; but had they not landed at Aliab—thirty miles from Fort Atbara—driven off the dervishes, and captured donkeys and loot? The loot was being unladen at the moment—an angareb or two and odd garments, especially many bundles of rough riverside hay. "Take that up to my old horse," said the lieutenant in command, satisfaction in his tones. "Is there any polo this afternoon?"

It was hard to say whether this work best suited the young naval officer or the young naval officer best suited the work. Steaming up and down the river in command of a ship of his own, bombarding here, reconnoitring there, landing elsewhere for a brush with the dervishes, and then again a little way farther to pick up loot,—the work had all the charm of war and blockade-running and poaching combined. If a dervish shell did happen to smash the wheel where would the boat be, perhaps seventy miles from any help? It was said the Sirdar was a little nervous about them, and to my inexperience it was a perpetual wonder that the boats came back from every trip. But somehow, thanks to just a dash of caution in their audacity, they always did come back. Impudently daring in attack, with a happy eye to catch the latest moment for retreat, they were just the cutting-out heroes of one's youth come to life. They might have walked straight out of the 'Boy's Own Paper.'

Every returning boat brought fresh news of the advance. Dervishes at Aliab, even if not in force, could not but mean a movement towards attack. It was quite impossible to wear out the hospitality of

Fort Atbara, but duty began to wonder what the rest of the army was doing. So I recaptured my camel—peacefully grazing in the nearest area of dervish raid, and very angry at being called on to work after three days of idleness—and bumped away north towards Berber.

X.

THE MARCH OUT.

ALAS for the Berber season—for the sprightly promise of its budding, the swift tragedy of its blight!

It would have been the most brilliant social year the town has ever known. Berber is peculiarly fitted for fashionable display: its central street would hold four Regent Streets abreast, and the low mud walls, with one-storeyed mud-houses just peeping over them, make it look wider yet. On this magnificent avenue the merchant princes of Berber display their rich emporia. Mortimer, Angelo, Walker, and half-a-dozen ending in -poulo, had brought caravans over the desert from Suakim, until you could buy oysters and asparagus, table-napkins and brilliantine, in the middle of the Sudan. Then there are the *cafés,*— "Officers' Club and Mineral Waters" is the usual title of a Sudan *café,*—where you could drink mastik and kinds of whisky, and listen to limpid streams of modern Greek from the mouths of elegants who shave twice and even three times a-week. There at sun-

down sat the native officers on chairs before the door,
every breast bright with the ribbons of hard victorious
campaigns, talking their ancestral Turkish and drinking drinks not contemplated by the Koran.   There
were five regiments in garrison, and more outside;
the town was alive with generals, and the band played
nightly to the Sirdar's dinner.

There was flavour in the sensation of sitting at
dinner under the half-daylight of the tropic moon,
kicking up black-brown sand, looking into a little
yard with an unfenced sixty-foot undrinkable well in
one corner and a heat-seamed mud wall all round it,
and listening to a full military orchestra wailing for
the Swanee Ribber, or giggling over the sorrows of
Mr Gus Elen's friend, who somehow never felt 'isself
at 'ome.   For myself, I was just beginning to be very
much at home indeed.   It was a splendid house to
share among three, one of the most palatial in Berber
—two rooms as high as an English double-storeyed
villa, doorway you could drive a hansom through, two
window-holes in one room and one in the other, bricks
of the finest quality of Nile mud, and roof of mats
that never let in a single sunbeam.   A fine house; and
we had further embellished it with two tables—they
cost a couple of pounds apiece, timber and carpenters
being scarce in Berber—five shelves, a peg, and eight
cane-bottomed bedroom chairs, brought across the
desert in sections.   In a fortnight our entertainments
would have been the talk of Berber, and now——

To-night the High Street was as bare and bald, Berber as desolate and forlorn, as old Berber itself. Old Berber, you must know, is the Berber which was before the Mahdists came and took it and besomed it with three days' massacre. It stands, or totters, some half mile south of the present dervish-built town. Palms spread their sunshades over it, and it is embosomed in the purple-pink flower, white-green bush, and yellow-green fruit of Sodom apples. At a distance it is cool luxury; ride into it, and it is only the sun-dried skeleton of a city. In what was once the bazaar the bones are thickest: here are the empty sockets out of which looked the little shops—all silent, crumbling, and broken. Altogether there are acres and acres of Old Berber—quite dead and falling away, not a single soul in the whole desolation. But when the Egyptian army first came last year there were bodies—bodies left thirteen years unburied, and dry wounds yawning for vengeance.

New Berber to-day was hardly less forlorn. On the morning of March 15, the few passengers down the High Street all carried arms. Here was a man on a fleet camel: he would have sold it the day before for £20; now no price would tempt his Arab covetousness into parting with his possible salvation. Here strode a tall man with white gown kilted up above black legs: he carried a Remington rifle, and with his free hand pushed before him a donkey bearing a bundle and a bed. An angareb is the first

luxury of the Sudan: Egyptian soldiers, when angarebs are looted, can hardly be restrained from
taking them away on their backs. This man was
removing wardrobe and furniture together on one
donkey. Down at the riverside every boat was busy;
the natives were crossing over to the islands and to
the western bank. Down at the landing-stage, three
miles north of the town, where the hospital was and
the post-office, and whither the telegraph was now
removed, the 1st Battalion, now to form all the garrison of Berber, was building a fort.

And in their stores and *cafés* in the High Street,
with twitching faces, sat the Greeks. They explained
in half-voices that they could not move their stock
because they had 400 camel-loads, and there were not
ten camels to be bought in all Berber. They com-
mented on the strange strategy that aims at beating
the enemy rather than at protecting property. They
even made a deputation to the Sirdar on the point;
but his Excellency pursued his own plan, and merely
served out Remingtons to the traders. Whereat the
Greeks pointed out that the rifles and a few cases of
wine and tinned meat against their doors would make
them impregnable; and then fell to twitching again.

What it was all about, nobody among the outsiders
knew. But we presumed that the gradual crescendo
of intelligence as to the dervish advance had resulted
in the decision that it was better to be in position too
early than too late. The Sirdar left early on the 15th;

the greater part of the garrison—Macdonald's fighting
brigade of blacks—had cleared the town the evening
before and marched for Kenur, the point of concentration, when the moon rose at one in the morning.
I saw the start of the 9th, the first black battalion
raised; and fine as are many of our British regiments,
these made them look very small. The Sudanese
battalions, as has been said, are enlisted for life, and
every black, wherever he may be found, is liable, as
such, for service. I have seen a man who was with
Maximilian in Mexico, in the Russo - Turkish War,
across Africa with Stanley, and in all the later
Egyptian campaigns, and who marches with his
regiment yet. However old the black may be, he
has the curious faculty of always looking about eighteen: only when you thrust your eyes right in his
face do you notice that he is a wrinkled great-grand-
father of eighty. But always he stands as straight as
a lance.

Not that the 9th average that age, I take it; or if
they do, it does not matter. Their height must
average easily over six feet. They are willowy in
figure, and their legs run to spindle-shanks, almost
ridiculously; yet as they formed up on parade they
moved not only with the scope that comes from
length of limb, but the snap of self - controlled
strength as well.

They love their soldiering, do the blacks, and take it
very seriously. When they stood at attention they

might have been rows of black marble statues, all
alike as in the ancient temples, filling up the little
square of crumbling mud walls with a hole in its
corner, so typical of the Berber landscape. Then the
English colonel snapped out something Turkish: in an
instant the lines of each company had become fours;
all turned with a click; the band crashed out a
march—barbaric Ethiopian, darky American, or English music-hall, it is all the same to the blacks—and
out swung the regiment. They moved off by companies through a narrow alley, and there lay four new-
killed goats, the sand lapping their blood. Every
officer rode, every man stepped, over the luck token;
they would never go out to fight without it. Then
out into the main street, every man stepping like a
conqueror, the band blaring war at their head; with
each company a little flag—blue, black, white, amber,
or green, or vermilion—on a spear, and half-way down
the column the colour the Camerons gave them when
they shared the glory of Ginnis. Boys trailed behind
them, and their women, running to keep up, shot after
them the thin screams that kindle Sudanese to victory.
A black has been known to kill himself because his
wife called him a coward. To me the sight of that
magnificent regiment was a revelation. One has got
accustomed to associate a black skin with something
either slavish or comical. From their faces these men
might have been loafing darkies in South Carolina or
minstrels in St James's Hall. But in the smartness

of every movement, in the pride of every private's bearing, what a wonderful difference! This was quite a new kind of black—every man a warrior from his youth up. "Lu-u-u, lu-u-u," piped the women; the men held up their heads and made no sound, but you could see the answer to that appeal quivering all down the column. For "we," they say, "are like the English; we are not afraid."

And is it not good to think, ladies and gentlemen, as you walk in Piccadilly or the Mile End Road, that every one of these niggers honestly believes that to be English and to know fear are two things never heard of together? Utterly fearless themselves, savages brought up to think death in battle the natural lot of man, far preferable to defeat or disgrace, they have lived with English officers and English sergeants, through years of war and pestilence, and never seen any sign that these are not as contemptuous of death as themselves. They have seen many Englishmen die; they have never seen an Englishman show fear.

XI.

THE CONCENTRATION.

AT the time I was disposed to blame the Mess Presi-
dent, but on calm reflection I see that the fault lay
with the nature of the Arab. We knew that the
Sirdar was to start early on the 15th on the eighteen-
mile ride to Kenur, and it was our purpose to travel
shortly behind him. The only restrictions, I may say
at once, laid upon correspondents during this campaign
were that they were not to go out on reconnaissances,
and especially not to go near the Sirdar. They were
advised not to stand in front of the firing line during
general actions, but even this was not insisted upon.
It did indeed require a fair deal of tact and agility to
keep out of the Sirdar's eye, since his Excellency had
a wearing habit of always appearing at any point
where there was anything of interest going on. But
practice soon brought proficiency, and for the rest the
correspondent, except when he had to work, enjoyed
by far the most enviable position in the army.

Therefore we had planned to start as soon as the

Sirdar was out of sight, and arrive just after he had disappeared into his quarters. We rose up at five and gloomily began to dismantle our home. We carted the tables and the chairs into the yard; we tore down the very shelves: who could tell when they would not be useful? By seven breakfast was over; the horses and camels were grouped around our door in the High Street; the bags and cases were fastened up and lying each on the right side of its right camel. There was nothing left but the chairs and the tables and the shelves and a bucket, and the breakfast things and a case to put them in. At eight I went out to see how things were looking; they were looking exactly the same, a question of precedence having arisen as to whose duty it was to wash up. At nine they were still the same, and we expostulated with the men: they said they were just ready. At ten the chairs and tables and breakfast things and camels were still lying about, and the men had disappeared. At eleven they had not returned. At twelve they condescended to return, and, adjourning the question of washing up, began packing the breakfast things dirty. At this point each man separately was called a dog, fined a pound, and promised fifty lashes. They received the judgment with surprised and wounded but respectful expostulation: what had they done? They had merely been in the bazaar a very little while, O thou Excellency, to buy food. By this time we were getting hungry; so, rather than delay the loading up, we went

to a Greek *café* and lunched on ptomained sardines
and vinegar out of a Graves bottle. When we got
back things were exactly as we had left them: the
men suavely explained that they had been lunching
too. At last at half-past one every camel had been
loaded and stood up; and then it was discovered that
all the chairs were being left behind. It became
necessary to catch camels one by one, climb up them,
and, standing on neck or hump, to tie two chairs
apiece on to them. While the second was being done,
the first walked away and rubbed himself against a
wall, and knocked his chairs off again. Every one of
the men rushed at him with furious yells; the second
camel, left to himself, waddled up to the wall with an
absent-minded air, and rubbed off his chairs.

At this point—about two in the afternoon, six hours
after the contemplated start — human nature could
bear it no longer. With curses and blows we told
them to follow immediately if they valued their lives,
and rode on. That was all they wanted. Looking
back after a hundred yards we saw every camel loaded
up and starting. If we had stayed behind we should
never have got off that night. If we had ridden on
six hours before we should not have been delayed.
One time is as good as another to the Arab as long as
he feels that he is wasting it. Give him half an hour
and he will take an hour; allow him six hours and he
will require twelve.

But of course by this time it was hopeless to expect

that the baggage would make eighteen miles by dark.
At Essillem, a dozen miles out, we found Colonel
Maxwell's brigade with all its baggage packed, waiting
only camels to move on too. At Darmali we found
exactly the same state of things. General Gatacre's
never-failing hospitality produced dinner, after which
we fell in with the disposition of the rest of the army,
and waited for camels too. At ten, just as we were
going to sleep in the sand in the middle of the main
street of the village, they loafed up, very cheerful, and
feeling quite sure that they would be neither fined
nor flogged. Had they not covered thirteen miles in
a trifle under eight hours?

Then suddenly I was awake again, at the shy meeting of a quarter-moon and dawn. The beginning of
what I knew, after my boy came to my chilly bed-
chamber under a wall and said reveille was about to
sound, was a monstrous confusion of camels. You
could see that the ground was strewn with vague,
shapeless, swaying lumps, with smaller, more agile
shadows crawling over them. What they were was
very plain from the noises: the camels had arrived.
The camel, when it is a question of either working or
leaving off work — so magnificently impartial is his
stupidity—can protest in any voice from a wolf's snarl
to the wail of an uncomforted child. As each camel
was loaded it jerked up its towering height and towering load—one of ours this time, I blush to say, was
two sacks of barley, a deal table, and all the eight

cane-bottomed chairs, waving their legs at the moon; and a weirdly disreputable sight it was—and then it was the next camel's turn to howl. It is a wonderful sight camels being loaded up, with buckets and table-legs and baths and tea-kettles, hung round them as if they were Christmas-trees; but one soon has enough of it. So I left them trying to eat the hospital stores, and rode slowly out into the twilight.

Outside the zariba a heavy black snake was forging slowly along the desert road; when I came nearer it changed into a centipede; then the centipede had a kilt on, and finally it divided into the Cameron High-landers. In front of them were the Warwicks, behind them the Maxim battery—four guns with carriages and three mules tandem, two on tripods and one mule to carry the whole gun—and the Lincolns; the whole brigade was on the march. Only seventy-five men of each regiment remained, to their indignation, as guard for the stores that the camels must make a second journey to fetch. As for the heavy baggage, that was put in the houses of the village and left to its fate. Officers started with 30-lb. kit, and men with 9-lb. Scarcity of camels perhaps justified the abandonment, but with the thermometer already 100° in the shade, it meant a lot of hardship.

After a month and a half of General Gatacre, five miles with rifle and ammunition and 9-lb. kit is very much the same to the British soldier as walking down-stairs to breakfast is to you. They were just getting

into their stride when the sun rose. The orange ball
stepped up over the desert sky-line briskly and all in
one piece, plainly intending to do a good day's work
before he lay down again—and behold, we were at
Kenur. Behold, also, the Sirdar's flag, white star and
crescent on red, borne by one of three orderlies. Before it rode the Sirdar himself, in white apparel, fresh
and cool, also like one who has his work before him
and knows how it is done, and means to do it. The
British halted. There was a word and a rattle, and
the battalions which had been formed in one long
column, four abreast, were marching off at right angles
in columns of a company apiece. In no space and
no time the whole brigade had tucked itself away
and taken up its quarters. And hardly had the
British left the road clear than in swung the second
black brigade from Essillem.

These were different, many of them, from the lank
soldiers of the 9th—short and stubby, plainly of other
tribes; but whether the black has seventy-eight inches
or sixty, every one of them is a soldier. They tramped
past with their untirable bands drumming and blowing beside them; in a couple of hours they had cut
their mimosa and made their zariba, and all the Dervishes in the Sudan would not be too many for them.
The British, too, were out all day in the sun, at the
same work, every man with his rifle on his back. It
had warmed up a little more now—though 100° in
the dry Sudan is not near so hot as it would be in

England—but the British stuck to their work like men, and their zariba, a word unknown to them two months back, was every bit as straight, and thick, and prickly as the natives'.

And now we were concentrated, and only waited for them to come on. And, wonderful beyond all hope, they were coming on. The indispensable gunboats, tirelessly patrolling the river, kept the Sirdar fully informed of everything. On Shebaliya Island, forty miles south of the Atbara, they had slung an angareb aloft between a couple of spars. The Dervishes' route led within twelve hundred yards of it. There they passed everlastingly — men, women, and children; horses, goats, and donkeys, singing and braying, flying their banners, thrumming their war-drums, booming their melancholy war - horn. And on the angareb, under an umbrella, sat a man and counted them. There was reason to hope that they were little short of 20,000.

Conformably with the traditions of the gunboat service, things did not stop at counting. On the 13th Bimbashi Sitwell and a section of the 4th Egyptians landed from the *Fatha*, Lieutenant Beatty's boat, and attacked a large force which had crossed to the island. There were about 1000 Dervishes and 40 Egyptians, but neither of the united services saw anything irregular in the proceedings. In face of the swarm of enemies Bimbashi Sitwell led his men into a ditch, whence they kept up a steady fire. Suddenly he felt

a tremendous blow on his shoulder; he thought one
of the soldiers had let his rifle out of hand, but turning round to swear, found himself on his back.   Then
he heard the voice of Lieutenant Beatty, R.N.: " It's
all right," it said; " we're doing 'em proper."   " Make
it so," he replied nautically, and then, hearing a new
burst of fire from the right, " You'd better order up a
few more file, and turn them out of that."   The next
thing he knew, after the blank, was that they were
turned out of that, and that 38 of them were dead,
which was very nearly one each for the 40 Egyptians.

Bimbashi Sitwell had a well-furnished pair of shoulders.   The bullet ran through both, but missed the
spine.   Four days after, he was receiving visitors at
Fort Atbara in pyjamas and a cigarette.   Which was
a happy issue to perhaps the most staggeringly auda-
cious of all the audacities perpetrated by the gunboats
on the Nile.

XII.

AT KENUR.

THE first thing I saw of the social life of Kenur was
the Press censor shaving himself: he said that anybody might take any quarters that nobody else had
taken. As he spoke my eye fell on a round tukl
between the Sirdar's quarters, the Censor's, and the
telegraph tent—plainly an ideal residence for correspondents. It appeared empty. True, it was not
much bigger than a 'bus-driver's umbrella; but you
could just get three men and a table into it. It
would do very well for to-day: to-morrow we expected to fight. As it turned out, we stayed at Kenur
four days, during which the tukl contracted hourly,
till in the end it seemed nearly half big enough for one
person. Moreover, it turned out to be tenanted after
all—by enormous bees, which had dug out the inside
of the wooden framework till the whole place was one
large hive. Honour and prudence alike seemed to call
for an attack on them. But on reflection I pointed
out that the truest courage lay in sitting quite still

when a large bee settled on the back of your neck, and
that the truest precaution lay in smoking tobacco.
So we sat down quite still and smoked tobacco for
four days.

Kenur was like all the villages in this part of the
world, only if possible longer. All are built along
the Nile, that the inhabitants may have as short a
way as possible to go for water: Kenur was from two
to three miles long, and the camp stretched the whole
length of it. Between the camp and the river was
nearly a mile of land once cultivated, now overgrown
with Sodom apples. Nervous critics pointed out that
dervishes might attack the long line of the zariba,
and slip in between the force and its water. But
most people knew that nothing of the sort would
happen. The Sirdar is not the man to wait to be
attacked, and the long, open camp was beautifully
adapted for bringing out the whole army in fighting-
line at a moment's notice.

The first afternoon at Kenur was enlivened by the
advent of the first four companies of the Seaforths.
They came by steamer, smiling all over, from colonel
to private, to find they were in time. Down by the
river to meet them was an enormous band drawn from
all the blacks, bristling with half-jocose, half-ferocious
swagger as the darlings always are. The Seaforths
formed up into column, deep-chested, upstanding, un-
deniable, a delight to look upon ; the Sirdar fell in by
the colonel, the band began to wail out "Hieland

Laddie" and "Annie Laurie," and anything else it
thought would make them feel at home, and off they
swung towards the southern horn of the zariba.   All
round it they marched, every regiment, white, black,
and yellow, lining the route in its turn, following its
colonel in "Hip, hip, hip, hurrah!"   Does not every
native soldier know that the Highlanders have sworn
to wear no trousers till they put them on in Khartum?

The second four companies came in next day, with
an equal ear-splitting.   Colonel Lewis's brigade at
Fort Atbara was only five miles off, connected by
telegraph, so that now we were complete.   Meanwhile
the days at Kenur were not wasted—days seldom are
with the Sirdar about.   Every morning at half-past
six or so the whole force paraded and manœuvred.
The first day's exercise was an attack in line, British
on the right, Maxwell's in the centre, M'Donald's on
the left.   The two latter used the attack formation of
the Egyptian army—four of each battalion's six companies in line and two in support.   The British had
three battalions in line and the four companies of the
Seaforths in support: on each flank were guns, and
the extreme battalion in each case was in column of
companies.   This was the formation in which the
Sirdar advanced on Dongola in '96, except that the
place of the flanking columns was there taken on the
right by the cavalry—who now were of course reconnoitring all day—and on the left by the Nile with
the gunboats.

The next day the force manœuvred in brigade
squares in echelon, and the day after formed one
square of the whole army, skeleton companies repre-
senting the Third Brigade. It was in the first of these
formations that we did all the subsequent marching
up the Atbara—a stately spectacle. On the right,
and leading, was the British brigade—an advancing
wave of desert-coloured khaki, with a dash of dark
for the kilts of the Highlanders. They marched in
columns of fours, that being a handy and flexible formation, and easily kept in line: the officer has only
to see that four men are keeping a proper front with
the rest of the brigade instead of fifty; and at the
word all can wheel up into line in less than a minute.
Next, leftward and clear in rear, so that an attack on
its front or the British flank would meet a cross-fire,
marched Maxwell's brigade. Leftward and in rear
of that came Macdonald. The Egyptian forces, marching in line for the front and rear of the square,
and in column for its flanks, and having darker uniform, made a denser blotch on the desert than the
British. But dark or light, when you looked along
the force it was tremendous, going forward wave by
wave irresistibly, devouring the desert.

Thus, on the morning of Sunday, March 20, the
force broke up from Kenur. The camp went wild,
for the news said that Mahmud was actually on the
Atbara at last. He had seized Hudi ford, it was said,
seven miles from the junction of the rivers; and to

Hudi we were to march straight across the desert. The Intelligence Department more than half disbelieved the native stories. The native has no words for distance and number but "near" and "far," "few" and "many"; "near" may be anything within twenty miles, while "many" ranges from a hundred to a hundred thousand. However we marched—eleven miles at two miles an hour, in a choking sand-storm that muffled the sun to a pale winter moon, till at three in the afternoon we struck the river at Hudi. Here we found three battalions of Lewis's brigade, the 15th being left to garrison Fort Atbara; but devil a dervish.

XIII.

ON THE ATBARA.

COMING down to the Atbara after the desert was like entering the gates of heaven. To you in England, fields pulsing with green wheat and gardens aflame with tulips, it might have seemed faded. To us it was paradise.

The north bank drops twenty feet plumb to the sky-blue river. A stone's-throw across, the other bank is splashed with grass that struggles against jaundice; but it is real grass, and almost greenish, and after the desert we are very grateful for it. Beyond that shelves a bare white-brown beach, thirsty for flood-time; beyond that a wall of white-green new-fledged mimosa topped with turrets of palm. Over it all the intense blue canopy of midday, the fires of sunset, or the black roof of midnight pierced with innumerable stars, so white and clear that you almost hold up your hand to touch them — it was worth a couple of marches of sand-storm to come into such a land.

Our side, too, was thick with mimosa and dom-
palm, and tufted with grass—great coarse bunches,
mostly as thick as straw and as yellow; but a few
blades maintained a bloodless green, and horses and
camels went without their sleep to tear at them. The
camels eat the mimosa too—elsewhere a bush that
grows thorns and little yellow honey-breathing fluff-
balls, but on the fruitful Atbara a cedar-spreading
tree, with young leaves like an acacia's. The camels
rear up their affected heads, and ecstatically scrunch
thorns that would run any other beast's tongue
through; their lips drop blood, but they never notice
it. And the blacks eat the dom-nuts—things like
petrified prize apricots, whose kernel makes vegetable
ivory, and whose husks, they say, taste like ginger-
bread; though, having no ore-crusher in my kit, I
cannot speak to that. But lanky Sambo was never
tired of shying at them as they clustered just above
the dead leaves and just below the green, and Private
Atkins lent a hand with enthusiasm. Then Sambo
would grin all round his head and crack the flinty
things between his shining teeth, and Thomas would
stand staring at him, uncertain whether he was a
long-lost brother-in-arms or something out of a circus.

They might well chew mimosa, and halfa-grass,
and dom-nuts, for even on the river we were in a
desert. We marched and camped in an utterly empty
land. Atbara banks are green, birds whistle and coo
in the tree-tops, now and again a hare switchbacks

across the line of march; but along all the river there
was not one living man. Here on the Atbara there
were but rare traces of population—a few stones, half
buried, standing for salt-workings, or a round, half
washed-out mud-bank for a wall.

In the empty Nile villages their bones were long
ago gnawed white by jackals and hyenas, their sons
were speared and thrown into the river, their wives
and daughters led away to the harems of Omdurman.
It is good land for the Sudan in this corner of the
two rivers, worth, in places, perhaps as much as a
penny an acre; and the Khalifa has swept it quite
clean, and left it quite soulless.

And soulless it seemed to stay. We slept one
night at Hudi in a sand-floored quadrangle of zariba,
and you could hear the men expecting battle through
their sleep. Next day, still looking to see black heads
and spears rise over every sky-line, we marched to
Ras el Hudi, six miles farther. Both Hudis were
fords over the Atbara, and where one ended the
other began: as the river was already nearly all ford,
and the whole place contained not a single hut,
you could call anywhere anything you liked. That
same day (March 21st) the cavalry found the enemy.
Perhaps it would be more strictly correct to say that
the enemy found them: they were halted and dismounted when the Dervish horse suddenly attacked
the sentries. The troopers were in their saddles and
out at the enemy smartly enough, and after a short

scuffle the Dervishes sheered off into the bush. The
cavalry lost seven troopers killed and eight wounded,
of whom two died next day. These were the first
fatalities of the campaign.

Next day, the bulk of the force remaining in Ras
Hudi camp, a stronger reconnaissance went out—all the
cavalry, with Maxims and the 13th Sudanese in support. Just as we were sitting down to breakfast we
heard heavy firing up river. On the sound rang out
bugles; syces could be seen frantically slamming
saddles on to horses, and tugging them over to the
Sirdar's headquarters. Ten seconds later the whole
force was getting under arms. I pushed a tinned
sausage down my throat and a biscuit into my holster,
looked that my water-bottle was both full and well-
corked — of course it was neither — and blundered
through tussocks and mimosa - thorns out of camp.
Already the long columns of khaki were combining
into brigade-squares; in a matter of minutes the army
was riveted together and rolling majestically over the
swaying desert towards the firing. This time, by a
variation on the usual order, Macdonald's brigade was
on the right, its front level with Gatacre's, while Maxwell was echeloned on the left, and Lewis in support:
the reason for this was that half a mile of bush fringed
the Atbara, and the blacks were expected to be handier
in it than the British. So we marched and marched.
The British officers had had no breakfast, but they
were used to that by now: officers and men—white,

black, and brown—all tingled with the exultant anticipation of battle. At last, four miles or so out of
camp, we halted before a mile-wide slope of stony
gravel—a God-sent field of fire. On the brow we
could see a picket of cavalry: presently a rider
detached himself, and came bucketing towards the
Sirdar's flag. The order was given to load, and the
sigh of contentment could be heard above the clatter
of locks. It had come at last!

But it hadn't. We had noted it as ominous that no
more firing had beckoned us as we advanced. The
reconnaissance and the fight alike seemed to have
faded in front of us like a mirage. The sun was
getting hot overhead: to go on indefinitely without
any kind of baggage was not to be thought of. "Rise
up, men, and prepare to go home," came the reluctant
order. The army rose up and faced about, and cursed
its way into camp again. It turned out afterwards
that the enemy's cavalry had appeared in force, and
that ours led them back to the 13th. Collinson Bey
formed square, and gave them a volley or two at half
a mile or so. A few Dervishes came out of their
saddles; and that was all, for they fell back and reappeared no more.

After that came to-morrow and to-morrow and to-
morrow. Some days there was a little shooting, other
days there was not; and we in camp heard and saw
nothing in either case. Every morning one or two
native battalions with Maxims went out, support-

ing the cavalry. They went out about three, and
frizzled through morning, midday, and afternoon at a
genial spot called Khor Abadar, five or six miles out:
a khor is a dry desert watercourse, but this one was no
more—nor less—than about a mile of what looked like
rather rough sea solidified into clay. Having frizzled
duly there all day, they would swing in again at seven
or so, striding into camp bolt upright and with a
jaunty snap, as if they had been out a quarter of an
hour for a constitutional. You could always tell when
the reconnaissance was coming in by the rolls of dust
that blotted out the camp. At the corner where they
stepped inside the zariba, Blackfriars on a November
night was midday to it. You caught at a black face
and the top of a shouldered rifle floating past from one
eye to the other; you felt, rather than beheld, a loom-
ing horse-head and lance-butt over your shoulder.
You neither saw nor heard, but were aware of regiments and squadrons as in the dream of a dog-sleep.
And as lazy day sweated after lazy day, the whole
camp and the whole army began to dim into the
phantom of a dream. The vivacious, never-sleepy
bugles became a singing in your ear, the ripple of sun
on bayonets was spots before the eyes, the rumour of
the crouching enemy was the echo of a half-remembered
fairy tale very, very far away.

For, to be quite truthful, during that long succes-
sion of to-morrows at Ras el Hudi, nobody quite knew
where the Dervishes were. It was quite certain they

were somewhere near, for their cavalry was seen almost daily; and they must be camped on the Atbara, for there was nowhere else whence they could get water. We were quite confident that they were there, and that the fight was coming, and we invented all sorts of stories to explain their delay in coming on. They started down the Nile fast; they have slackened now—so we assured ourselves—to wait for their rear-guard, or to reconnoitre, or to knock down dom-nuts, or for any of a thousand reasons, and we were here a day sooner than was necessary. A day too soon, of course, was nothing—or rather it would be nothing after we had fought; at present an extra day certainly meant a little longer discomfort. You must remember that the army was nearly 1400 miles from the sea, and about 1200 from any place that the things armies want could possibly come from. It had to be supplied along a sand-banked river, a single line of rail, which was carrying the material for its own construction as well, and various camel-tracks. That 13,000 men could ever have been brought into this hungry limbo at all shows that the Sirdar is the only English general who has known how to campaign in this country. The real enemy, he has seen, is not the Dervishes, whom we have always beaten, but the Sudan itself.

He was conquering it; but for the moment the Sudan had an opening, and began trying us rather high. Not me personally, who had three camels and two blankets and much tinned meat. To me and my likes the Sirdar's refusal of transport— most natural and proper, after all—had been a blessing; it had made correspondents self-supporting, and therewith rich. But for the moment the want of transport and Mahmud's delay in coming on was hard on the troops—especially hard on the British brigade, and hardest of all on their officers. Officers and men came alike with one blanket and no overcoat. Now you must know that, though the Sudan can be live coals by day, it can be aching ice by night. It is the healthiest climate in the world if you have shade at noon and many rugs an hour before reveille; but if you have not, and especially if you happen to be a kilted Highlander, it interferes with sleep.

You must further remember that we left Kenur with the intention of fighting next day or the next. The British took the expectation seriously; the Egyptian officers did not. "You see," said one, "I've been in this bally country five years; so when I was told to bring two days' kit, I brought a fortnight's." He was now sending his private camel back to Fort Atbara for more; the officers of the British brigade had no private camels. The officers had brought only what could go into a haversack, which includes, roughly, soap and a sponge, and a toothbrush and a towel, but not a clean shirt, nor a handkerchief, nor shaving-tackle; so that the gilded popinjays were a little tarnished just at present. One of them said, most truly, that an English tramp in summer, with a sweet haystack to sleep under, and sixpence a-day for bread and cheese and beer at wayside inns, was out of reckoning better off than a British officer on the banks of the Atbara. He slept on a pillow of dusty sand, which worked steadily into his hair; he got up in the middle of the night to patrol; then he lay down again and shivered. The men could sleep three together under a triple layer of blanket; the officers must sleep each in his position on the flank or in the centre of his company. When he got up in the morning he had nothing to shave with, and lucky if he got a wash. The one camel-load of mess stores was wellnigh eaten up by now; he received the same ration as the men. His one shirt was no longer clean; he hardly dared pull out his one handkerchief; he went barefoot inside his boots while his socks were being washed. And always—night or day, on fatigue or at leisure, relatively clean or unredeemedly dirty, when he had borrowed a shave and felt almost like a gentleman again, or when he lay with his head in the dust and the black private doubted whether he should salute or not—his first paternal thought was the wellbeing of his men.

When we found Mahmud he should pay for it. But in the meantime where was he? There was a perpetual series of cavalry reconnaissances, and a perpetual stream of scallywags coming in from his camp. Any day from dawn to dark you might see

H

half - clothed black men squatting before Colonel
Wingate. Some were fairly fat; some were bags of
bones. But all stated with one consent that they
were hungry, and having received refreshment felt
that they could do no less than tell Colonel Wingate
such tidings as they conceived he would like to hear.
There was no such thing as a place on the Atbara,
as I have explained: there were names on the map,
but as they named nothing in particular you could
put them anywhere you liked within ten miles or
so. Also, there is no such thing as distance in the
native mind, so that the native also could locate anything anywhere that seemed convenient.

On the 27th Bimbashi Haig reconnoitred the opposite bank of the Atbara up to Manawi—say eighteen
miles—and saw no trace of the enemy. Combining
that fact with the precipitate from the scallywags'
stories, we came to the conclusion that Mahmud and
Osman were on the southern bank, somewhere near
the spot marked on the map as Hilgi. It was believed
that on the first news of the first cavalry contact they
entrenched themselves there in a four-mile belt of
scrub. Now General Hunter had made a reconnaissance up the Atbara last winter as far as Adarama—
indispensably informative it turned out—and the Staff
know what sort of scrub it is. It is an impenetrable,
flesh-tearing jungle of mimosa-spears and dom-palm
and stumbly halfa-grass and hanging ropes of creeper:
no army in the world could possibly attack through it.

That being so, the Sirdar's course appeared to be to wait at Ras el Hudi until Mahmud came out. Hunger might bring him out—only as yet it had not. The more trustworthy of the deserters said that there was still a certain store of food. You must know that the Dervishes have honeycombed the Sudan with caches of buried grain: many have been found and opened by the Egyptian army, but it is possible that some remain to draw on. Moreover, men who were at Toski told how, in the starving army of Wad-el-Nejumi, the fighting men were well fed enough: it was the women and the children and the followers whose ribs broke through the skin. The scallywags were starved, of course: that is why they came in, and being starved themselves they saw the whole army in like case. But it seemed by the best information that what with food they brought, and stores they found, and dom-nuts they knocked off the trees, the dervishes had a few days of fairly filled stomach before them yet.

Then how to fetch them out? The situation called for a bold stroke, and the Sirdar answered it, after his wont, with a bold and safe one. On the morning of March 24 the 15th Egyptians left Fort Atbara in the three gunboats for Shendi. Left at Shendi were all the women of Mahmud's force, and with his women gone the Sudani is only half a man. It might draw him and it might not; it was worth trying.

XIV.

THE RAID ON SHENDI.

I HAD stepped out in the morning to pick fruit from the *sanduk* for breakfast. Below me, in the shallow river, a damson-skinned black was bathing and washing his white Friday clothes and whistling "The British Grenadiers." The sun was just up; but in the Sudan he begins to blister things the moment he is over the horizon. The *sanduk* lay on the south side of the north wall of our zariba. Greengages were glittering in the young sunshine; but to pull up misapprehension, I may as well say at once that *sanduk* is the Arabic for provision-case, and that our greengages glittered through glass bottles. It may be that you were never much attracted by bottled fruits. But they taste of fruit a good deal more than tinned ones; and when your midday is six hours of solid 110 in the shade, you will find bottled fruits one of the things least impossible to eat that you are likely to get.

Therewith entered the Mess-President's head camel-

man. He was a Jaali by tribe; his name meant
"Powerful in the Faith"; and in this wilderness I
liked to think that if he were not black, and had no
moustache, and no razor-cut tribal marks on his cheeks,
his tilted nose and smiling teeth, and erect, sprightly
carriage would make him a rather pretty-ugly French
girl. He approached his lord's bed before the tent
door and pattered Arabic faster than I can keep up
with. But the sum of his tale was this: that the raid
on Shendi had been a great success, many Dervishes
were slain, and many taken, with many women
and children; that his fellow-Jaalin had done best
part of the execution, and that the 15th Battalion was
already back again at Fort Atbara.

Then let us go to Fort Atbara, said we, and hear all
about it. We are going mouldy for want of exercise
—and, to be quite open with you, the liquor famine
here is getting grave. Last night the boy came up
with a couple of bottles: "Only two wine more," said
he, and mournfully displayed one Scrubbs's Cloudy
Ammonia — try it in your bath, but not in your
drinking-cup — and one Elliman's Embrocation. So
saddle up; it is 1000 to 5 against a fight here to-day,
and it is better to sweat a-horseback in the desert
oven-blast than fry in sand and camp-smells here.

So the Mess-President and I picked our way over
the spongy ground outside camp where the water lies
in flood time, and then swung out, quarter of an hour
canter and ten minutes walk, over the hard sand and

gravel of the desert. The way from Fort Atbara was trodden already into a road as broad as Berber High Street, and almost as populous—now a white-under-clothed Jaali scallywag with a Remington and a donkey, now a lolloping convoy of camels, now a couple of Greeks with stores. For the Jew, as we know him, is a child for commercial enterprise along-side the Sudan Greek. A Greek had his ovens going on Ferkee field before the last shot was fired; the moment the Suakim road was opened the Greek's camels were on it. The few English merchants here were hard and enterprising, and they had good stuff—only just when you wanted it, it was usually just a day's journey away. The Greek gets his stuff up every-where: it is often inferior stuff, and he caravans it with a double-barrelled rifle on his shoulder and visions of Dervishes behind every mimosa bush; but he gets it up. He charges high for it, but he deserves every piastre he gets.

At Fort Atbara there stood already a small bazaar of tukls, and a pink shirt-sleeved, black-stubble-chinned Greek in each among his wares. There we laid in every known liquor except claret and beer; there we even got six dozen Pilsener-bottles of soda-water — of such are the privations of the Sudan. Most of the Greeks seemed to confine their energies to sardines, many degrees over proof. But one had planted a little salad-garden; another knew where he could get tomatoes; a third specialised in scented

soap and stationery. Remember, we were twelve
hundred miles from the nearest place where people
buy such things in shops; remember, too, that not
an inch of Government truck or steamer could be
spared for private dealers; and then you will realise
what a Nansen of retail trade is the Sudan Greek.

But a correspondent cannot live by soda-water and
tabasco sauce alone: let us try to acquire some information. In the commanderia—that stable house
of mud, six-roomed and lofty roofed, the stateliest
mansion of the Sudan—sits Hickman Bey, who swept
out Shendi. In the English army it would be almost
a scandal that an officer of his service should go anywhere or do anything. The Egyptian army is an
army of young men, with the red-hot dash of a boy
tempered by responsibility into the fine steel of a
man at his best for both plan and deed.

But about the raid. To listen to any one of the
men who conducted it you would think that he had
been a passenger, and that all the others had done all
the work: that is their way. The three gunboats
with their naval officers—now you observe the full
significance of the fact that the British Navy's command of the sea runs up to the Sixth Cataract—with
the 15th Battalion, guns, and 150 friendly Jaalin,
left Fort Atbara on March 24. They were to have
surprised Shendi in the morning of the 26th; but
luck was bad, though it turned out not to matter
much. One of the boats went aground, as boats will

on a daily falling Nile. It took some hours to get her off, and then, as it was too late for Saturday morning, and an afternoon attack would leave no light for pursuit, it was decided to make it Sunday. So the boats went slow, stopping here and there to wood up on the depeopled banks; but at one place it fell out that the landing-party came on three Dervishes. One of them got away with his skin and the alarm. When he came to Shendi the garrison—700 men with many women and children — were tom-tomming a fantasia on account of an alleged victory whereof Mahmud had advertised them. The fantasia broke up hurriedly, and all the best quality women were sent away on camels to Omdurman. That meant, of course, the Baggara Arab women. The women of the black riflemen and spearmen were left to shift.

At ten on Sunday morning Colonel Hickman and his raiders duly appeared and landed. They found the enemy drawn up between the bank and rising ground; there were four forts—one sunken, three circular earth walls—but Mahmud took away the guns with him. The Fifteenth formed column of fours and marched placidly in front of the enemy, taking not the least notice of their fire—which indeed hurt nobody— till it outflanked their left. The two forces were then more or less like a couple of L's lying on their backs, one inside the other. The dervish L was the inside one—the stem of it fighting men and the foot scally-

wags carrying bundles; the Egyptian L's stem was
the Fifteenth, and its foot, stretching inland towards
the loot, the Jaalin.

Bimbashi Peake, of the Artillery, let off two rounds
of shrapnel over the scallywags, and the fight was
over. Instantly the plain was quite black with the
baggage the dervishes dropped — bundles of clothes,
angarebs, chairs, big war-drums, helmets, spears, gibbas, bags of dhurra, donkeys, horses, women, children.
Every dervish was making for Omdurman as hard as
his legs would let him.

Now came the Jaalin's chance. The Jaalin used to
be a flourishing tribe, and inhabited the island of
Meroe—the country between the Atbara and the Blue
Nile. A few years ago the tribe had a difference of
opinion with the Khalifa: there are not many Jaalin
now, and what there are inhabit where they can.
The survivors are anxious to redress the balance by
removing a corresponding proportion of Baggara, and
they began. After a time they came to Hickman
Bey, panting, but only half happy. "It is very good,
O thou Excellency," they cried; "we're killing them
splendidly. They're all out in the desert, only we
can't get at them to kill them enough. Can't we have
some of the donkeys to pursue on?" "Take the lot,"
said his Excellency.

So the island of Meroe beheld the novel sight of
Baggara cavalry, on brood mares with foals at foot,

fleeing for their lives before Jaalin on donkeys. Most of the five-and-twenty horsemen got away to tell the news to the Khalifa; by this time probably their right hands and right feet were off. The footmen the Jaalin pursued till ten at night, and slew to the tune of 160; also there were 645 prisoners, mostly women. They got a tremendous reception from the women at Fort Atbara when they reached it, and joined in it themselves quite unaffectedly. By now they are probably the wives of such black soldiers as are allowed to marry; as like as not many of them actually had husbands, brothers, sons, fathers in one Sudanese battalion or another. A Sudan lady's married life is full of incident in these days; it might move the envy of Fargo, North Dakota. But when all is said and done, a black soldier with a life engagement at 15s. a-month minimum, with rations and allowances, is a more brilliant catch than any Baggara that ever came out of Darfur.

It was a raid that for neatness and thoroughness might teach a lesson to Osman Digna himself. What Osman and Mahmud said when they heard their men's women were gone, and that their own retreat along the Nile could be harried for a hundred miles as far as Shabluka, I do not pretend to know. I should be sorry to meet any of the ends they must have invoked upon all the Sirdar's relatives.

And when we got back, and the camels seesawed

in with the *sanduks*, the cook, for all his new wealth, was very angry. " You have brought no curry-powder, O thou Effendim," he said. " You didn't say you wanted any curry-powder," the Mess-President defended himself. " Yes I did," said the cook, sternly ; " I said we were short of *all* vegetables."

XV.

REST AND RECONNAISSANCES.

THE force remained in camp at Ras el Hudi till April
3. Mahmud's exact position was still undetermined,
his intentions yet more so. It was a queer state of
things—two armies within twenty miles of each other,
both presumably wishful to fight, both liable to run
short of provisions, yet neither attacking and neither
quite sure where the other was. But the Sirdar had
always the winning hand. While he sat on the Atbara Mahmud was stale-mated. It may be supposed
that he came down the Nile to fight: very well, here
was the Sirdar ready to fight and beat him. Osman
Digna probably had raiding in his head. But he could
not raid Berber while the Sirdar was below him on
the Atbara: that would have meant seventy miles
across the desert, with wells choked up—though he
may not have known this—and the Sirdar always
liable to attack him on flank or to get to Berber before
him. One day we had a report that he had started on
a journey the other way, towards Adarama; but, if he

ever went at all, it was probably to dig up grain:
there was nothing worth raiding about Adarama.
Finally, now that Shendi was destroyed, to go back
meant ruin; the blacks, irritated by the loss of their
women, would desert; the gunboats would harry the
retreat as far as Shabluka; it was even possible that
the whole Anglo-Egyptian force would get to the Nile
before they did. And if he stayed where he was, then
in the end he must either fight or starve.

Mahmud was stale-mated, no doubt, whatever course
he took; only in the meantime he took none. He did
not move, he did not fight, and he did not starve.
And we were still not quite sure where he was. The
army stayed a fortnight in Ras Hudi camp, reconnoitring daily, with an enemy within twenty miles,
whose precise position it did not know. It hardly
seems to speak well for the cavalry. Yet it would be
most unjust to blame them: the truth is that the
Egyptian cavalry was hopelessly outnumbered and
outmatched. Broadwood Bey had eight squadrons—
say 800 lances — with eight Maxims and one horse
battery. There were also two companies of camel-
corps, but these were generally wanted for convoys.
Against this Mahmud, as he said afterwards himself,
had 4000 Baggara horse.

Furthermore, it cannot be said that the Egyptian
cavalry were above criticism. They were enormously
improved, as will shortly be seen: ever since the Dongola campaign they had come on greatly, but it is

doubtful whether they will ever have the dash of the best European or Indian cavalry. They have great merits: in an empty land they will live on almost nothing, and no stretch of work can subdue their iron bodies to fatigue. They are no longer open to suspicion on the score of courage. But in reconnaissance work they want smartness and intelligence. It could not be imputed to them as a fault that they did not ride through five times their force and see what was behind. But it was a fact that the Baggara worked better in the bush than they did. Day after day they would ride out and see nobody or only a vedette or two; as soon as they began to retire they were followed by dervishes, who had apparently been seeing them all the time. An officer told me that one day, walking out from Fort Atbara, he saw a returning patrol under a native lieutenant. He stood still under a tree to see if they would see him: they passed him by like men asleep. In a word, the Egyptian trooper is what it is inevitable he should be. You cannot breed a light quick-witted scout out of a hundred centuries of drudgery and serfdom. He will improve with time; meanwhile he is still a fellah

Considering the quantity and quality of their material, it was wonderful that Broadwood Bey and his British officers did as much as they did. To work the weakest arm of a force cannot be inspiriting work, but they stuck to it with unquenchable courage and inexhaustible patience. If it be

asked why the cavalry was not strengthened with
British or Indian regiments, the answer is very easy.
It was almost a miracle that so large a force had been
got up to the Atbara and fed there; to bring up more
horses into a country almost naked of fodder was a
physical impossibility, too impossible even for Sir
Herbert Kitchener.

But if the cavalry was for a while unsuccessful in
localising Mahmud's entrenchment, it was wholly successful in keeping his scouts from coming near us, and
that was no small achievement. The Baggara might
have made things very unpleasant for us even at Ras
el Hudi.   But for the patrols of the unwearying
cavalry they could easily have crept up in the bush
across the river and fired into camp all night every
night. They might have got below the camp and cut
up convoy after convoy till hunger drove the Sirdar
down to Fort Atbara again and opened the way to
Berber. We sat day after day and wondered why
they never did it; but they never did.

At last, on March 30, General Hunter went out.
With him went the cavalry, the horse-battery, and
four Maxims, while two battalions of infantry and
a field battery were advanced in support to Khor
Abadar. When he got back that evening everybody
knew that Mahmud's stronghold was found. He had
gone on until he came to it. He had ridden up to
within 300 yards of it and looked in. What he saw,
of course, the Intelligence Department knew better

than I did, but some things were common property.
The position faced the open desert—we all breathed
freely at this—and went right back through the scrub
to the river. Round it ran a tremendous zariba three
miles long, and in the centre, on an eminence, were
trenches affording three tiers of fire. This proved to
be an exaggeration as regarded size, and a misunder-
standing otherwise : the triple trench ran nearly round
the position. What was certain and to the point was
that the place was trimmed with black heads, but
that their owners seemed reluctant to come out. The
horse-battery gave them a score of rounds or so, but
they made no answer, and in their thick bush any
casualties they may have had were safely concealed.

However, here at last was Mahmud marked down.
To be precise, he was at Nakheila, eighteen miles away,
as the cavalry and Staff said, though, when the infantry came to foot it, they made it well over twenty :
every infantry man knows how cavalry and Staff will
underrate distances. Wherever he was, we knew the
way to him, and we could take our time. Now what
would the Sirdar do ?

For the next two days the camp buzzed with
strategy and tactics. It was no longer what Mahmud
would do: Mahmud, as we have seen, could do nothing. But would the Sirdar wait for him to starve into
attack or dispersal, or would he go for Nakheila ?
Many people thought that, being a careful man, he
would wait and not risk the loss an attack would

cost; but they were wrong. On the evening of April
1 it became known that we were moving on the
morning of the 3rd four miles forward to Abadar.
Some theorists still held out that the change of camp
was a mere matter of health; and indeed sanitation
had long cried for it. Others held that the Sirdar was
not the man to lengthen his line of communication
for nothing: the move meant attack.

What considerations resolved the Sirdar to storm
Mahmud's zariba, I do not pretend to know. But
many arguments for his decision suggested themselves
at once. It was true that the Dervishes could not
stay at Nakheila for ever, but as yet there was no sign
of starvation from them. On the other hand, it was no
joke to supply 12,000 men even seventeen miles from
Fort Atbara by camel-transport alone: as time wore
on and camels wore out, it became less and less easy.
Secondly, the white brigade was beginning to feel the
heat, the inadequate shelter, and the poor food: up to
now its state of health had been wonderful—only
two per cent of sick or thereabouts—but now began to
appear dysentery and enteric. Finally, it was hardly
fitting that so large a British force should sit down
within twenty miles of an enemy and not smash him.
There was a good deal of lurking sympathy with
Mahdism in some Egyptian quarters far enough away
not to know what Mahdism was: to shrink from a
decisive attack would nourish it. The effect on the
troops themselves would be disheartening, and dis-

heartenment spells lassitude and sickness. And to
the Dervishes themselves a battle would be a far
more killing blow than a dispersal and retreat. In
all dealings with a savage enemy, I suppose the
rule holds that it is better and cheaper in the end
to attack, and attack, and attack again. All considerations of military reputation pleaded unanimously
that Mahmud must be destroyed in battle; and at
last the army was on the direct road to destroy
him.

XVI.

CAMEL-CORPS AND CAVALRY.

"CAMEL-CORPS luck," said the Bimbashi, and smiled bitterly, then swore. "O my God, if this is the big show!"

Climbing up over sand-bags on to one of the gun-platforms of Fort Atbara, we crouched in the embrasure and listened. Boom—boom—boom; very faint, but very distinct, and at half-minute intervals. We had ridden in the day before from the Sirdar's camp up the Atbara to buy more bottled fruit and, alas! more gin from the Greek shanties on the Nile beach. A convoy, on a similar errand, had been attacked by Dervishes half an hour after we had passed it, yet we heard not a shot. To-day, all this way off, we heard plainly: it must be an action indeed. Our own army, we knew, was not to move. Could it be that Mahmud had come down and was attacking us at Abadar? And we eighteen miles away at Fort Atbara, and down there in the sand-drift roadway the wobbling, grousing camels, that were to be conveyed

out at two miles an hour! We joined the Bimbashi,
and cursed miserably on the chance of it.

But no, we struggled to persuade ourselves, it
couldn't be so bad as that. It must be a battalion
come out to clear the road for our convoy. Or it
must be the reconnaissance that was going up to the
dervish zariba at Nakheila. Correspondents are not
allowed to go with reconnaissances, so that if it is
only that, there's no great loss after all. Anyhow it
is eleven o'clock now. The baggage camels have
lolloped out under the mud guard-house, through the
fort-gate, through the gap in the mimosa-thorn
zariba. The camel-corps escort is closing up in rear:
we are off.

Half a mile ahead ride five blacks, their camels
keeping perfect line. The sun flashes angrily on their
rifle-barrels, but they look him steadily in the face,
peering with puckered eyes over the desert below
them: in this land of dust and low scrub a camel's
hump is almost a war balloon. Far out on their right
I see a warily advancing dot, which is four more; a
black dot on the rising leftward skyline, three more;
out on the right flank of the baggage camels, shaving
the riverside thickets, gleam white spider legs, which
are a couple of camel-troopers more. They stop and
examine a track; they break into a trot and disappear
behind a palm clump; they reappear walking. But
the main force of the two companies rides close about
the swinging quadrangle of baggage camels—in front,

on flank, in rear. Slowly and sleepily the mass of beasts strolls on into the desert, careless what horsemen might be wheeling into line behind the ridge, or what riflemen might be ambushed in the scrub. But the scouts in front are looking at every footprint, over every skyline, behind every clump of camel-thorn.

To be out of an exciting action is camel-corps luck; this is camel-corps work. The Bimbashi missed his part in the reconnaissance to ride all night and guard the menaced convoy; he slept one hour at dawn, and now returns in the sun. He is quite fresh and active. This is his usual work; but he is not happy because this also is his usual luck. Only the Egyptian army would have found it very difficult to do without him and his desert cavalry in the past, and even now, with all the desert roads except the Bayuda behind it finds plenty of work for the camel-corps still. And one day they say, " Take out twenty camels," and the next day, "Take out the rest." The next day "Those twenty that weren't out yesterday can't possibly be tired"—but the Bimbashi goes out every day. The skin is scaled off his nose with sun, and his eyes are bloodshot with sand, and the hairs of his moustache have snapped off short with drought, and his hair is bleaching to white. All that is the hall-mark of the Sudan.

Getting into the saddle had been like sitting down suddenly in a too hot bath; by this time you could not bear your hand upon it. Out in the desert

gleamed the steel-blue water and black reflected trees
of the mirage; even in mirage there is no green in
the midday sun of the Sudan.   What should be green
is black; all else is sun-coloured.   It is torment to
face the gaudy glare that stabs your eyes.   If you
lift them to the sky it is not very blue—I have seen
far deeper in England; but it is alive all over with
quivering passionate heat.   Beating from above and
burning from below, the sun strikes at you heavily.
There is no way out of it except through the hours
into evening.   No sound but boot clinking on camel-
stirrup: you hear it through a haze.   You ride along
at a walk, half dead.   You neither feel nor think, you
hardly even know that it is hot.   You just have
consciousness of a heavy load hardly to be borne,
pressing, pressing down on you, crushing you under
the dead weight of sun.

We met the usual people — a Greek with four
camels, a bare-legged boy on a donkey, a bare-
breasted woman under a bundle — the second and
third-class passengers of the desert.   We questioned
them with alternate triumph and despair, as they
answered alternately after their kind.   One said it
was two squadrons, a battery, and a battalion fighting
in our old camp at Ras Hudi; another said Mahmud
had come down to Abadar and had fought the Sirdar
for four hours; another said Mahmud had gone right
away, and that the whole Anglo-Egyptian army had
gone after him.   Every story was wholly false, be-

gotten only of a wish to please; whence you perceive the advantages enjoyed by him who would collect intelligence in the Sudan.

Slowly the minutes crawled on; the camels crawled slower. On days like this you feel yourself growing older: it seemed months since we heard the guns from the parapet; it would have hardly seemed wonderful if we had heard that the campaign had been finished while we were away. We had ridden awhile with the Bimbashi, but conversation wilted in the sun; now we had ambled ahead till even the advanced guard had dropped out of sight behind. One servant with us rode a tall fast camel; from that watch-tower he suddenly discerned cases lying open on the sand about a hundred yards off the trampled road. Anything for an incident: we rode listlessly up and looked. A couple of broken packing-cases, two tins of sardines, a tin of biscuits, half empty, a small case of empty soda-bottles with "Sirdar" stencilled on it, and a couple of empty bottles of whisky. Among them lay a cigarette-box with a needle and a reel of cotton, a few buttons, and a badge—A.S.C.— such as the Army Service Corps wear on their shoulder-straps.

We were on the scene of last evening's raid. Two camels, we remembered, had been cut off and the loads lost. We found the marks on the sand where the convoy-camels had knelt down in living zariba to wait for relief from Abadar, seven miles away. All the

time it took to fetch the camel-corps the Dervishes
must have lurked in the bush eating biscuits and
drinking the whisky of the infidel.   The Sirdar's
soda-water was plainly returned empties, so that they
would have found the whisky strong; the sardines,
not knowing the nature of tinned meats, they had
thrown away.   We waited to report to the Bimbashi.

Presently the convoy crept up, a confusion of vague
necks and serpent heads, waving like tentacles.   The
Bimbashi had given his horse to an orderly, and was
sleeping peacefully on his camel.   Now we had found
among the scattered camel-loads a wineglass, broken
in the stem, but providentially intact in the bowl.
Also we had bought for a great price at Fort Atbara
four eggs, and had whisky wherein to break them.
So the Bimbashi slipped off his camel all in one piece,
and we lunched.

By now the damned sun was taking his hand off
us.   We were slipping through his fingers; he was
low down behind us, and his rays sprawled into
larger and longer shadows.   Then he went down in
a last sullen fusion of gold.   The camels, feeling themselves checked, flopped down where they stood; the
drivers flopped down beside them, and bobbed their
heads in the approximate direction of Mecca.   They
might well give thanks; with sunset the world had
come to life again.   A slight air sprang up, and a
gallop fanned it to a grateful breeze.   Soon the
eastern sky became a pillar of dust; the horses in

camp were being led to water. The great fight was
still timed for the day after to-morrow, and another
twelve hours of sunlessness were before us.

The camp was just as we had left it, all but for
one piece of news: the cavalry had had a fight, and
had fought well against every arm of the enemy. It
was their guns, not our own, we had heard nearly forty
miles away at Fort Atbara. General Hunter was in
command of the reconnaissance, and when General
Hunter goes out to look at the enemy you may be
sure he will look at him if he has to jump over his
zariba to do it. Leaving the supporting battalion of
infantry behind, the eight squadrons of cavalry with
eight Maxims rode to the front of Mahmud's entrenchment. Last time he had made no sign of life. This
time the first appearance brought out 700 cavalry.
These were pushed back, but next came infantry,
swarming like ants out of the zariba till the desert
was black with them. They were estimated at some
1500; they opened fire, not effectively. Then came
a bang to the rearward: he was firing his guns. And
on each flank, meanwhile, emerged from the bush beside the entrenchment his encircling cavalry to cut
ours off.

"It was Maiwand over again, only properly done,"
said one of the men who saw it. The Maxims opened
fire on both cavalry and infantry, knocking many over,
though the Dervishes were always in open order. And
when it was time to go the Baggara horsemen were

by this time across our true line of retirement. Broad-wood Bey ordered his troopers to charge. Behind his English leaders—the Bey himself, who always leads every attack, and Bimbashis le Gallais and Persse—the despised unwarlike fellah charged and charged home, and the Baggara lord of the Sudan split before him. Bimbashi Persse was wounded in the left forearm by a bullet fired from horseback; six troopers were killed and ten wounded. The loss of the Dervishes by lance, and especially by Maxim bullet, was reckoned at near 200.

Our seventeen casualties were a light price to pay for such a brilliant little fight, to say nothing of the information gained, and above all, the vindication of the Egyptian trooper. That the fellah was fearless of bullet and shell all knew; now he had shown his indifference to cold steel also. The cavalry mess was a hum of cheerfulness that night, and well it might be. The officers were all talking at once for joy: the troopers riding their horses down to the pool moved with a swing that was not there before. For the dogged, up-hill, back-breaking, heart-breaking work of fifteen years had come to bear fruit.

And cheerfulness spread to the whole army also: next morning—the 5th—we were off again, this time to Umdabieh, seven miles across the desert. The bush at Abadar was almost jungle — full of green sappy plants and creepers, a refreshment to camels, but a prospective hotbed of fever for men. Everybody was getting very sick of the Atbara, which had been such a paradise of green when we first camped on it. We missed the ever-blowing breeze of the Nile: the night was a breathless oven and the day a sweaty stewpan. The Atbara seemed even getting sick of itself: day by day it dropped till now it was no river at all, but a string of shallow befouled pools. All longed for the fatherly Nile again.

So once more the squares marched forth before day-light, and black dusk lowered under the rising sun. Umdabieh was a novelty for an Atbara camp, in that a few mud huts marked the place whence the Dervishes had blotted out a village. The river was punier than ever and the belt of bush thin ; lucky was the man whose quarters included a six-foot dom-palm to lay his head under. I spent both afternoons at Umdabieh chasing a patch of shadow round and round a tree. We did nothing on the 6th, for on the evening of the 7th we were to march, and to fight on Good Friday.

XVII.

THE BATTLE OF THE ATBARA.

As the first rays of sunrise glinted on the desert
pebbles, the army rose up and saw that it was in
front of the enemy. All night it had moved blindly,
in faith. At six in the evening the four brigades
were black squares on the rising desert outside the
bushes of Umdabieh camp, and they set out to march.
Hard gravel underfoot, full moon overhead, about them
a coy horizon that seemed immeasurable yet revealed
nothing, the squares tramped steadily for an hour.
Then all lay down, so that the other brigades were
swallowed up into the desert, and the faces of the
British square were no more than shadows in the
white moonbeams. The square was unlocked, and
first the horses were taken down to water, then the
men by half-battalions. We who had water ate some
bully-beef and biscuit, put our heads on saddle-bags,
rolled our bodies in blankets, and slept a little.

The next thing was a long rustle about us, stealing
in upon us, urgently whispering us to rise and mount

and move. The moon had passed overhead. It was
one o'clock. The square rustled into life and motion,
bent forward, and started, half asleep. No man spoke,
and no light showed, but the sand-muffled trampling
and the moon-veiled figures forbade the fancy that it
was all a dream. The shapes of lines of men—now
close, now broken, and closing up again as the ground
broke or the direction changed—the mounted officers,
and the hushed order, "Left shoulder forward," the
scrambling Maxim mules, the lines of swaying camels,
their pungent smell, and the rare neigh of a horse,
the other three squares like it, which we knew of
but could not see,—it was just the same war-machine
as we had seen all these days on parade. Only this
time it was in deadly earnest, moving stealthily but
massively forward towards an event that none of us
could quite certainly foretell.

We marched till something after four, then halted,
and the men lay down again and slept. The rest
walked up and down in the gnawing cold, talking to
one and another, wondering in half-voices were we
there, would they give us a fight or should we find
their lines empty, how would the fight be fought, and,
above all, how were we to get over their zariba. For
Mahmud's zariba was pictured very high, and very
thick, and very prickly, which sounded awkward for
the Cameron Highlanders, who were to assault it.
Somebody had proposed burning it, either with war-
rockets or paraffin and safety matches; somebody else

suggested throwing blankets over it, though how you throw blankets over a ten by twenty feet hedge of camel-thorn, and what you do next when you have thrown them, the inventor of the plan never explained. Others favoured scaling-ladders, apparently to take headers off on to the thorns and the enemy's spears, and even went so far as to make a few ; most were for the simpler plan of just taking hold of it and pulling it apart. But how many of the men who pulled would ever get through the gap ?

Now the sun rose behind us, and the men rose, too, and we had arrived. Bimbashi Fitton had led the four brigades in the half-light to within 200 yards of the exact positions they were to take in the action. Now, too, we saw the whole army — right of us Macdonald's, right of him, again, Maxwell's, to our left rear Lewis's in support, far away leftward of them the grey squadrons of the cavalry. The word came, and the men sprang up. The squares shifted into the fighting formations: at one impulse, in one superb sweep, near 12,000 men moved forward towards the enemy. All England and all Egypt, and the flower of the black lands beyond, Birmingham and the West Highlands, the half-regenerated children of the earth's earliest civilisation, and grinning savages from the uttermost swamps of Equatoria, muscle and machinery, lord and larrikin, Balliol and the Board School, the Sirdar's brain and the camel's back—all welded into one, the awful war machine went forward into action.

We could see their position quite well by now,
about a mile and a half away—the usual river fringe
of grey-green palms meeting the usual desert fringe
of yellow-grey mimosa. And the smoke-grey line in
front of it all must be their famous zariba. Up from
it rolled a nimbus of dust, as if they were still busy
at entrenching; before its right centre fluttered half a
dozen flags, white and pale blue, yellow and pale
chocolate. The line went on over the crunching
gravel in awful silence, or speaking briefly in half-
voices—went on till it was not half a mile from the
flags. Then it halted. Thud! went the first gun,
and phutt! came faintly back, as its shell burst
on the zariba into a wreathed round cloud of just
the zariba's smoky grey. I looked at my watch,
and it marked 6.20. The battle that had now
menaced, now evaded us for a month — the battle
had begun.

Now, from the horse battery and one field battery
on the right, from two batteries of Maxim-Nordenfelts
on the left, just to the right front of the British, and
from a war-rocket which changed over from left to
right, belched a rapid, but unhurried, regular, relentless shower of destruction. The round grey clouds
from shell, the round white puffs from shrapnel, the
hissing splutter of rockets, flighted down methodi-
cally, and alighted on every part of the zariba and of
the bush behind. A fire sprang and swarmed redly
up the dried leaves of a palm - tree; before it sank

another flung up beside it, and then another. When
the shelling began a few sparse shots came back; one
gunner was wounded. And all over the zariba we
saw dust-clothed figures strolling unconcernedly in
and out, checking when a shell dropped near, and
then passing contemptuously on again. The enemy's
cavalry appeared galloping and forming up on our
left of the zariba, threatening a charge. But tut-tut-
tut-tut went the Maxims, and through glasses we
could see our cavalry trembling to be at them. And
the Baggara horsemen, remembering the guns that
had riddled them and the squadrons that had shorn
through them three days before, fell back to cover
again. By now, when it had lasted an hour or more,
not a man showed along the whole line, nor yet a
spot of rifle smoke. All seemed empty, silent, lifeless,
but for one hobbled camel, waving his neck and
stupid head in helpless dumb bewilderment. Presently the edge of the storm of devastation caught
him too, and we saw him no more.

An hour and twenty minutes the guns spoke, and
then were silent. And now for the advance along the
whole line. Maxwell's brigade on the right — 12th,
13th, and 14th Sudanese to attack and 8th Egyptian
supporting—used the Egyptian attack formation,—
four companies of a battalion in line and the other
two in support. Macdonald,—9th, 10th, and 11th
Sudanese in front and 2nd Egyptian supporting,—his
space being constricted, had three companies in line

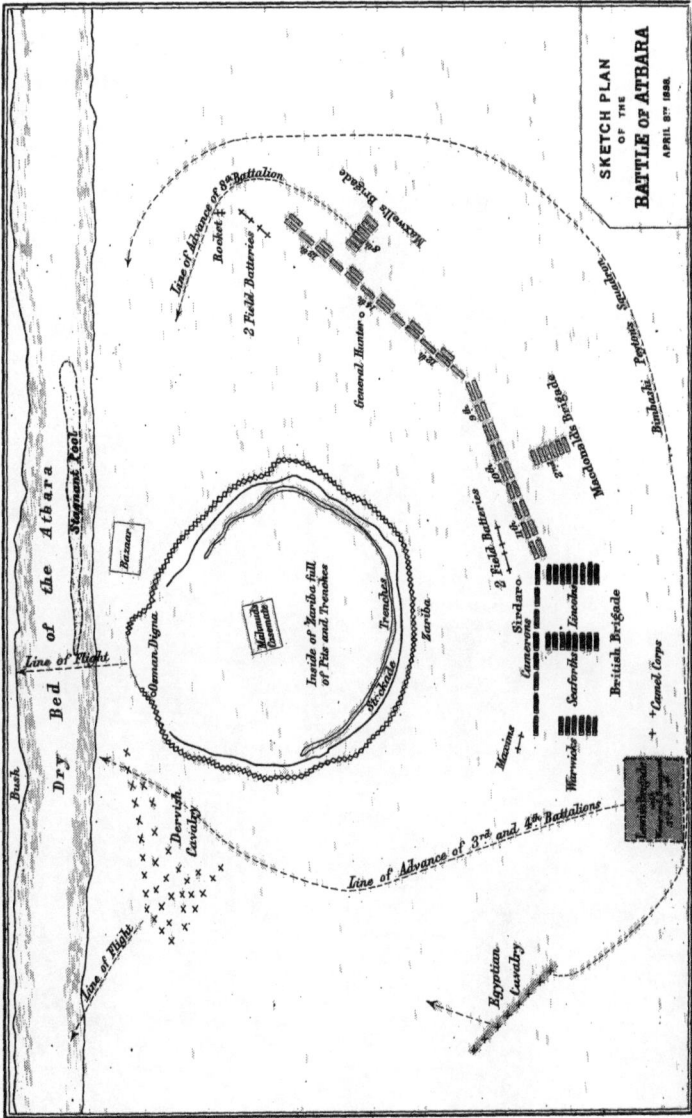

SKETCH PLAN
OF THE
BATTLE OF ATBARA
APRIL 8TH 1898.

Dry Bed of the Atbara

Stagnant Pool

Bank

Bush

Line of Flight

Line of Flight

Dervish Cavalry

Egyptian Cavalry

Line of Advance of 3rd and 4th Battalions

Line of Advance of 8th Battalion

Rocket

2 Field Batteries

Maxwell's Brigade

General Hunter

Macdonald's Brigade

Bimbashi Foster's Squadron

2 Field Batteries

Sirdaro

Osman Digna

Bazaar

Mahdist Commands

Inside of Zariba full of Pits and Trenches

Stockade

Trenches

Zariba

Cameroons

Seaforths

Lincolns

British Brigade

Maxim

Warwicks

Camel Corps

The Edinburgh Geographical Institute

and three in support. The British had the Camerons
in line along their whole front; then, in columns of
their eight companies, the Lincolns on the right, the
Seaforths in the centre, and the Warwicks, two companies short, on the left : the orders to these last were
not to advance till it was certain the dervish cavalry
would not charge in flank. Lewis's three-battalion
brigade—3rd, 4th, and 7th Egyptian—had by this
time two battalions to the British left rear and one
forming square round the water - camels. All the
artillery accompanied the advance.

The Camerons formed fours and moved away to the
left, then turned into line. They halted and waited
for the advance. They were shifted back a little to
the right, then halted again. Then a staff officer
galloped furiously behind their line, and shouted something in the direction of the Maxim battery. "Advance ? " yelled the major, and before the answer
could come the mules were up to the collar and the
Maxims were up to and past the left flank of the
Camerons. They stood still, waiting on the bugle—a
line of khaki and dark tartan blending to purple, of
flashing bayonets at the slope, and set, two-month-
bearded faces strained towards the zariba. In the
middle of the line shone the Union Jack.

The bugle sang out the advance. The pipes screamed
battle, and the line started forward, like a ruler drawn
over the tussock-broken sand. Up a low ridge they
moved forward : when would the Dervishes fire ? The

K

Camerons were to open from the top of the ridge, only 300 yards short of the zariba; up and up, forward and forward: when would they fire? Now the line crested the ridge—the men knelt down. " Volley-firing by sections "—and crash it came. It came from both sides, too, almost the same instant. Wht-t, wht-t, wht-t piped the bullets overhead: the line knelt very firm, and aimed very steady, and crash crash, crash they answered it.

O ! A cry more of dismayed astonishment than of pain, and a man was up on his feet and over on his back, and the bearers were dashing in from the rear. He was dead before they touched him, but already they found another for the stretcher. Then bugle again, and up and on: the bullets were swishing and lashing now like rain on a pond. But the line of khaki and purple tartan never bent nor swayed; it just went slowly forward like a ruler. The officers at its head strode self-containedly—they might have been on the hill after red-deer; only from their locked faces turned unswervingly towards the bullets could you see that they knew and had despised the danger. And the unkempt, unshaven Tommies, who in camp seemed little enough like Covenanters or Ironsides, were now quite transformed. It was not so difficult to go on—the pipes picked you up and carried you on—but it was difficult not to hurry; yet whether they aimed or advanced they did it orderly, gravely, without speaking. The bullets had whispered to raw

youngsters in one breath the secret of all the glories
of the British Army.

Forward and forward, more swishing about them
and more crashing from them. Now they were
moving, always without hurry, down a gravelly incline. Three men went down without a cry at the
very foot of the Union Jack, and only one got to
his feet again ; the flag shook itself and still blazed
splendidly. Next, a supremely furious gust of bullets,
and suddenly the line stood fast. Before it was a
loose low hedge of dry camel-thorn—the zariba, the
redoubtable zariba. That it ? A second they stood
in wonder, and then, " Pull it away," suggested somebody. Just half-a-dozen tugs, and the impossible
zariba was a gap and a scattered heap of brushwood.
Beyond is a low stockade and trenches ; but what of
that ? Over and in ! Hurrah, hurrah, hurrah !

Now the inside suddenly sprang to life. Out of
the earth came dusty, black, half-naked shapes, running, running and turning to shoot, but running
away. And in a second the inside was a wild confusion of Highlanders, purple tartan and black-green,
too, for the Seaforths had brought their perfect columns
through the teeth of the fire, and were charging in at
the gap. Inside that zariba was the most astounding
labyrinth ever seen out of a nightmare. It began with
a stockade and a triple trench. Beyond that the bush
was naturally thick with palm stem and mimosa-
thorn and halfa-grass. But, besides, it was as full of

holes as any honeycomb, only far less regular. There
was a shelter-pit for every animal—here a donkey
tethered down in a hole just big enough for itself and
its master; beside it a straw hut with a tangle of
thorn; yawning a yard beyond, a larger trench, choke-
full of tethered camels and dead or dying men. There
was no plan or system in it, only mere confusion of
stumbling-block and pitfall. From holes below and
hillocks above, from invisible trenches to right and
innocent tukls to left, the bewildered bullets curved,
and twisted, and dodged. It took some company-
leading; for the precise formations that the bullets
only stiffened were loosening now. But the officers
were equal to it: each picked his line and ran it, and
if a few of his company were lost—kneeling by green-
faced comrades or vaguely bayoneting along with a
couple of chance companions—they kept the mass
centrèd on the work in hand.

For now began the killing. Bullet and bayonet
and butt, the whirlwind of Highlanders swept over.
And by this time the Lincolns were in on the right,
and the Maxims, galloping right up to the stockade,
had withered the left, and the Warwicks, the enemy's
cavalry definitely gone, were volleying off the blacks
as your beard comes off under a keen razor. Farther
and farther they cleared the ground—cleared it of
everything like a living man, for it was left carpeted
thick enough with dead. Here was a trench; bayonet
that man. Here a little straw tukl; warily round

to the door, and then a volley. Now in column
through this opening in the bushes; then into line, and
drop those few desperately firing shadows among the
dry stems beyond. For the running blacks—poor
heroes—still fired, though every second they fired less
and ran more. And on, on the British stumbled and
slew, till suddenly there was unbroken blue overhead,
and a clear drop underfoot. The river! And across
the trickle of water the quarter-mile of dry sand-bed
was a fly-paper with scrambling spots of black. The
pursuers thronged the bank in double line, and in two
minutes the paper was still black-spotted, only the
spots scrambled no more. "Now that," panted the
most pessimistic senior captain in the brigade—"now
I call that a very good fight."

Cease fire! Word and whistle and voice took a
little time to work into hot brains; then sudden
silence. Again, hurrah, hurrah, hurrah! It had lasted
forty minutes; and nobody was quite certain whether
it had seemed more like two minutes or two years.
All at once there came a roar of fire from the left;
the half-sated British saw the river covered with a
new swarm of flies, only just in time to see them stop
still as the others. This was Lewis's half-brigade of
Egyptians at work. They had stood the heavy fire
that sought them as if there were no such things as
wounds or death; now they had swept down leftward
of the zariba, shovelled the enemy into the river-bed,
and shot them down. Bloodthirsty? Count up the

Egyptians murdered by Mahdism, and then say so if you will.

Meanwhile, all the right-hand part of the zariba was alive with our blacks. They had been seen from the British line as it advanced, ambling and scrambling over rise and dip, firing heavily, as they were ordered to, and then charging with the cold bayonet, as they lusted to. They were in first, there cannot be a doubt. Their line formation turned out a far better one for charging the defences than the British columns, which were founded on an exaggerated expectation of the difficulty of the zariba, and turned out at rifle unhandy. And if the zariba had been as high and thick as the Bank of England, the blacks and their brigaded Egyptians would have slicked through it and picked out the thorns after the cease fire. As against that, they lost more men than the British, for their advance was speedier and their volleys less deadly than the Camerons' pelting destruction that drove through every skull raised an inch to aim.

But never think the blacks were out of hand. They attacked fast, but they attacked steadily, and kept their formation to the last moment there was anything to form against. The battle of the Atbara has definitely placed the blacks—yes, and the once contemned Egyptians — in the ranks of the very best troops in the world. When it was over their officers were ready to cry with joy and pride. And the blacks, every one of whom would beamingly charge the bottomless pit after his Bey, were just as joyous and proud of their officers. They stood about among the dead, their faces cleft with smiles, shaking and shaking each other's hands. A short shake, then a salute, another shake and another salute, again and again and again, with the head-carving smile never narrowed an instant. Then up to the Bey and the Bimbashis— mounted now, but they had charged afoot and clear ahead, as is the recognised wont of all chiefs of the fighting Sudan when they intend to conquer or die with their men — and more handshakes and more salutes. "*Dushman quaïss kitir*," ran round from grin to grin; "very good fight, very good fight."

· Now fall in, and back to the desert outside. And unless you are congenitally amorous of horrors, don't look too much about you. Black spindle-legs curled up to meet red-gimbleted black faces, donkeys head- less and legless, or sieves of shrapnel, camels with necks writhed back on to their humps, rotting already · in pools of blood and bile-yellow water, heads without faces, and faces without anything below, cobwebbed arms and legs, and black skins grilled to crackling on smouldering palm-leaf,—don't look at it. Here is the Sirdar's white star and crescent; here is the Sirdar, who created this battle, this clean-jointed, well-oiled, smooth-running, clockwork-perfect masterpiece of a battle. Not a flaw, not a check, not a jolt; and not a fleck on its shining success. Once more, hurrah, hurrah, hurrah!

XVIII.

LOSSES AND GAINS.

IT was over. It was a brilliant, crushing victory, and the dervish army was destroyed: so much everybody knew. But no more. The fight had gone forward in a whirl: you could see men fall about you, and knew that there must be losses on our side; but whether they were 100 or 1000 it was impossible even to guess. Then, as the khaki figures began to muster outside the zariba, it was good to meet friend after friend—dusty, sweaty, deep-breathing, putting up a grimed revolver—untouched. It was good to see the Tommies looking with new adoration to the comfort of their rifles, drunk with joy and triumph, yet touched with a sudden awe in the presence of something so much more nakedly elemental than anything in their experience. Two hours had sobered them from boys to men. Just then there was nothing in the world or under it to which the army would not have been equal. Yet, in that Godlike moment, I fancy every man in the force thought first of home.

Now to see what we had done and suffered. And
first, for a new fillip to exultation, Mahmud was a
prisoner. Some soldiers of the 10th Sudanese had
found him as they swept through the zariba—found
him sitting on his carpet, his weapons at his side, after
the manner of defeated war-chiefs who await death.
He was not killed, and presently he was brought bare-
headed before the Sirdar—a tall, dark-brown com-
plexioned man of something between thirty and forty.
He wore loose drawers and a gibba—the dervish
uniform which still mimics the patched shirt of the
Mahdi, but embroiders it with gold. His face was
of the narrow-cheeked, high-foreheaded type, for he
is a pure-bred Arab: his expression was cruel, but
high. He looked neither to right nor to left, but
strode up to the Sirdar with his head erect.

"Are you the man Mahmud?" asked the Sirdar.

"Yes; I am Mahmud, and I am the same as you."
He meant commander-in-chief.

"Why did you come to make war here?"

"I came because I was told,—the same as you."

Mahmud was removed in custody; but everybody
liked him the better for looking at his fate so straight
and defiantly.

But small leisure had anybody to pity Mahmud:
the pity was all wanted for our own people. Hardly
had the Camerons turned back from the river-bank
when it flew through the companies that two of the
finest officers in the regiment were killed. Captains

Urquhart and Findlay had both been killed leading
their men over the trenches. The first had only
joined the battalion at Rus Hudi; he had newly
passed the Staff College, and only two days before
had been gazetted major; after less than a fortnight's
campaigning he was dead. Captain Findlay's fortune
was yet more pathetic: he had been married but a
month or two before, and the widowed bride was not
eighteen. He was a man of a singularly simple, sincere,
and winning nature, and the whole force lamented
his loss. Probably his great height — for he stood
near 6 feet 6 inches — had attracted attack besides
his daring: he was one of the first, some said the
first, to get over the stockade, and had killed two of
the enemy with his sword before he dropped. Both
he and Captain Urquhart had got too far ahead of
their men to be protected by rifle fire; but they were
followed, and they were avenged.

Second-Lieutenant Gore of the Seaforths was also
killed while storming the trenches: he had not yet,
I think, completed one year's service. Among the
wounded officers were Colonel Verner of the Lincolns
and Colonel Murray of the Seaforths, both slightly:
the latter was very coolly tied up by Mr Scudamore,
the 'Daily News' correspondent, inside the zariba
under a distracting fire. More severely hit were
Major Napier (Camerons) and Captain Baillie (Seaforths): both were excellent officers and good companions; both afterwards died. Besides these the

Seaforths had three officers wounded, the Lincolns two, and the Warwicks one. Most of the casualties occurred in crossing the trenches, which were just wide enough for a man to stand in and deep enough to cover him completely. As our men passed over, the blacks fired and stabbed upwards; most of the wounds were therefore below the belt.

The Seaforths happened to have most officers hit among the four battalions of the British brigade; as they advanced in column against the hottest part of the entrenchment, this was quite comprehensible. But the Camerons, who led the whole brigade in line, lost most in non-commissioned officers and men. Counting officers, they had 15 killed and 46 wounded. The Seaforths lost (again with officers) 6 killed and 27 wounded; the Lincolns 1 killed and 18 wounded; and the Warwicks 2 killed and 12 wounded. Of these several afterwards died. Staff-Sergeant Wyeth, A.S.C., and Private Cross of the Camerons, were both mentioned in despatches. The first carried the Union Jack, which was three times pierced; the other was General Gatacre's bugler. Wyeth was severely wounded, and Cross presently seized with terrible dysentery: both died within a few days. Private Cross had bayoneted a huge black who attacked the general at the zariba, and it was said he was to be recommended for the V.C. A similar feat was done by a colour-sergeant of the Camerons, whose major was entangled in the stockade, and must have been

killed. The colour-sergeant never even mentioned
the service to his officer, who only discovered it by
accident. Of course there were scores of hair-breadth
escapes, as there must be in any close engagement.
One piper was killed with seven bullets in his body;
a corporal in another regiment received seven in his
clothing, one switchbacking in and out of the front
of his tunic, and not one pierced the skin. Another
man picked up a brass box inside the zariba, and
put it in his breast pocket, thinking it might come
in useful for tobacco. Next instant a bullet hit it
and glanced away. The Maxim battery had no
casualties — very luckily, for it was up with the
firing - line all the time; probably nobody could
stand up against it. Altogether the British brigade
lost 24 killed and 104 wounded, of whom perhaps
20 died.

The Egyptian loss was heavier. They had advanced
more quickly, and by reason of their line formation
had got to work in the trenches sooner than the
British; but they had not kept down the enemy's fire
with such splendid success. The 11th Sudanese,
which had the honour of having been one of the first
inside the zariba, lost very heavily—108 killed and
wounded out of less than 700. The total casualties
were 57 killed, and 4 British and 16 native officers,
2 British non - commissioned officers, and 365 non-
commissioned officers and men wounded. The white
officers were Walter Bey and Shekleton Bey, com-

manding the 9th and 14th Sudanese respectively,
and Bimbashis Walsh and Harley of the 12th
Sudanese. The former lost his leg. The instructors
were Sergeants Handley of the 9th and Hilton of the
12th. Thus, out of five white men, the 12th had three
hit. More officers would probably have been hit, but
that none except the generals were allowed to ride.
Generals Hunter, Macdonald, and Maxwell all rode
over the trenches at the head of their men.

The total of casualties, therefore, works out at 81
killed and 493 wounded, out of a strength probably a
little short of 12,000. It was not a wholly bloodless
victory, but beyond question it was a wonderfully
cheap one. For the results gained could not be over-
stated: Mahmud's army was as if it had never been.
These two short hours of shell and bullet and bayonet
had erased it from the face of the earth.

A scribe taken prisoner at Shendi said that the force
which marched north had been officially reported to
the Khalifa as 18,941 fighting men. The report may
or may not have been true: in any case Mahmud had
not this strength on Good Friday. Some had been
shot from the gunboats or by the 4th Battalion on
Shebaliya Island as they came down the river; some
had been killed in the skirmishes at Khor Abadar, or
in General Hunter's reconnaissances outside Nakheila.
Many had deserted. Mahmud himself said that his
strength on the 8th was 12,000 infantry and 4000
cavalry, with 10 guns. Some days afterwards he

asserted that his cavalry had left him the day before, but that was the brag of returning confidence. We all saw his cavalry.

To be sure, the cavalry did get away; and Osman Digna, who never fights to a finish, got away with them. The cavalry did nothing and behaved badly, which is significant. For the cavalry were Baggara— the cattle-owning Arabs of the Khalifa's own tribe, transplanted by him from Darfur to the best lands round Omdurman. They are the lords of the Sudan —and ingloriously they ran away. On the other hand, the Jehadia, the enlisted black infantry, fought most nobly. If their fire seemed bad to us, what hell must ours have been to them! First an hour and a half of shell and shrapnel—the best ammunition, perfectly aimed and timed, from some of the deadliest field-pieces in the world; then volley after volley of blunted Lee-Metford and of Martini bullets, delivered coolly at 300 yards and less, with case and Maxim fire almost point-blank. The guns fired altogether 1500 rounds, mostly shrapnel; the Camerons averaged 34 rounds per man. A black private, asked by his Bimbashi how many rounds he fired, replied, "Only 15." "Why, you're not much of a man," said his officer. "Ah, but then, Effendim," he eagerly excused himself, "I had to carry a stretcher besides." If the black bearer-parties fired 15 rounds, what must the firing-line have done! Mahmud said that his people had only laughed at the shrapnel, but that the infantry fire was *Sheitun tam-*

am — the very devil. Mahmud, however, admitted that, having been round the position, he lay close in his stockade during the bombardment; and as his stockade, or casemate, was the strongest corner in the place, he can hardly speak for the rest. And I saw scores and hundreds of dead goats and sheep, donkeys and camels, lying in pits in the part of the zariba stormed by the British. Now Thomas Atkins does not kill animals needlessly, even when his blood is hottest. The beasts therefore must have been killed by shrapnel; and if so many beasts, we may presume that many men, no better protected, were killed too. And so, I am afraid, unavoidably, were many women, for the zariba was full of them.

Yet the black Jehadia stood firm in their trenches through the infernal minutes, and never moved till those devilish white Turks and their black cousins came surging, yelling, shooting, and bayoneting right on top of them. Many stayed where they were to die, only praying that they might kill one first. Those who ran, ran slowly, turning doggedly to fire. The wounded, as usual, took no quarter; they had to be killed lest they should kill. For an example of their ferocious heroism, I cite a little, black, pot-bellied boy of ten or so. He was standing by his dead father, and when the attackers came up, he picked up an elephant-gun and fired. He missed, and the kicking monster half-killed him; but he had done what he could.

In the zariba itself Bimbashi Watson, A.D.C. to the
Sirdar, counted over 2000 dead before he was sick of
it. There were others left: trench after trench was
found filled with them. A few were killed outside the
zariba; a great many were shot down in crossing the
river-bed. Altogether 3000 men must have been
killed on the spot; among them were nearly all the
Emirs, including Wad Bishara, who was Governor of
Dongola in 1896. But this was not half the significance of the victory. Now you began to comprehend
the perfection of the Sirdar's strategy. If he had
waited for Mahmud on the Nile, fugitives could have
escaped up-stream. If he had waited low down the
Atbara, they could still have got across to the Nile.
But by giving battle up at Nakheila, he gave the
escaping dervish thirty miles of desert to struggle
across before he could reach water and such safety
as the patrolling gunboats would allow him. A few
may have got back to Omdurman — if they dared;
some certainly were afterwards picked off by the
gunboats in the attempt. Others fled up the Atbara;
many were picked up by the cavalry through the
afternoon: some got as far as Adarama or even near
Kassala, and were killed by the friendly levies there.
For the wounded the desert was certain death. In
a word, the finest dervish army was not. Retreat
was impossible, pursuit superfluous; defeat was annihilation.

XIX.

THE TRIUMPH.

"Catch 'em alive O !   Catch 'em alive O !
If they once gets on the gum
They'll pop off to kingdom come ;
Catch 'em alive O !   Catch 'em alive O !
For I am the flyest man around the town."

BACK swung the blacks from battle. The band of the
Twelfth specialises on Mr Gus Elen : it had not been
allowed to play him during the attack—only the regimental march till the bandsmen were tired of it, and
then each instrument what it liked—but now the air
quoted came in especially apposite.

They had caught 'em alive O. Hardly one but had
slung behind him a sword or a spine-headed spear, a
curly knife, or a spiky club, or some other quaint
captured murdering-iron. Some had supplemented
their Martini with a Remington, an inch calibre
elephant-gun with spherical iron bullets or conical
shells, a regulation Italian magazine rifle, a musket
of Mahomet Ali's first expedition, a Martini of '85, or

L

a Tower Rifle of '56 with a handful of the cartridges the sepoys declined to bite. Some had suits of armour tucked inside them; one or two, Saracen helmets slung to their belts. Over one tarbush waved a diadem of black ostrich plumes. The whole regiment danced with spear-headed banners blue and white, with golden letters thereupon promising victory to the faithful. And behind half-a-dozen men tugged at one of Mahmud's ten captured guns; they meant to ask the Sirdar if they might keep it.

The band stopped, and a hoarse gust of song flung out. From references to Allah you might presume it a song of thanksgiving. Then, tramp, tramp, a little silence, and the song came again with an abrupt exultant roar. The thin-legged, poker-backed shadows jerked longer and longer over the rough desert shingle. They had been going from six the bitter night before, and nothing to eat since, and Nakheila has been 111° in the shade, with the few spots of shade preoccupied by corpses. That being so, and remembering that the British and wounded had to follow, the Second Brigade condescended to a mere four miles an hour. And "By George! you know," said the Bey, "they're lovely; they're rippers. I've seen Sikhs and I've seen Gurkhas, and these are good enough for me. This has been the happiest day of my life. I wasn't happier the day I got the D.S.O. than I've been to-day."

It was the happiest day of a good many lives. But forty all but sleepless hours on your feet or in your

saddle tell on the system in a climate that seesaws
between a grill and an ice-machine. By the time I got
in I was very contented to tie my horse by some whity-
brown grass and tumble to sleep with my head on the
saddle. At midnight dinner was ready; then solid
sleep again. Awaking at five, I found an officer of
Colonel Lewis's brigade in his spurs and demanding
tea. He had got in from Nakheila but two hours
before, which brought his fast well over twenty-four
hours and his vigil to close on forty-eight.

For it isn't everybody that tramps back into camp
from battle with bands and praises of Allah. Some
stay for good, and it pricks you in your joy when you
catch yourself thinking of that swift and wicked injus-
tice. Why him? Also some come home on their
backs, or wrenched and moaning in cacolets bumping on baggage-camels. Lewis's never-weary, never-
hungry Egyptians had been bringing in the wounded—
carrying stretchers across twelve black miles of desert
at something over a mile an hour. And General
Hunter, who in the morning had been galloping bare-
headed through the bullets, waving on the latest-raised
battalion of blacks, now chose to spend the night playing guide to the crawling convoy. General Hunter
could not do an unsoldierlike act if he tried.

It was difficult after all to be sorry for most of the
men who were hit, they were so aggressively not sorry
for themselves. The afternoon of the fight they lay
in a little palm-grove northward of the zariba under

tents of blanket—a double row of khaki and grey flannel shirt, with more blankets below them and above. One face was covered with a handkerchief; one man gasped constantly—just the gasp of the child that wants sympathy and doesn't like to ask for it; one face was a blank mask of yellow white clay. The rest, but for the red-splashed bandages and the importunate reek of iodoform, might have been lying down for a siesta. Their principal anxiety — these bearded boys who had never fired a shot off the range before — was to learn what size of deed they had helped to do to-day. "A grahn' fight? The best ever fought in the Sudan? Eh, indeed, sir; ah'm vara glahd to hear ye say so." "Now, 'ow would you sy, sir, this 'd be alongside them fights they've been 'avin' in India?" "Bigger, eh? Ah! Will it be in to-morrow's pyper? Well, they'll be talkin' about us at 'ome." It was not the unhappiest day in these men's lives either.

The morrow of the fight brought a quiet morning —for all but correspondents, who had now to pay for many days of idle luxury—and in the afternoon we all marched off to the old camp at Abadar. Thence on Sunday the brigades were to march to their old quarters—British to Darmali, 1st to Berber, 2nd to Essillem, and 3rd to Fort Atbara. Everybody was agasp for the moving air and moving water of the Nile. But the British got very late into camp on Saturday night, and there was no longer any hurry, as there was no longer any enemy. So instead we had an Easter Sunday church-parade—men standing reverently four - square in the sand; in the middle the padre, square-shouldered and square-jawed, with putties and square boots showing under the surplice; a couple of drums for lectern, and "Thanks be to God, who giveth us the victory," for text.

On Monday, the 11th, the Sirdar rode into Fort Atbara, and the Egyptian brigades followed him. The British marched to Hudi, and thence across the desert to Darmali, their summer quarters. There began to be talk about leave. But before the campaign closed there was one inspiriting morning—the return to Berber.

It was more like a Roman triumph than anything you have ever seen—like in its colour, its barbarism, its intoxicating arrogance. The Sirdar reached Berber an hour or so after sunrise; the garrison—Macdonald's brigade—had bivouacked outside. The Sirdar rode up to the once more enfranchised town, and was there received by a guard of honour of the 1st Egyptians, who had held the town during the campaign. The guns thundered a salute. Then slowly he started to ride down the wide main street — tall, straight, and masterful in his saddle. Hunter Pasha at his side, his staff and his flag behind him, then Lewis Bey and some of his officers from Fort Atbara, then a clanking escort of cavalry. At the gate he passed under a triumphal arch, and all the street was Vene-

tian masts and bunting and coloured paper, and
soldiers of the 1st presenting arms, and men and
women and children shrieking shrill delight.

Well might they ; for they have tried both rules, and
they prefer that of Egypt. So they pressed forward
and screamed " Lu, lu," as they saw returning the
Sirdar and their Excellencies, these men of fair
face and iron hand, just to the weak and swiftly
merciless to the proud. And when these had passed
they pressed forward still more eagerly. Farther
behind, in a clear space, came one man alone, his
hands tied behind his back. Mahmud! Mahmud,
holding his head up and swinging his thighs in a
swaggering stride—but Mahmud a prisoner, beaten,
powerless. When the people of Berber saw that,
they were convinced. It was not a lie, then: the
white men had conquered indeed. And many a dark-
skinned woman pressed forward to call Mahmud
" Dog " to his face: it was Mahmud, last year, who
massacred the Jaalin at Metemmeh.

By this time the Sirdar had come almost to the
bazaar, at the north end of the town ; and there was a
small platform with an awning. He dismounted, and so
did the officers ; then took his stand, and in came the
troops. At their head the brigadier—" old Mac,"
bronzed and grizzled, who has lived in camp and
desert and battlefield these twenty years on end.
Then the blacks, straight as the spears they looted at
Nakheila, quivering with pride in their officers and

their own manhood—yet not a whit prouder than when they marched out a month before. Then the cavalry and the guns and the camel-corps—every arm of the victorious force. And Berber stood by and wondered and exulted. The band crashed and the people yelled. "Lu-u-u, lu-u-u-u" piped the black women, and you could see the brave, savage, simple hearts of the black men bounding to the appeal. And the Sirdar and General Hunter and the others stood above all, calm and commanding; below Bey and Bimbashi led battalion or squadron or battery, in undisturbed self-reliance. You may call the show barbaric if you like: it was meant for barbarians. The English gentleman, if you like, is half barbarian too. That is just the value of him. Here was this little knot of white men among these multitudes of black and brown, swaying them with a word or the wave of a hand upraised. Burned from the sun and red-eyed from the sand, carrying fifteen years' toil with straight backs, bearing living wounds in elastic bodies. They, after all, were the finest sight of the whole triumph—so fearless, so tireless, so confident.

XX.

EGYPT OUT OF SEASON.

THERE was no difference in Port Said. Ships want coal in July as in December: the black dust hung over the Canal in sullen fog, and the black demons of the pit wailed as they tripped from lighter to deck under their baskets. In the hotel the Levantine clerks and agents took their breakfast in white ducks under a punkah, but that was all the change. Black island of coal, jabbering island of beggars and touts, forlorn island cranked in by sea and canal and swamp and sand, Port Said in summer was not appreciably more God-forsaken than in the full season.

Ismailia was not appreciably deader than usual. If anything, with half-a-dozen French summer gowns and a French bicycle club, in blue and scarlet jerseys, doing monkey-tricks in front of the station, it was a shade more alive.

In Cairo came the awful change. Cairo the fashionable, the brilliant, was a desolation. When you run into the station in the season, the platform is lined with names of hotels on the gold-laced caps of under-porters: you can hardly step out for swarms of Arabs, who fight for your baggage. On the night of July 12, the platform showed gaunt and large and empty. The streets were hardly better—a few listless Arabs in the square outside the station, and then avenue on avenue of silent darkness.

By daylight Cairo looked like a ball-room the morning after. One hotel was shamelessly making up a rather battered face against next season. The verandah of Shepheard's, where six months ago you could not move for tea-tables, nor hear the band for the buzz of talk, was quite empty and lifeless; only one perspiring waiter hinted that this was a hotel. The Continental, the centre of Cairene fashion, had a whole wing shuttered up; the mirrors in the great hall were blind with whiting, and naked suites of bed-room furniture camped out in the great dining-room. Some shops were shut; the rest wore demi-toilettes of shutter and blind; the dozing shopkeepers seemed half-resentful that anybody should wish to buy in such weather. As for scarabs and necklaces and curiosities of Egypt, they no longer pretended to think that any sane man could give money for such things. As you looked out from the Citadel, Cairo seemed dazed under the sun; the very Pyramids looked as if they were taking a holiday.

All that was no more than you expected: you knew that no tourists came to Egypt in July. But native

Egypt was out of season too.   The streets that clacked
with touts and beggars, that jingled with every kind
of hawker's rubbish—you passed along them down
a vista of closed jalousies and saw not a soul, heard
not a sound.   The natives must be somewhere, only
where ?   A few you saw at road-making, painting, and
the like jobs of an off-season.   But every native was
dull, listless, hanging from his stalk, half dead.   Eyes
were languid and lustreless : the painter's head drooped
and swayed from side to side, and the brush almost
fell from his lax fingers.   In the narrow bevel of
shadow left under a wall by the high sun, flat on back
or face, open-mouthed, half asleep, half fainting, gasped
Arab Cairo—the parasite of the tourist in his holiday,
the workman leaving his work, donkey-boy and donkey
flat and panting together.

Well might they gasp and pant ; for the air of
Cairo was half dead too.   You might drive in it at
night and feel it whistle round you, but it did not
refresh you.   You might draw it into your lungs, but
it did not fill them.   The air had no quality in it, no
body : it was thin, used up, motionless, too limp to
live in.   The air of August London is stale and close,
poor ; exaggerate it fifty-fold and you have the air of
July Cairo.   You wake up at night dull and flaccid
and clammy with sweat, less refreshed than when you
lay down.   You live on what sleep you can pilfer
during the hour of dawn.   As you drive home at night

you envy the dark figure in a galabeah stretched on
the pavement of Kasr-en-Nil bridge; there only in
Cairo can you feel a faint stirring in the air.

To put all in one word, Egypt lacks its Nile. The
all-fathering river is at his lowest and weakest. In
places he is nearly dry, and what water he can give
the cracked fields is pale, green, unfertile. He was
beginning to rise now, slowly; presently would come
the flood and the brown manuring water. The night
wind would blow strongly over his broadened bosom,
the green would spring out of the mud, and Egypt
would be alive again.

Only in one place was she alive yet—and that was
the Continental Hotel. Here all day sat and came
and went clean-limbed young men in flannels, and
at dinner-time the terrace was cool with white mess-
jackets. Outside was the only crowd of natives in
Cairo—a thick line of Arabs squatting by the opposite
wall, nursing testimonials earned or bought, cooks
and valets and grooms—waiting to be hired to go up
the Nile. Up at the citadel they would show you the
great black up-standing 40-pounder guns with which
they meant to breach Khartum. Out at Abbassieh
the 21st Lancers were changing their troop-horses for
lighter Syrians and country-breds. The barrack-yard
of Kasr-en-Nil was yellow with tents, and under a
breathless afternoon sun the black-belted Rifle Brigade
marched in from the station to fill them. The wilted

Arabs hardly turned their heads at the band; the
Rifles held their shoulders square and stepped out
with a rattle.

The Egyptian may feel the sun; the Englishman
must stand up and march in it. You see it is his
country, and he must set an example. And seeing
Egypt thus Nileless, bloodless, you felt more than
ever that he must lose no time in taking into firm
fingers the keys of the Nile above Khartum.

XXI.

GOING UP.

On the half-lit Cairo platform servants flung agonised arms round brothers' necks, kissed them all over, and resigned themselves to the horrors of the Sudan. Inside the stuffy carriages was piled a confusion of bags and bundles, of helmet-cases and sword-cases, of canvas buckets cooling soda, and canvas bottles cooling water,—of Beys and Bimbashis returning from leave. It was rather like the special train that takes boys back to school. A few had been home—but the Sirdar does not like to have too many of his officers seen in Piccadilly ; it doesn't look well. Some had been to Constantinople, to Brindisi and back for the sea, to San Stefano, the Ostend of Egypt, to Cairo and no farther. Like schoolboys, they had all been wild to get away, and now they were all wild to get back. Thank the Lord, no more Cairo—sweat all the night instead of sleep, and mosquitos tearing you to pieces. Give me the night-breeze of the desert and the clean sand of the Sudan.

But first we had to tunnel through the filthiest seventeen hours in Egypt. The servants had spread our blankets on the bare, hard leather seats of the boxes that Egyptian railways call sleeping - cars; a faint grateful air began to glide in through the windows. And then came in the dust. Without haste —had it not seventeen hours before it?—it streamed through every chink in a thick coffee-coloured cloud. It piled itself steadily over the seats and the floor, the bags and bundles and cases; it built up walls of mud round the soda-water, and richly larded the half-cold chicken for the morrow's lunch. We choked ourselves to sleep; in the morning we choked no longer, the lungs having reconciled themselves to breathe powdered Egypt. Our faces were layered with coffee-colour, thicker than the powder on the latest fashionable lady's nose. Hair and moustaches, eyebrows and eye-lashes, and every corner of sun-puckered eyes, were lost and levelled in rich friable soil. And from the caked, sun-riven fields of thirsty Egypt fresh clouds rose and rolled and settled, till in all the train you saw, smelt, touched, tasted nothing but dust.

At Luxor came the first novelty. When I came down the practicable railway stopped short there: now a narrow-gauge railway ran through to Assuan. It is not quite comprehensible why the gauge should have been broken,—perhaps to make sure that the line should be kept exclusively military. It can easily be altered afterwards to the Egyptian gauge;

meanwhile the journey is done by train in twelve hours against the post-boat's thirty-six.

Assuan was the same as ever. Shellal, at the head of the cataract, the great forwarding station for the South, was the same, only much more so. The high bank was one solid rampart of ammunition and beef, biscuit and barley; it clanged and tinkled all night through with parts of steamers and sections of barges. Stern-wheelers came down from the South, turned about, took in fuel, hooked on four barges alongside, and thudded off up-river again. No hurry ; no rest. And here was the same Commandant as when I came up before. He had had one day in Cairo ; his hair was two shades greyer; he was still being reviled by everybody who did not have everything he wanted sent through at five seconds' notice; he was still drawing unmercifully on body and brain, and ripping good years out of his life to help to conquer the Sudan. Victory over dervishes may be won in an hour, may be cheap; victory over the man-eating Sudan—the victory of the railway, the steamer, the river—means months and years of toil and so much of his life lost, to every man that helps to win it.

The steamer tinkered at her fourteen-year-old boiler for twenty hours, and then trudged off towards Halfa. She did the 200 odd miles in 77 hours, so that it would have been almost as quick to have gone by road in a wheelbarrow. But then the nuggars along-side were heavy with many sacks of barley, to be turned later into cavalry chargers. Moreover, on the second morning, rounding a bend, we suddenly saw a line drawn diagonally across the river. All the water below the line was green; all above it was brown. And the brown pressed slowly, thickly forward, driving the green before it. This was the Nile-flood,—the rich Abyssinian mud that comes down Blue Nile and Atbara. When this should have floated down below the cataract, Egypt would have water again, air again, bread again, life again. And the Sudan would have gunboats and barges of cartridges and gyassas of food and fodder, and the Sirdar thundering at the gates of Khartum.

Next windy, green-treed Halfa—only this time it was less windy than last, and the trees, though still the greenest on the Nile, were not so green. Last time there had been melons growing on the sandy eyot opposite the commanderia, and the eyot had grown higher daily; this time it was all dry sand and no melons,—only it grew daily smaller in the lapping water. But spring or summer, Halfa's business is the same—the railway and the recruits. That line was finished now up to the Atbara, and the fore-shore was clear of rails and sleepers. But instead they were forcing through stores and supplies, choking the trucks to the throat with them. The glut had only begun when the line reached its terminus; it would be over before the new white brigade came through. Everything in the Sirdar's Expedition has its own time — first material, then transport, then troops; and woe unto him who is behind his time.

The platform was black and brown, blue and white with a great crowd of natives. For drawn up in line opposite the waiting trucks were rigid squads of black figures in the familiar brown jersey and blue putties, and on the tarbushes the badges, green, black, red, yellow, blue, and white, of each of the six Sudanese battalions. Thin-shanked Shillúks and Dinkas from the White Nile, stubby Beni-Helba from Darfur and the West,—they were just the figures and huddled savage-smiling faces that we had last seen at Berber. Only—the last time we had seen those particular blacks they were shooting at us. Every one had begun life as a dervish, and had been taken prisoner at or after the Atbara. Now, not four months after, here they were, erect and soldierly, with at least the rudiments of shooting, on their way to fight their former masters, and very glad to do it. They knew when they were well off. Before they were slaves, half-clothed, half-fed, half-armed, good to lose their women at Shendi, and to stay in the trenches of Nakheila when the Baggara ran away. Now they are free soldiers, well paid, well clothed, well fed, with weapons they can trust and officers who charge ahead and would rather die than leave them. Their women—who, after all, only preceded them into the Egyptian army—are as safe from recapture at Halfa as you are in the Strand. No wonder the blacks grinned merrily as

M

they bundled up on to the trucks, and the women
lu-lu-lued them off with the head-stabbing shrillness
of certain victory.

The first time I travelled on the S.M.R. I enjoyed
a berth in the large saloons; the second time in one
of the small saloons; this time it was a truck. But
the truck, after all, was the most comfortable of the
three. It was a long double-bogie, with a plank roof,
and canvas curtains that you could let down when
the sun came in, and eight angarebs screwed to the
floor. Therein six men piled their smaller baggage,
and set up their tables, and ate and drank and slept
and yawned forty-eight hours to the Atbara. Of all
the three months' changes in the Sudan, here were the
most stupefying. Abeidieh, where the new gunboats
had been put together, had grown from a hut and two
tents to a railway station and triangle and watering-
plant and engine-shed, and rows of seemly mud-
barracks, soon to be hospital. But the Atbara was
even more utterly transformed. I had left it a fortified camp; I found it a kind of Nine Elms. Lewis
Bey's house, then the pride of the Sudan, now cowered
in the middle of a huge mud-walled station-yard.
Boxes and barrels and bags climbed up and over-
shadowed and choked it. Ammunition and stores,
food and fodder—the journey had been a crescendo
of them, but this was the fortissimo. You wandered
about among the streets of piles that towered overhead, and lost yourself in munitions of war. Along

the Nile bank, where two steamers together had been a rarity, lay four. Another paddled ceaselessly to and fro across the river, where the little two-company camp had grown into lines for the cavalry and camel corps. Slim-sparred gyassas fringed all the bank; lateen sails bellied over the full river.

Of troops the place was all but empty; the indispensable Egyptians were away up the river cutting and stacking wood for the steamers or preparing depots. In mid-April the Atbara was the as yet unattained objective of the railway; in mid-July the railway was ancient history, and the Atbara was the port of departure for the boats. Just a half-way house on the road to Khartum. What a man the Sirdar is—if he is a man! We got out and pitched our tents; and here we found the men who had not been on leave—the railway and the water transport and the camel transport and the fatigues in general—working harder, harder, harder every day and every night. We drank a gin-and-soda to the master-toast of the Egyptian army: "Farther South!"

XXII.

THE FIRST STEPS FORWARD.

AT the beginning of August the military dispositions were not, on paper, very different from those of the end of April. The Sirdar's headquarters had been moved to the Atbara in order that the vast operations of transport at that point might go on under his own eye. Of the four infantry brigades which had fought against Mahmud, three were still in their summer quarters. Neither of the two additional brigades had yet arrived at the front.

The force destined for Omdurman consisted of two infantry divisions, one British and one Egyptian; one regiment of British and ten squadrons of Egyptian cavalry; one field and one howitzer battery, and two siege-guns of British artillery and one horse and four field batteries of Egyptian, besides both British and Egyptian Maxims; eight companies of camel-corps; the medical service and the transport corps; six fighting gunboats, with eight transport steamers and a host of sailing boats.

The Egyptian infantry division was commanded, as before, by Major-General Hunter; but it now counted four brigades instead of three. The First, Second, and Third (Macdonald's, Maxwell's, and Lewis's) were constituted as in the Atbara campaign.

The commanding officers of battalions were the same except for the 13th Sudanese. Smith-Dorrien Bey, who originally raised the regiment, now commanded in place of Collinson Bey. The latter officer had been promoted to the command of the Fourth Brigade. It was entirely Egyptian—the 1st (Bimbashi Doran), 5th (Borhan Bey, with native officers), 17th (Bunbury Bey), and the newly-raised 18th (Bimbashi Matchett). Of these the first was at Fort Atbara; the 17th and 18th were coming up from Merawi, hauling boats over the Fourth Cataract. They reached Abu Hamed by the beginning of August. The 5th was half at Berber and half on the march across the desert from Suakim. The Third Brigade was at various points up-river, cutting wood for the steamers.

The two Egyptian battalions (2nd and 8th) attached to the First and Second Brigades were at Nasri Island, ten miles or so from the foot of the Shabluka Cataract, forming a depôt for supplies and stores. The six black battalions left Berber on July 30, and arrived at the Atbara in the small hours of August 1. Taking the strength of an Egyptian battalion at 750, the division would number 12,000 men.

Major - General Gatacre commanded the British Division. Of its two brigades the First—the British Brigade of the last campaign, now under Colonel Wauchope — was still in summer quarters. Head-quarters, Camerons, Seaforths, and Maxim battery at Darmali; Lincolns and Warwicks at Essillem. The last two had changed commanding officers — Lieu-tenant-Colonel Louth now had the Lincolns, Lieu-tenant - Colonel Forbes the Warwicks. The latter officer had arrived at Umdabieh two days before the Atbara fight to relieve Lieutenant - Colonel Quale Jones, ordered home to command the 2nd Battalion of the regiment; with rare tact and common-sense it was arranged that Colonel Jones should lead the bat-talion he knew. Colonel Forbes went into the fight as a free-lance, and I saw him enjoying himself like a schoolboy with a half - holiday. The Warwicks rejoiced once more in the possession of their two companies from the Merawi garrison. Casualties in action, and deaths and invalidings from sickness, had brought down the strength of this brigade, though officers and men had stood the climate exceedingly well. The sick-rate had never touched 6 per cent. There were not fifty graves in the cemetery; and most of the faces at the mess-tables were familiar. The Lincolns, who had come up over 1100 strong, still had 980; the other three battalions were each about 750 strong, and the Warwicks were expecting a draft of sixty men. With the Maxims, A.S.C., and Medical

Service the strength of the brigade would come to nearly 3500. The Second Brigade had not yet come up from Egypt. Colonel Lyttelton was to command. The four battalions composing it were the 1st Northumberland Fusiliers (5th, Lieutenant-Colonel Money) and 2nd Lancashire Fusiliers (20th, Lieutenant-Colonel Collingwood) from the Cairo garrison, the 2nd Rifle Brigade (Colonel Howard) from Malta, and the 1st Grenadier Guards from Gibraltar. Each battalion was to come up over 1000 strong. The 1st Royal Irish Fusiliers, from Alexandria, were sending up a Maxim detachment with four guns, so that the whole division would number well over 7500.

Broadwood Bey's nine squadrons of cavalry had concentrated during the last week of July on the western bank opposite Fort Atbara. They were to march up, starting on August 4, and to be joined at Metemmeh by a squadron from Merawi. The 21st Lancers (Colonel Martin) were expected up from Cairo about 500 strong; the total of the cavalry would be about 1500. British and Egyptian were to be separate commands.

The whole of the artillery, on the other hand, was under Long Bey, of the Egyptian Army. The arrival of Bimbashi Stewart's battery from Merawi had completed the strength of the Egyptian artillery; both this battery and Bimbashi Peake's had been re-armed with 9-pounder Maxim-Nordenfeldts, so that all the field guns were now the same. These, with the horse battery, began to go up the Nile at the beginning of August—the pieces by boat, the horses and mules marching. The 32nd Field Battery R.A. (Major Williams), the 37th Field Battery with 5-inch howitzers and Lyddite shells and two 40-pounder siege guns, were coming up from Cairo. This would give a total of forty-four guns, besides twenty British and Egyptian Maxims.

Two companies of camel corps were at the Atbara, timed to march on August 2. One was coming over from Suakim. The other five, under Tudway Bey, commanding the whole corps, were to start with the Merawi squadron of cavalry, about the same time, and march by Sir Herbert Stewart's route across the Bayuda Desert to Metemmeh. The strength would be about 800. The land force was thus over 22,000 men.

The three new gunboats—Malik, Sheikh, and Sultan —were put together at Abeidieh, the work beginning immediately after the battle of the Atbara, as soon as the railway reached that place. They carry two $12\frac{1}{2}$-pounder Maxim-Nordenfeldt quick-firers fore and aft, and three Maxims, two on the upper deck and one on a platform above. They are lightly armoured, being bullet-proof all over, and the screw is protected by being sunk in a plated well a few feet forward of the stern. As fighting boats they might be expected to show superior qualities to the vessels of the Zafir class; but as beasts of burden with barges they were inferior to these. Drawing only 18 inches against the older boat's 30 inches, they could not get grip enough of the water to make good headway against the full Nile.

From the disposition of the force, extended along the Nile from Shabluka to Alexandria, and across the desert from Korti to Suakim, it was evident that the campaign had not yet opened by the beginning of August. The army was only entering on the movements preparatory to concentration. The point of concentration was Wad Habashi, a dozen miles or so south of Shabluka; the time was as yet uncertain. Transport was so far forward that we might easily get to Omdurman the first week in September. All depended on the weather. Up to now there had been hardly any rain. But the real rainy season—said Slatin Pasha, who is the only white man with real opportunity of knowing—runs from August 10 to September 10. It might be sooner or later, heavier or lighter. A swollen river, a flooded, torrent-riven bank, malaria and ague, would hold us back. A dry season would pass us gaily through.

And when we advanced from Wad Habashi? It was utterly impossible to say what would befall. If the Khalifa wanted to give us trouble, he would leave without fighting. That would probably mean that he would get his throat cut by one of the innumerable enemies he has made; certainly it would mean the collapse of his empire. But it would also mean a

costly expedition with no finality at the end of it;
it would mean years of anarchy, dacoity from Khartum to the Albert Nyanza, from Abyssinia to Lake
Chad.   Only there was always the relieving thought
that Khalifa Abdullahi would aim not so much at
giving trouble to us as at avoiding it for himself.
With Mahmud's experience before his eyes he might
think it safest to be taken prisoner.   He might, just
possibly, even decide to die game.

Granting that he fought, it was still hopelessly uncertain where and how he would fight.   It might be
at Kerreri, sixteen miles north of his capital; it might
be inside his wall.   We could speculate for days; we
did; but to come to any conclusion more likely than
any other was beyond any man in the army.

XXIII.

IN SUMMER QUARTERS.

SCENE of the dialogue, a mess-room in a village on the Nile. Time, nearly lunch-time. A subaltern is discovered smoking a cigarette under the verandah. Enter I.

Subaltern. Hallo, Steevens! when did you come up? Get down and have a drink. Hi, you syce! Take this *hawaga's hoosan* and take the *sarg* and bridle off and *dini* a drink of *moyyah.* What'll you drink? . . . Oh no: this isn't so bad—better than Ras Hudi, anyhow. You're looking at our pictures—out of the 'Graphic,' you know—coloured them ourselves—helps you through the day, you know: that's a well-developed lady, isn't it? Have a cigarette, will you? We're all getting pretty well fed up with this place by now.

Enter a Captain. Hallo, Steevens! when did you come up? Have you got anything to drink? I suppose you've been at home all this time. No, I haven't been farther north than Berber. Had a very jolly ten days up the Atbara, though. Two parties

went—one with the General, one afterwards. Seven
guns got a hundred and sixty-five sand-grouse in one
day. Went up right beyond our battlefield. High?
Never smelt anything like it in my life. The bush
gets very thick above. No; no lions.

Subaltern. We got a croco down here, though, and a
bally great fish with a head on him three feet six long,
the head alone. No, I haven't been down either. I
went down with a boat party to Geneineteh, though—
ripping. There was a grass bank just six inches above
the water, and you could bathe all day. The men
loved it, if they were pretty fit to begin with; if they
weren't, you see, what with bully beef and dirty
water——

Captain. But we're all getting fed up, as the
Tommies say, with this place by now.

Enter a Senior Captain. Hallo, Steevens! I heard
you'd come up. In this country it isn't "Have a
drink," but "What'll you drink?" Well, here we are
still in this filthy country. Yes, I got ten days in
Cairo, but I was at the dentist's all the time. Gad,
what a country! When I think of all the lives that
have been lost for this miserable heap of sand they
call the Soudan—ugh!—it's—it's——

Subaltern. Ripping sport: everybody was wondering
how the Pari Mutuel was done so well. The truth
was, it was run by the same men of the Army Pay
Department that do it at the races in Cairo. Devilish
good race, too, the Atbara Derby. We thought we

hadn't got a chance against all these Egyptian army fellows, and Fair won it by a head, Sparkes second, a bad third.

Enter a Major. Well, Steevens, how are you? Been up long? Have a—— I see you've got one. Good to see all you fellows coming out again; means business. River's very full to-day, isn't it?

Captain. Risen three feet and an inch since yesterday. The Atbara flood, I suppose. You were at Atbara; did you see it?

I. Rather. It came down roaring, hit the Nile, and piled up on end. Brought down trees, beams, dugouts——

Major. Well, now, shall we go in to lunch? You didn't see the First British Brigade field-firing to-day, did you? Nothing will come within 800 yards of that alive. Do you think we shall have a fight?

Enter a Colonel. Good morning, Mr Steevens: have you been up long? Are you being attended to? Yes, now; shall we have a fight? What will he do now? I can't bear to think we aren't going to have a fight.

Senior Captain. Fight? wh——

Major. If he'd only come out into the open——

Captain. No; he'll stick behind his——

Subaltern. Wall: then we shall have——

Major. Two days' bombardment; but then, you know——

Colonel. Well, I wish we'd another brigade in reserve to stay at——

Senior Captain. Another brigade, sir? Why, it makes me sick to see all this preparation against such an enemy. We had 1500 men at Abu Klea, and now we've got 20,000. Fanatics? Look at those men we fought at the Atbara, those miserable scally-wags. Do you call these fanatics? Sell their lives? give 'em away. Despise the enemy; yes, I do despise them; I despise them utterly. Rifles are too good for them. Sticks, sir, we ought to take to them—sticks with bladders on the end. Why, the moment we came to their zariba they got up and ran—got up like a white cloud and ran. And then all these prepara-tions and all this force? They're a contemptible enemy—a wretched, despicable enemy. Why won't the Sirdar let the gunboats above Shabluka? Because Beatty would take Khartum.

Colonel. Come, come now. But what'll you have to eat now?

General Conversation. Going to the Gymkhana this afternoon. . . . Squat on his hunkers inside his wall . . . won't sell you a drop of milk, the surly devils, when we're saving their country . . . the houses at Omdurman are outside the wall, you know . . . not a bad notion of jumping, that bay pony . . . street-to-street fighting, we should lose a devil of a lot of men . . . did you hear the Guards cabled to ask what arrangements had been made for ice on the cam-paign? . . . but then he can't defend his wall; it hasn't got a banquette, and it's twelve feet high . . .

gave the recruit their water-bottles to fill at the lake. "Here, Jock," they said, "take mine too." So the wretched man started off with the water-bottles of the whole half-company to fill them at the mirage . . . have another drink . . . rather; fed up with it; railway fatigues, too, and field-days twice a-week . . . it was their Colonel kept them from coming up, they say: damned fine regiment all the same . . . weakest Government of this century, sir . . . stowasser gaiters . . . go under canvas a couple of days before we start . . . ripping sport . . . fed up . . . drink . . .

Colonel (*rising*). Well, now, will you have a cigarette?

Senior Captain. A miracle of mismanagement. . . .

Voice of Tommy (*outside*). Whatcher doin'?

Second voice. Cancher see? stickin' 'oods on these 'ere cacolets.

Voice of Tommy. Whatcher doin' that for?

Second voice. Doncher know? To kerry the bleed'n' Grenadier Gawds to Khartum.

XXIV.

DEPARTURES AND ARRIVALS.

ON the 3rd of August the six Sudanese battalions left Fort Atbara for the point of concentration at Wad Habashi. Most people who saw them start remarked that they would be very glad to hear they had arrived.

You may have seen sardines in tins; but you will never really know how roomy and comfortable a tinned sardine must feel until you have seen blacks packed on one of the Sirdar's steamers. Nothing but the Sirdar's audacity would ever have tried it; nothing but his own peculiar blend of luck and judgment would have carried it through without appalling disaster.

Dressed in nothing but their white Friday shirt and drawers, the men filed on to the boats. Every man carried his blanket, for men from the Equator have tender chests, but it was difficult to see how he was ever to get into it. On each deck of each steamer they squatted, shoulder to shoulder, toe to back, chin to knee. Fast alongside each gunboat were a couple of double-decked roofed barges, brought out in sections from England for this very purpose. Both decks were jammed full of black men till you could not have pushed a walking-stick between them: the upper deck bellied under their weight like a hammock. At the tail of each gunboat floated a gyassa or two gyassas: in them you could have laid your blanket and slept peacefully on the soldiers' heads. Thus in this land of impossibilities a craft not quite so big as a penny steamer started to take 1100 men, cribbed so that they could not stretch arm or leg, 100 miles at rather under a mile an hour.

The untroubled Nile floated down brim-full, thick and brown as Turkish coffee, swift and strong as an ocean. The turbid Atbara came down swishing and rushing, sunk bushes craning their heads above the flood, and green Sodom apples racing along it like bubbles, and flung itself upon the Nile. Against the double streams the steamers—seven in all, bigger and smaller, with over 6000 men—pulled slowly, slowly southward. The faithful women, babies on their hips, screamed one more farewell: their life is a string of farewells, threaded with jewels of victorious return. The huddled heaps of white cotton and black skin began to blend together in the blurring sunlight. They started before breakfast; by lunchtime all but one had vanished round the elbow a

N

mile or two up-stream. The blacks were gone out
to conquer again.

Blacks gone, whites came. The Headquarters and
first four companies of the Rifle Brigade were in camp
before the steamers were under way. These things
fit in like the joints of your body till you take them
for the general course of things; only when you go
to Headquarters and see Chiefs-of-Staff and D.A.A.G.S.
and orderly-officers and aides-de-camp calculating and
verifying and countersigning and telegraphing and
acknowledging, do you realise that the staff-work of
an army is the biggest and most business-like business in the world.

The Rifles' first morning of Sudan was not endear-
ing. They were shot out on to a little hillock or platform at half-past one in the morning, in the middle
of one of the best dust-storms of the season. Through
the throttled moonlight they might have seen, if they
had cared to look at anything, the correspondent of
the 'Daily Mail' hammering at his uptorn tent-pegs
with a tin of saddle-soap, and howling dismally to a
mummified servant to bring him the mallet. Tack,
tack, tack went the mallets all over camp. But
the Rifles had neither tents nor angarebs nor bags:
they were dumped down among their baggage and sat
down for five hours to contemplate the smiling Sudan.
Then they disinterred themselves and their belongings
and marched into camp.

But this new brigade was to have a Cook's tour by

comparison with the other. They had abundant kit and abundant stores. From the sea to Shabluka they hardly needed to put foot to the ground: thence it was a matter of half-a-dozen marches to Khartum and Omdurman. Fight there—then into boats again and down to the rail-head at the Atbara; train to Halfa, boat to Assuan, train to Cairo or Alexandria—the two new battalions, Rifles and Guards, might be up and down again, in and out of the country inside a couple of months. The sarcastic asked why they were not brought up in ice, unpacked at Omdurman to fight, and then packed in ice again. But that was unjust. Either you must give a regiment time to get fit and weed out its weaklings, or else you must cocker it all you can till you want it. The Rifles and Guards would never be as hard as the splendid sun-dried battalions of the First Brigade—there was not time to harden them. The next best thing was to keep them fresh and fit by sparing them as much as possible.

So the Rifles made their camp on the Atbara bank —cool, airy, and relatively free from dust-drift. Next day—the 4th—the second half of the battalion came in; next day Brigadier-General Lyttelton with his staff and the 32nd field battery; next day the first half of the Grenadier Guards. So they were timed to go on —half a battalion or a battery or a squadron nearly every morning till the whole second brigade was on the Atbara. Before the tail of it had arrived the head would be off again—men and guns by boat, beasts by road—to Wad Habashi.

To transport 5000 men, 600 horses, two batteries with draught cattle, and two siege-guns some 1300 miles along a line of rail and river within four weeks is not, perhaps, on paper, a very astounding achievement. But remember last time we came the same way. Remember 1884—the voyageurs and the Seedee boys, the whalers and the troopers set to ride on camels and fight on foot, and all the rest of the Empire-ballet business—the force that left Cairo about the time of year these were leaving, that began to leave Halfa at the opening of September and struck the Nile at Metemmeh late in January, while most of it never got beyond Korti. It is exactly the difference between the amateur and the professional.

Remember, furthermore, that the railway from Luxor to Assuan and the railway from Halfa to the Atbara are both quite new: at home, with every engineering facility which is lacking in the Sudan, a new line is allowed a few months' trial to settle and mature before heavy traffic is run over it. The track is single, the engines are many of them old, the native officials are all of them incapable. The steamers are few and in great part old. The wind for the sailing boats was mostly contrary. The country is a howling red-hot depopulation. Yet every arriving vessel was not merely up to its time but a little before it. It wanted for nothing by the way, and when it arrived found provision for just three times as long as it was likely to need it.

And all the time, remember, just the same thing was going on up the river. While the trains were bringing the British, the boats were taking the blacks. The gyasses sank their low waists awash with the Nile-flood under groaning loads of supplies : the streets of boxes and sacks at the Atbara never seemed to grow less, but similar streets were rising at Nasri Island. Above us the bank was being stacked with wood for the steamers; below us Egyptian battalions were hauling at more boats to take more supplies forward. All one steady pull along a rope 1300 miles long—a pull without a stumble, without a slack. And the Sirdar ran his eye along the whole tension of it, knowing every man's business better than he did himself. Only furious because the wind was south or west instead of north. He was not accustomed to such luck, and he did not deserve it. But neither did he succumb to it. The sailing boats went south all the same. The Sirdar told them to go south; and somehow, tacking, towing, punting, Allah knows how, south it was.

XXV.

THE PATHOLOGY OF THIRST.

IF it had not been for the drink I should never have come twice to the Sudan.

It is part of the comprehensive uselessness of this country that its one priceless production can never be exported. If the Sudan thirst could be sent home in capsules, like the new soda-water sparklets, it would make any man's fortune in an evening. The irony of it is, that there is so much thirst here — such a limitless thirst as might supply the world's whole population richly : on the other side there are millions of our fellow - creatures, surrounded by every liquor that art can devise and patience perfect, but wanting the thirst to drink withal. Gentlemen in England now abed will call themselves accursed they were not here. And even the few white men who vainly strive to do justice to these stupendous depths and intensities, these vast areas and periods of thirst— how utterly and pitiably inadequate we are to our high opportunity.

I wonder if you ever were thirsty ? Probably not.
I never had been till I came to the Sudan, and that
is why I came again. If you have been really thirsty,
and often, you will be able to distinguish many vari-
ations of the phenomenon. The sand-storm thirst I
hardly count. It is caused by light soil forming in
the gullet; wash the soil away and the thirst goes
with it: this can be done with water, which you do
not even need to swallow.

The desert thirst is more legitimately so called: it
arises from the grilling sun on the sand, from the
dancing glare, and from hard riding therein. This
is not an unpleasant thirst: the sweat evaporates on
your face in the wind of your own galloping, and
thereby produces a grateful coolness without, while
throat and gullet are white-hot within. The desert
thirst consists in this contrast: it can be satisfied by a
gulp or two of really cool water which has also been
evaporating through a canvas bottle slung on your
saddle.

But in so far as it can be satisfied, it is no true
Sudan thirst. The true Sudan thirst is insatiable.
The true Sudan thirst—which, to be sure, may be
found in combination with either or both of the
others, and generally is—is born of sheer heat and
sheer sweat. Till you have felt it, you have not
thirsted. Every drop of liquid is wrung out of your
body: you could swim in your clothes; but, inside,
your muscle shrinks to dry sponge, your bones to dry

pith. All your strength, your substance, your self is draining out of you; you are conscious of a perpetual liquefaction and evaporation of good solid you. You must be wetted till you soften and swell to life again.

You are wetted. You pour in wet, and your self sucks it in and swells—and then instantly it gushes out again at every pore, and the self contracts and wilts. You swill in more, and out it bubbles before you even feel your inside take it up. More—and your pores swish in spate like the very Atbara. Useless: you must give it up, and let the goodness sluice out of you. There is nothing of you left; you are a mere vacuum of thirst. And that goes on from three hours after sunrise till an hour before sundown.

You must not think that we are idle all this while —not even correspondents. The real exercise of yourself and your ponies you have begun before breakfast, and intend to continue after tea. For the rest, at Fort Atbara, you can go down to the railway station. If there is a train there, there will be troops getting out of it; if there is not, you can ask when one is expected, and read chalked on a notice-board the latest bulletin of the health of every engine on the road between there and Halfa. On the platform, too, is the post-office. You can ask when the next post goes out or comes in: the dirty Copt boy they call postmaster will answer, " To-morrow." The postal service is not good at Fort Atbara. They say the Sirdar does not allow it room enough; as the room he does allow is entirely filled with the angarebs of the officials, and as they seldom arise from them, there is doubtless much justice in the complaint.

There are other diversions for the correspondent in the heat of the day. He may walk in the *nuzl*, or station yard. *Nuzl* is the Arabic for a place where things are dumped down—and dumped down in this *nuzl* they certainly are. Streets and streets and streets of them, —here a case of pepper, there the spare wheel of a gun, there jars of rum, there piles of Remington rifles for issue to more or less friendly tribes—everything that an army should or would or could want. There you see the men who do the real hard work of the army—not the men who work hard and then rest, but the men who work hard and never rest—the Director of the Water Transport, the Staff Officer for Supplies and Stores, the Director of Telegraphs. And there, with the hardest worked, you see the tall white-clad Sirdar working— now breaking a man's heart with curt censure, now exalting him to heaven with curt praise. Now ante-dating a movement, now hastening an embarkation, now increasing the load of a barge—for where the Sirdar is there every man and every machine must do a little better than his best.

All this you may see, and sweat, between the hour before sunrise and the hour before sunset. It goes on always, but usually after sunset you look at it no more.

For then the Sudan thirst has spent itself and it is at your mercy. You begin with a bombardment of hot tea. The thirst thinks its conquest assured; it takes the hot tea for a signal of surrender, and hurls the first cup arrogantly out again through your skin. You fire in the second cup—and you find that you have gained some ground. It may be that tea is nearer the temperature of your body than a merely tepid drink; it may be some divine virtue in the herb; but you feel the second cup of tea settle within you. You feel yourself a degree less torrid, a shade more substantial.

If you are wise you will rest content for the moment with this advantage. Order your pony and gallop an hour in the desert. You will sweat, of course; you need not expect to escape that at any time. But the sweat cools off you, and you ride in with a fresh skin. Take your tub in your tent: the Nile cools faster than the land, and oh the deliciousness of the cold water licking round you!

Now comes the sweet revenge for all the torments of the day. It is quite dark by now, unless the moon be up, leaning to you out of a tender blue immensity, silver, caressing, cool. Or else the sprightly candles beckon from your dinner-table, spread outside the tent, a halo of light and white in the blackness, alert, inviting, cool. You, too, by now are clean and cool. You quite forget whether the day was more than warm or no.

But you remember the thirst. You are cool, but within you are still dry, very dry and shrunken. Take

a long mug and think well what you will have poured
into it; for this is the moment of the day, the moment
that pays for the Sudan. You are very thirsty, and
you are about to slake your thirst. Let it be alcoholic,
for you have exuded much life in the day; let it above
all be long. Whisky-and-soda is a friend that never
fails you, but better still something tonic. Gin and
soda? Gin and lime-juice and soda? Gin and bitters
and lime-juice and soda? or else that triumphant
blend of all whetting flavours, an Abu Hamed—gin,
vermouth, Angostura, lime-juice, soda?

Mix it in due proportions; put in especially plenty
of soda—and then drink. For this is to drink indeed.
The others were only flushing your body with liquid
as you might flush a drain. But this! This splashes
round your throat, slides softly down your gullet till
you feel it run out into your stomach. It spreads
blessedly through body and spirit — not swirling
through, like the Atbara, but irrigating, like the Nile.
It is soil in the sand, substance in the void, life in
death. Your sap runs again, your biltong muscles
take on elasticity, your mummy bones toughen. Your
self has sprung up alive, and you almost think you
know how it feels to rise from the dead.

Thenceforward the Sudan is a sensuous paradise.
There is nothing like that first drink after sunset, but
you are only half irrigated yet: the first drink at
dinner—yes, and the second and the culminating
whisky - and - soda—can give rich moments. Then

your angareb stands ready, the sky is your bed-chamber, and the breath of the desert on your cheek is your good-night kiss. To-morrow you will begin to sweat again as you ride before breakfast. To-morrow —to-night even—there may be a dust-storm, and you will wake up with all your delicious moistness furred over by sand.   But that is to-morrow.

For to-night you have thirsted and you have drunk. And to-morrow will have an evening also.

XXVI.

BY ROAD, RIVER, AND RAIL.

GRADUALLY Fort Atbara transformed itself from an Egyptian camp to a British.

Parts of the Fourth Egyptian Brigade came in from the north, but started south again almost immediately. The steamers which had taken up the blacks began to drop down to the Atbara; as soon as they tied up, new battalions were packed into them, and they thudded up-river again.

Of the four battalions of Collinson Bey's command, the 1st left in detachments on August 8, and the first instalment of the 17th had preceded them on August 7. Three companies of the 5th, with a company of camel corps, reached Berber from Suakim on August 3; they had marched the 288 miles of desert in fifteen days. This was the record for marching troops, and it is not likely that anybody but Egyptians will ever lower it. One day, after a thirty-mile stage, the half-battalion arrived at a well and found it dry. The next was thirty miles farther. Straightway the men

got up and made their march sixty miles before they
camped. They say that when, as here, native officers
are in command of a desert march, they put most of
their men on the baggage-camels: no doubt they do,
but the great thing is that the troops get there.

The 5th joined its other half in Berber and marched
in to Fort Atbara on August 6; on August 7 it was
packed into steamers and sent up to Wad Habashi.
On August 9 arrived the first half of the newly-raised
18th and two companies of the 17th. These had been
pulling steamers and native boats up from Merawi;
they too had broken a record, doing in twenty days
what last year had taken twenty-six at the least and
forty at the most. Among their steamers was the
luckless Teb, which had run into a rock just before
Dongola, and in '97 had turned turtle in the Fourth
Cataract. The Sirdar had now taken the precaution
of renaming her the Hafir.

The four steamers had, of course, arrived days before, and were already broken to harness. The gyassas
were still behind, fighting with the prevailing south
wind; between Abu Hamed and Abeidieh the trees
on the bank were sunk under the flood, so that it was
almost impossible to tow. One day the wind would
be northerly, and that day the boats would sail forty
miles; the next it would be dead contrary, and,
sweating from four in the morning to ten at night,
they would make five. But it had to be done, and it
was done. The first arrivals of the 17th and 18th

were picked up by train south of Abu Hamed; on August 11th and 13th the rest came in to find their comrades already gone. This completed the Fourth Brigade, and with its completion the whole strength of the Egyptian army was at the Atbara or forward.

So that the camp became British. The two halves of the Rifle Brigade, the first half of the Guards, and the 32nd Battery had come up on successive days; after that there was a lull. But on August 9 we had an exciting day—exciting, at least, by the standard of Fort Atbara. Late the night before had come the balance of the British artillery—the 37th Field Battery, with six howitzers, a detachment of the 16th Company, Eastern Division, Garrison Artillery, with two 40-pounders, and a detachment of the Royal Irish Fusiliers, with four Maxims.

They were getting the 40-pounders into position for shipment on the bank. All gunners are fine men, and garrison gunners are the finest men of all gunners; these were pushing and pulling their ungainly darlings in the tire-deep sand as if they were a couple of perambulators. They are old guns, these 40-pounders; their short barrels tell you that. They were in their second decade when they first came to Egypt in 1882, and, once in Khartum, they are like to spend the rest of their lives there. But for the present they were the heaviest guns with the force, and they must be nursed and cockered till they had knocked a hole or two in the Khalifa's wall. So the gunners had laid out ropes, and now solid figures in grey flannel shirts, khaki trousers, and green-yellow putties — braces swinging from their waists, according to the ritual of cavalry and gunners and all men who tend beasts— were hammering away at their pegs and establishing their capstan with which the enormous babies were to be lowered into their boats.   Before they breakfasted all was in order; before they dined the guns were in the boats specially made to take them; before they supped they were well on the waterway to Khartum.

The Irish Fusiliers were picked from a fine regiment which had very hard luck in not being brought up in the Second Brigade. Set faces, heavy moustaches, necks like bulls, the score or so of men were the admiration of the whole camp. But most curiosity went naturally to the howitzers. They were hauling them out of the trucks when I got down—little tubby 5-inch creatures, in jackets like a Maxim's, on carriages like a field-gun's, carriage and gun-jacket alike painted pea-soup colour. The two trucks full of them were backed up to a little sand platform; the gunners wheeled out gun and limber and limbered up; a crowd of Egyptians seized hold, and — hallah hoh! hallah hoh!—they tugged away with them. The cry of the Egyptian when doing combined work is more like that of Brünnhilde and her sisters in the "Walküre" than any civilised noise I can remember to have heard.

The howitzers were to fire a charge of lyddite whose

bursting power is equal to 80 lb. of gunpowder.
With a very high trajectory the effect would be something like that of bombs dropped from a balloon.
Lyddite appears to be an impartial as well as an ener-
getic explosive; if you stand within 800 yards behind
it, it is as like as not to throw back a bit of shell into
your eye; after which you will use no other. When
they tried it in Cairo at knocking down a wall, it did
indeed knock down a good deal of it, but left a good
deal standing. That, however, was because percussion
fuses were used; the delay fuses were all sent up the
Nile. By delaying the explosion the smallest fraction
of a second, till the shell has penetrated, its devilish-
ness, they trusted, would be increased a hundredfold.
This was lyddite's first appearance in war: we all
looked forward to it with keen anticipation. The
further forward I looked, personally, the better I
should be pleased.

On the afternoon of this same less-uneventful-than-
usual 9th, a train snorted in with the second four
companies of the Guards. The Guards paraded in
their barrack square fill the beholder with admiration,
tempered with a sense of his own unworthiness;
emerging from roofed trucks they were less imposing.
Of course it was the worst possible moment to see
them, and the impression formed was less good than
that of other corps. Falling in beside the train they
were certainly taller than the average British soldier,
but hardly better built. They were mostly young,

O

mostly pale or blotchy, and their back pads—did you
know before that it was possible to get sunstroke in
the spine?—were sticking out all over them at the
grotesquest angles. Many of the officers wore thick
blue goggles, and their back pads were a trifle restive
too. The half-battalion marched limply. Only remember that they had hardly stretched their legs since
they embarked at Gibraltar just three weeks before.
The wonder was that they could march at all.

A very different show was that of the 10th, when
the first half of the Northumberland Fusiliers came
in. To be sure, they appeared with advantages. The
Guards' band played in three companies, and you
do not know how a band drives out limpness until
you have tried. But allowing for that, the 5th still
made a very fine entry. The men were not tall, but
they were big round the chest, and averaged nearly
six years' service. They swung up in a column of
dust with their stride long, heads up, shoulders squared,
soldiers all over. The officers were long-limbed, firmly
knit, straight as lances. There are not many more
pleasing sights in the world than the young British
subaltern marching alongside his company, his long
legs moderating their stride to the pace of the laden
men, his wide blue eyes looking steadily forward,
curious of the untried future, confident in the traditions of his service and his race. From the look of
the 5th Fusiliers you might guess with safety that

the young soldier's confidence was not likely to be abashed.

So that now the camp was all but English. A few Egyptians remained behind, indispensable for fatigues. But the Northumberland men were working away at their ammunition and baggage all the next morning, Tommy lugging at the camel's head-rope and adjuring him to "Come on, ol' man," and the old man, unaccustomed to friendly language, only snarling the more devilishly and tipping his load on to the sand. But Tommy had his revenge when he rode back to the station for another load; the baggage-camel had to trot, which he had never done before except to escape being saddled.

Englishmen working with camels, squads of shirt-sleeved Englishmen tramping to and fro on fatigues, Englishmen putting up hospital-tents, forty or fifty Englishmen with mild sun-fever in hospital, English bands, the crisp voice of the English sergeant, above all, silver-throated English bugles—reveille waking the dawn and last post floating up the silent night—Fort Atbara had seen one more incarnation.

XXVII.

THE LAST OF FORT ATBARA.

THUS at Fort Atbara we sat, and sat, and sat. When there were any troops to see, coming in or going out, we went to see them. When there were not, we galloped about in the desert, ate, drank, slept, and generally fulfilled the whole duty of correspondents. Why did you not make a dash for the front? the guileless editor will ask. But the modern war correspondent is not allowed to make unauthorised dashes, and the man who should commend the claims of his newspaper by slapping a British General's face would righteously be shot.

Besides, there was no front to speak of worth dashing for. The camp at Wad Habashi, we heard, had been encroached on by the ever-rising Nile, and it had been moved four miles up-stream to a spot in full view of the gorge of Shabluka. A Bimbashi of cavalry, who returned thence one day, pronounced the scenery finer than anything in Switzerland; but then you must remember that since seeing Switzer-

land he had seen the desert railway and Berber and
Fort Atbara and all the other dry dead levels of
the blank Sudan. More practical was the news that
as yet there had been only one storm of rain with
thunder and lightning. At Fort Atbara we had
cloudy days and rainy sunsets, whereas in the spring
we had never seen anything but hard blue for
weeks together. On the whole, too, it was cooler:
115° in the shade on one or two clear afternoons,
but often not so much as 100° all day. And the
farther south you went, they said, the cooler it became.

Indeed, the nearer we actually got to the beginning
of operations, the softer task the expedition seemed.
The only people who did not seem to find it so were
the two battalions that had the softest task of all—
the Rifles and the Guards. These came into hospital
in dozens. Both regiments had a bad reputation
for going sick—the Rifles because they are mostly
cockneys without constitutions, the Guards because
they are too much pampered. Anyhow, they de-
veloped more sickness between them in a week than
the whole of the First Brigade. Their failure to
stand the sun and the dust-storms was not for want
of officers' example—certainly in the Rifles, whose
officers were keen sportsmen, riding out to stalk
gazelle after lunch on the hottest afternoons. It was
not for want of amusement, as amusement goes in
standing camp, for the Rifles were alive with vocal

talent.   Almost every night, drifting down from their
camp, you might hear the familiar chorale—

> Jolly good song, jolly well sung,
> Jolly good comrades ev-ery one.
> If you can beat it you're welcome to try;
> Always remember the singer is dry.
>   Soop!

The Rifles were keeping their spirits up, and they
were as smart and keen as you could wish.   But they
were not acclimatised, nor were the Guards, so that
they sent nearly a hundred cases—mostly mild sun-
fever—into hospital in a week.

The first squadron of the 21st Lancers—they were
travelling as three squadrons to be re-formed into four
in the field—arrived on the 11th.   The second half of
the 5th Fusiliers came in on the 13th.   Everything
seemed strolling on satisfactorily and sleepily.   Then
suddenly the Sirdar aroused us with one of his lightning movements.   You will have formed an idea of
the sort of man he is—all patience for a month, all
swiftness when the day comes.   The day came on
August 13.   At eleven I saw him, grave as always,
gracious and courteous, volunteering facilities.   At
noon he was gone up the river to the front.

The waiting, the sudden start, the caution that
breathed no word of his intention, yet dictated an
official explanation of his departure before he left—it
was the Sirdar all over.   And with his departure

Fort Atbara took on yet another metempsychosis. It became all at once the deserted base-camp, a caravanserai for reinforcements, a forwarding depot for stores. True, most of the staff remained—nobody pretending to know what had taken the Sirdar away so astonishingly, unless it was merely his idiosyncrasy of sudden and rapid movement. If anybody had been told any other reason, it was just the man or two that would not tell again.

But curiosity is a tactless futility when you have to do with generals. It was enough that the advance had come with a rush. The detachments of the 17th and 18th Egyptian, sitting about on the bank till steamers arrived to let them complete the brigade, disappeared magically in the Sirdar's wake. With them went their Brigadier, Collinson Bey. On that same evening the leading steamers passed up with parts of the First British Brigade from Darmali. Four days' voyage to below Shabluka and then they would come down in one day for the Second. Then we should be complete and ready for Omdurman.

Meanwhile there was hardly a fighting man in Fort Atbara. The three battalions of the Second Brigade were in camp just south of it, on the Atbara. The first third of the Lancers were across the river; the second came in on the afternoon of the 14th. It wanted only the third squadron and the Lancashire Fusiliers to complete the force. The cavalry was to start on the 16th with every kind of riding and baggage animal to march up, and the more able-bodied of the correspondents were going with them.

So on the torrid Sunday morning of the 14th we filled the empty fort with a dress rehearsal of camels. In the Atbara campaign I had been part of a mess of three with nine camels: now it was a mess of four with twenty.   We marched them all up solemnly after breakfast and computed how much of our multitudinous baggage would go on to them.   Fourteen of them were hired camels: a hired camel is cheaper than a bought one, but it generally has smallpox, carries much less weight, and is a deal lengthier to load.

The twenty gurgling monstrosities sat themselves down on the sand and threw up their chins with the camel's ineffable affectation of elegance.   The men cast a deliberate look round and remarked, "The baggage is much and the camels are few."   Next they brought out rotten nets of rope and slung it round the boxes and sacks.   That is to say, one man slung it round one box and the others stood statuesque about him and suggested difficulties.   That done, the second man took up the wondrous tale, then the third, then the fourth.   This took about two hours.   Then they suggested that a camel could not without danger to its health carry more than two dozen of whisky, whereas anything worthy the name of a camel can carry four hundredweight.   Altogether they made some fifty camel - loads of the stuff.   And when we said we wouldn't have it, all the men stood round and gabbled, and half the camels girned and gnashed their teeth, and the neighbouring donkeys lifted up their voices and brayed like souls in torment, and when you moved to repulse an importunate Arab you kicked a comparatively innocent camel.   Allah was their witness that the camels—which, when we hired them two days before, were very strong—were very weak.

But little we cared.   We were going up to Omdurman and Khartum.   Camel - loads adjust themselves, but war and the Sirdar wait for nobody.   We were marching into lands where few Englishmen had ever set heel, no Englishman for fifteen years.   We were to be present at the tardy vengeance for a great humiliation.

XXVIII.

THE DESERT MARCH TO OMDURMAN.

THE column was to move out of camp at five in the morning. But at half-past, when our tardy caravan filed up to join it, dim bulks still heaved themselves up in the yellow smoke, half-sunrise, half-dust-cloud —masses of laden camels, strings of led horses proclaiming that the clumsy tail of our convoy was still unwinding itself. Threading the patchy mimosa scrub, we came out into a stretch of open sand; beyond it, straight, regular, ominous of civilisation, appeared the telegraph wire which crosses the Nile at Fort Atbara, and now ran on to beyond Metemmeh.

In two black bars across the sand, as straight as the wire itself, the flat rays of sunrise shadowed the 21st Lancers. Two travelling or nearly three campaigning squadrons, they were the first British cavalry in the Sudan since 1885. On their side it was their first appearance in war. They were relatively a young regiment, and the only one in the British army which has never been on active service. You may imagine whether they were backward to come.

To tell truth, at this first glimpse of British cavalry in the field, they looked less like horsemen than Christmas-trees. The row of tilted lances, the swing of heavy men in the saddle when they moved, was war and chivalry. The rest was picketing pegs lashed to carbines, feeds of corn hanging from saddles, canvas buckets opposite them, waterproofs behind, bulky holsters in front, bundles of this thing and that dangling here and there, water-bottles in nets under the horses' bellies, khaki neck screens flapping from helmets, and blue gauze veils hooding helmets and heads and all. The smallest Syrian—they had left their own big hungry chargers in Cairo—had to carry 18 stone; with a heavy man the weight was well over 20.

But though each man carried a bazaar, the impression of clumsiness lasted only a moment.

When they moved they rode forward solidly yet briskly,—weighty and light at the same time, each man carrying all he wanted as behoves men going to live in an enemy's country. The sight was a better lecture in cavalry than many text-books. It is not the weapons that make the cavalryman you saw, but the mobility; not the gallop, but the long, long walk; not the lance he charges with, but the horse that carries him far and fast to see his enemy in front and screen his friends behind. So much if you wished to theorise; if it was enough merely to look and listen, there was a fine piquancy in the great headpiece, the raking lance, all the swinging apparatus of the free-booter—and then, inside the casque, a round-faced English boy, and the reflection, " If I was to go and see my brother now, as keeps a brewery, it'd be just right." Masterpiece of under-statement, more telling than a score of superlatives—" just right !" But we must not hurry on too fast. Before the cavalry were well observed, before even thirst became appealing, it was necessary to wait for the whole force—column, or convoy, or circus, or whatever is the technical name for it—to form up in the open. By degrees it did. Leading, the cavalry with its scouts and advanced guard and flanking parties. Then a line of tarbushes on grey horses—Egyptian gun-teams, and with them a couple of Maxims scoring the desert with the first ruts of all its immemorial years. Then a ragged line of khaki and helmets, of blue and crimson and gold and green turbans and embroidered waistcoats—the officers' chargers and transport mules of the two British brigades some with soldier-grooms, some with Berberi syces. Is not the waistcoat of the groom the same radiant marvel whether he be of Newmarket or Kalabsheh ? Likewise there were British Maxim mules and the miscellaneous donkeys of all the army. Lastly, lolloping their apathetic two and a half miles an hour, the baggage camels lumbered up the plain—well-furnished Government beasts, with new sound saddles

THE NILE — METEMMEH TO KHARTUM

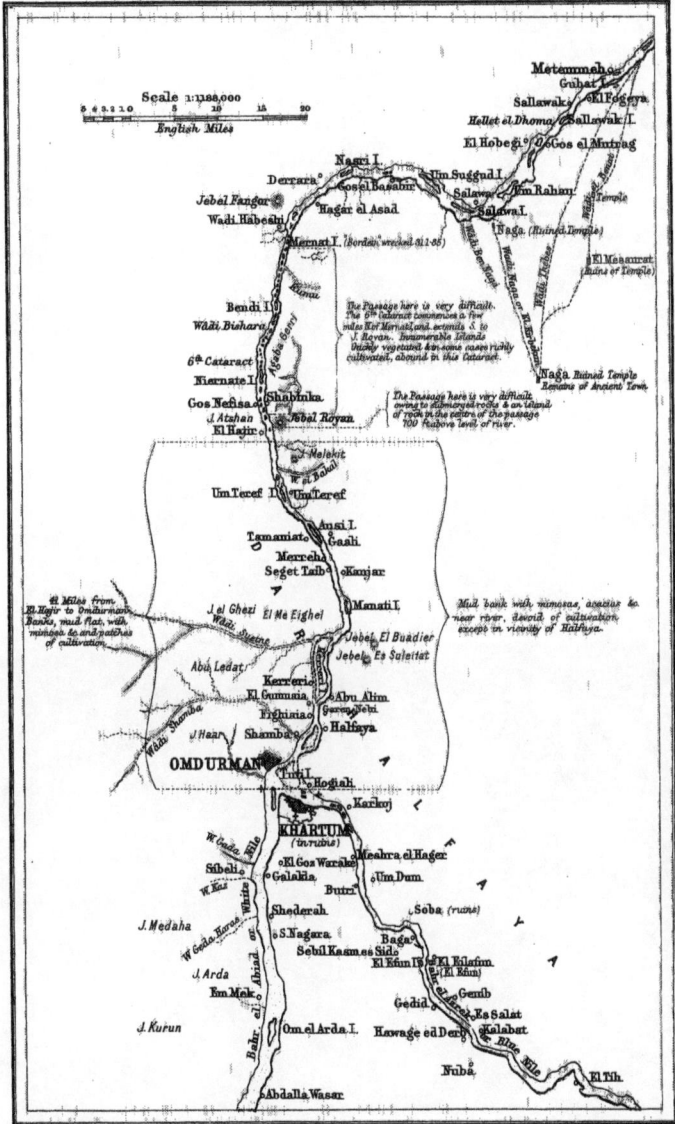

Scale 1:1,158,000

English Miles

Metemmeh
Gubat I.
Sallawaki o El Foggera
Hellet el Dhoma Sallawak I.
El Hobegi o Gos el Mutrag

Nasri I.
Derrara o
Gos el Basabir
Um Suggud I.
Um Rahin
Jebel Fangur
Hagar el Asad
Salawa
Salawa
Wadi Habeshi
Temple
Naga (Ruined Temple)

Mernat I. (Borden wrecked at 1-95)
El Mesaurat
(Ruins of Temple)

Bendi I.
The Passage here is very difficult.
The 6th Cataract commences a few
miles El Mernati, and extends 3 to
J. Royan. Innumerable Islands
thickly vegetated &in some cases richly
cultivated, abound in this Cataract.

Wadi Bishara

6th Cataract
Mernate I.
Gos Nefisa
Shabinka
J. Atshan
Jebel Royan
El Hajir
The Passage here is very difficult
owing to submerged rocks & an island
of rock in the centre of the passage
100 ft above level of river.

Naga Ruined Temple
Remains of Ancient Town.

Melakit

Um Teref I. Um Teref

Ansi I.
Tamaniato
Gasli
Merreh
Seget Taib
Kanjar

81 Miles from
El Hajir to Omdurman
Banks, mud flat, with
mimosa &c. and patches
of cultivation.

J. el Ghezi
El Ma Eighel
Mamati I.
Mud bank with mimosas, acacias &c.
near river, devoid of cultivation
except in vicinity of Halfaya.

Wadi Saeire
Jebel El Buadier
Jebel Es Suleitat

Abu Ledat
Kerreri
Haar
El Gummia
Abu Alim
Gerre Nebbi
Fighinian
Shamba
Halfaya

Wadi Shamba

OMDURMAN
Tuti I.
Hogiali
Karkoj

KHARTUM
(in ruins)
Meshra el Hager

W Gadim Nile
White Nile
El Gos Waraka
Galakia
Sibeli
Um Dum
Butri
Soba (ruins)
W End
Shederah
J. Medaha
S. Nagara
Baga
W Gedir Horas
Sebil Kasma es Sido
J. Arda
El Kfun I.
El Kilafun
(El Kfun)
Em Mek
Genib
Gedid
Es Salat
Kawage ed Derb
Galabat
Om el Arda I.
J. Kurun

Blue Nile
Nuba
El Tih

Abdalla Wasar

and little sun-bonnet pads over forehead and pate;
scraggier private camels with boxes of stores and
green trunks and baths; starveling, hired camels
banging whisky cases against their bare ribs. Add
to all a few goats already trailing stiff legs behind
them, a few sheep trampling their little flesh into
whipcord, a drove of brindled bulls at the same task
—and you have the caravan.

Every four-footed beast that was to go to Khartum
—saving only one-third of the 21st troop horses—
must march with this convoy or not at all. Every
man that went with it went simply as in charge of
a beast; every man was supposed to ride, and the
marches were cut out at nearly twenty miles a-day.
Horses, mules, donkeys, sheep, goats, oxen, camels—
the monstrous caravan sprawled over the desert, jost-
ling and swaying and bumping, jerking off in different directions at different rates, neighing and low-
ing and braying and bleating and grunting,—Military
Tournament, Lord Mayor's Show, Sanger's Circus, and
Noah's Ark all jammed into one. Then the multitudinous chaos straightened itself for a second, swayed,
crooked itself again, and began to totter towards
Khartum.

We tottered for five hours through sparse camel-
thorn, over ground mostly once flooded or once rained
on, a sieve of lurking holes. By that time many
thought we should be near the end of the thirteen miles
which was our day's ration, and I, who had idiotically

started without breakfast, wished that I had never
seen a horse or the Sudan or the light of day. At
last, when it was getting on for one, the head of the
column—by now a reeling ruin—turned Nileward.
We shook up our horses and licked our split lips.
Then we issued on to an old cotton-field—dry stalks,
and between them the earth wrinkled with foot-deep
cracks as close-grained as the back of your hand.
The cracks were just big enough for a horse to break
his leg in, and the islands between were just big
enough to collapse into the cracks when a horse put
his foot on them.   Over this we crawled timidly till
we came to a shallow yellow-ochre puddle.   There
we learned that this was our water, and the cracks
were our camp.

The cracks proved full of scorpions, and the respec-
tive legs of your table or angareb inclined themselves
at angles of 45° to the horizontal and to each other.
However, we pretended we were at sea going home
again, and consumed tinned spiced beef and peaches
and beer—may I never want a meal more or deserve
it less!—and slept.   The feature of next day's march
was a new form of vegetation — a bush with leaves
something like those of a canariensis, and really green,
a phenomenon hitherto not met in the Sudan.   And
whether we marched twenty-two miles that day as
was intended, or thirty-two as was asserted, or something in between as was concluded, I do not know
nor then cared: at eight I had called up a camel,

and breakfasted on tinned spiced beef and peaches
and beer.

But the important point that emerged was this : the
unusually high and ever-rising Nile flood was playing
the very deuce with us. The river was pushing up
what they call " khors "—broad, shallow depressions
which look like tributaries, only whose water runs
the wrong way. These planted themselves across the
track, and we had to fetch circuits round them. This
second day we arrived at a second puddle, which was
a second khor, and watered there. But the distressing
point in the situation was that the force was to draw
rations and forage every second day from depots on
the bank. This was the second day, and the depot
was duly on the bank ; only the khor had flooded up
in between. The Lancers had watered their horses,
and fed them—and then they had to saddle up at four
or so, and file off round the khor three miles to get
their rations. Some of the mules had not yet come
in ; without even off-saddling they had to follow ;
which made a march of nearly twelve hours on end.

You could not blame anybody for the vagaries of
the Nile, but it was natural that somebody would
suffer from them. Already at the first halting-place
four Egyptians carried in a comrade in a blanket with
a rude splint on his leg. The same day a trooper of
the Lancers went down. He had been advised not to
try the Sudan sun at all, but insisted on his chance
of service : after this first march he just got his

horse watered and fed, and then dropped insensible
with sunstroke.   He was but just conscious next
morning.   Four Egyptian gunners carried him on an
upturned angareb to Kitiab, the second halting-place.
Here he was left with others.   Next day and the
next there were others.

The horses, too, suffered.   Those of the squadron
which came up first, and the horses from Darmali
and Essillem, stood the marching almost perfectly.
Those which had started to tramp the morning after
the rail-river journey went down with fever in the
feet.   Twelve days' standing had sent all the blood to
their feet; the red-hot sand did the rest.

We left a dozen on the shore at Kitiab to be picked
up by a passing boat, if so it might befall.   The third
day we marched on through a park-like country, thick
with tall, spreading, almost green mimosa-trees; in
one place, where a khor lapped up, if sand were grass
you might almost have cried "The Serpentine."   We
camped at a ruined village on a sandhill—name unknown and uncared—and for the first time saw the
Nile, which we were supposed to be drinking.   He
was lying at the far end of a three-mile tangle of
bush.   The fourth day, guided by the brown-faced
cliffs on his farther bank, we came down on the
pleasantest camp I had yet seen on Nile or Atbara—
Magawieh.   There was no village but mud ruins; but
there were clusters and groves of real palms—date-
palms with yellow and scarlet clusters of ripe fruit.

We sat down on the very lip of the river, which came up flush with the grass bank, like a full tide. And there, on August 20, we halted to rest the horses. Half-a-dozen were sent down with fever in the feet; also a few soldiers, some bad, some not so bad as they said. The rest of us were very hard and sound by now, with the skin well peeled off our noses.

By now we had marched about halfway to Wad Habashi. And of population we had seen hardly a soul. Ruined villages we passed in plenty—so far back from the river that they must have lived from wells. Now, since Mahmud killed out the Jaalin, they did not live at all. We found evidences of some poor prosperity—the dry runnels of old irrigation, the little chequers of old fields, old, round, mud granaries, old crackling zaribas, old houses rocking on their mud foundations, old bones white in the sun. All the rest was killed out by the despot we were marching to try to kill. The fighting force of the Jaalin was ahead of us on the same errand, and with two more motives —revenge and loot. Behind us straggled the returning families—one man with a spear, a bevy of plum-bloom girls and old women and infants on donkeys, a goat or two for sole sustenance. They were returning; their ruins were their own again.

XXIX.

METEMMEH.

"Goom!" The hideous cry broke on to the night, and jarred on the white stars. "Mohammed! Ali! Hassan! Goom, goom!" I sat up on my angareb and groaned. Do not be frightened; "goom" is not the cry of a beast of prey. It is worse; it is the Arabic for "Wake," and it was three in the morning. We were moving out of our pleasant palm-shade at Magawieh on August 21, and taking the road south again.

The clumsy column formed up after its clumsy wont, and threaded sleepily desertward through the mimosa-thorns. After a few minutes we came, to our wonder, on to a broad flat road embanked at each side. It could hardly have been built by scorpions, and there were no other visible inhabitants. Then, at a corner, we came to a sign-post — a sign-post, by all that's astounding — with "To Metemmeh" inscribed thereon. We learned afterwards that the fertile-minded Hickman Bey, finding himself and his battalion woodcutting in the neighbourhood, had used up some of his spare energy and of his men's spare muscle in making the road and setting up the sign, the only one in the Sudan. At the time the thing was like meeting an old friend after a long parting, and the caravan set out at least half a mile an hour the better for it.

We trudged through the sand and scrub for the best part of five hours. Then suddenly it sank and died away. We had noticed already more than the usual number of mummied camels and donkeys by the road-side. The sun had tanned the skin and bleached the bones; hawks and vultures had seen to the rest; they might have been lying there days or years. The camels lay with their heads writhed back till the ears brushed the hump, the attitude in which a camel always dies. But all the donkeys had their throats cut — and that told us we were reaching Metemmeh.

Last year, about this time or a little earlier, the main force of the Egyptian army lay at Merawi, preparing to advance on Abu Hamed. The Khalifa ordered the Jaalin to advance against it; but the Jaalin had been in the fore - front of every dervish disaster since Abu Klea, and they sent secretly to the Sirdar for arms. But it was too late, and Mahmud fell upon the Jaalin as Hunter fell upon Abu Hamed. They fought hard, but Mahmud had too many rifles for them. Metemmeh was made

even as Khartum and old Berber; the branch of
Jaalin whose headquarters were Metemmeh was
blotted out of existence. The carcasses we saw were
the beasts that had dropped or been overtaken in
their flight.

The scrub sank and died away. We came on to a
bare level of old cultivated land, sparsely dotted with
dry twigs, seamed with rents and holes, and covered
thick with bones. Bones, skulls, and hides of camels,
oxen, horses, asses, sheep, goats—the place was carpeted with them, a very Golgotha. A sickening smell
came into the air, a smell heavy with blood and fat.
We off-saddled at a solitary clump of tall palms on the
bank, turned round, and across a mile of treeless desolation saw a forlorn line of black mud wall. The look
of the wall alone was somehow enough to tell you
there was nobody inside. That was the corpse of
Metemmeh.

Before we went in we looked at the forts and
trenches with which they had lined the bank against
the gunboats. It was to be presumed that they had
done the same at Omdurman, so we looked at them
out of more than idle curiosity. They were rude
enough, to be sure. Circular, of some 120 feet radius,
the forts were mud emplacements for a single gun with
three embrasures looking to front, half right and half
left; the guns—captured since at the Atbara—could
only be fired as they bore on a boat in line with one of
these. Yet, rough and crumbling as they were, it was

plain that the boats' fire had done them little harm.
The embrasures were chipped about a good deal,
and with very accurate shooting anybody trying to
serve the guns would probably have gone down.
But the mud work could shelter any man who
sat close enough under it, and common shell or even
shrapnel would do him little harm. The trenches
were not wholly contemptible either—deep and with
traverses.

The next thing was to ride over to Mahmud's old
camp. He had placed it behind the ridge on which
Metemmeh stands, in the open desert and out of
range, as he thought, of the boats; the time-fuse of
a 12½-pounder shell, picked up in the very centre of
the camp, seemed to suggest a subsequent disillusion-
ment. As you rode up you first saw nothing but four
mud huts. Then the soil looked redder than that of
the desert behind it; presently you saw that it had
been turned up in shallow heaps; the place looked
like a native cemetery. And when we got a little
nearer we found that this was his fortified camp. One
of the huts appeared to have been his dwelling-house;
another was a sort of casemate—mud walls 4 feet
thick and an arrangement of logs that looked as if it
had been meant as a stockade to shield riflemen.
But the rest of the position was merely childish—as
planless as his zariba on the Atbara, without any of
its difficulties. It was just a number of shelter-
trenches scattered anyhow over the open sand. Some

could have held twenty men, some two. They must
have spread over nearly a square mile, but they were
quite rare and discontinuous; in the circle of the camp
there was about twice as much firm ground as trench.
Add that the whole could have been shelled from the
Metemmeh ridge at half a mile or so, and that you
could thence have seen almost every man in the place
—well, if Omdurman was to be no harder nut than
this——

Now turn back to Metemmeh—poor, blind-walled,
dead Metemmeh. And first, between camp and town,
stand a couple of crutched uprights and a cross-bar.
You wonder what, for a moment, and then wonder
that you wondered. A gallows! At the foot of it a
few strands of the brown palm - fibre rope they use
in this country, and one, two, four, six, eight human
jaw-bones. Just the jaw - bones, and again you
wonder why; till you remember the story that when
Sheikh Ibrahim, of the Jaalin, came here a week
or two ago he found eight skulls under the gallows
in a rope - netting bag. When he took them up
for burial the lower jaws dropped off, and lie here
still.

If the jaws could wag in speech again—but we must
try not to be sentimental. If we are, we shall hardly
stand the inside of Metemmeh. So blank and piteous
and empty is the husk of it. These are not mere mud
hovels, but town houses as the Sudan understands
houses—mud, certainly, but large, lofty rooms with

wide window-holes and what once were matting roofs.
Two that I went into were even double-storied; no
stairs, of course, but a sort of mud inclined plane
outside the walls leading to the upper rooms. Another
house had a broad mud-bank forming a divan round
its chief room. Now the beams were cracked and
broken, and the divan had been rained on through
the broken roof; shreds of what once may have
been hangings were dangling limply in the breeze.
At the gateway of this house — once an arch, now
a tumble of dry mud — was a black handful of a
woman's hair.

In every courtyard you see the miserable emblems
of panic and massacre. Ride through the gate—there
lies a calabash tossed aside; a soiled, red, peak-toed
slipper dropped from the foot that durst not stop to
pick it up again; the broken sticks and decayed cords
of a new angareb that the butchers smashed because
it was not worth taking away. And in every courtyard you see great patches of black ashes spreading
up the wall. Those monuments are recent; they are
the places where, only days ago, they burned the
bones of the Jaalin. The dead camels and donkeys
lie there yet, across every lane, dry, but still stinking.
A parrot-beaked hairy tarantula scrambles across the
path, a lizard's tail slides deeper into a hole; that
is all the life of Metemmeh. Everything steeped in
the shadeless sun, everything dry and silent, silent.
The stillness and the stench merge together and soak

into your soul, exuding from every foot of this melancholy graveyard — the cenotaph of a whole tribe, fifteen years of the Sudan's history read in an hour. Sun, squalor, stink, and blood : that is Mahdism.

Press your bridle on the drooping pony's neck; turn and ride back to the river, the palms, and the lances.   God send he stays to fight us.

XXX.

A CORRESPONDENT'S DIARY.

Wad Hamed, Aug. 22. — The concentration of the force here is all but complete.

The British regiments have all arrived, whole or in part, with the exception of the Rifles and the 21st Lancers, of whom two squadrons are marching by the road. They are expected at mid-day to-morrow.

With almost the full strength of the Egyptian army added, the force is the largest ever seen in the Sudan, the composition of every arm being at least half as strong again as at the Atbara.

The cavalry and the convoy are going very well now. The beasts and men are hardened by marching, which is an invaluable training. We came twenty-five miles to-day in one march without effort.

Wad Hamed, Aug. 23. — The camp here is both compact and commodious. Though there are but little short of 20,000 men, in a zareba barely more than a mile long, nobody is crowded, and everywhere there is easy access to water.

The blacks are encamped at the south end in terraces of straw huts; next are the Egyptians under shelters extemporised from their blankets; at the north end the British are installed in tents. Their quarters are far more comfortable than at Atbara, though officers and men have to sleep in their boots for the sake of practice.

There is but little shade from the trees, but the camp is covered with tufts of coarse yellow grass, which keep down the dust.

The steamers lying along the shore, the guns, horses, mules, and camels, the bugle-calls, and the cries in English and Arabic, make up a little world full of life in the desert.

The concentration will not actually be effected here as General Hunter, with two Egyptian brigades, will march to-morrow to Hajir at the head of the Shabluka cataract, where there will be a new concentration within a few days. He will be followed in the evening by his other two brigades, which will march to various points up the river, and cut wood for the steamers ascending the rapids.

The Lancers will arrive here this evening, and the Rifles will come probably by boat early to-morrow. The force will then be complete. There was an imposing parade of the forces here this morning. The 1st, 2nd, 3rd, and 4th Egyptian Brigades and the

2nd and 1st British Brigades paraded in the above
order, counting from the right. The force advanced
in columns of companies, then turned half-right on
the extreme right brigade. It was difficult to get
a full impression of the manœuvres in consequence
of the dust.

News from Omdurman is abundant, and reconnaissances show that the top of the Shabluka cataract is definitely abandoned. It is rumoured that
the Khalifa intends to meet our force in the open;
but this story, as the story of the blowing-up of the
Khalifa's steamer in an attempt to lay a mine, must
be taken with the greatest caution. The Khalifa
probably does not know his own intentions yet.

The Egyptian troops and the seasoned British bri-
gade are in splendid condition. The 2nd British
Brigade is naturally not so inured to the climate.
Everybody is straining on the tiptoe of expectation.

Wad Hamed, Aug. 24 (4 p.m.)—Last night brought
us the best storm of the season.

It began, as its way is, savagely and without a
second's warning.

A flicker of silver lightning, a bloated drop of rain,
then the wind rushed down snorting and tearing at
the tent-ropes like an angry stallion.

It tore up the tents, and left them flapping in
agony, while the rain came down and completed the
conquest by drenching our kits at its leisure.

What was worse, the gyassa, laden with stores and spare kits, belonging to an Egyptian battalion which was just about to start forward, was blown clean over, and everything shot into the river.

At daylight you could see the disconsolate fatigue-party, which was left behind to tow the gyassa, wearily salvaging, with chocolate legs naked below the waist, but with irreproachable uniform above.

The lightning flared and the wind bombarded us till the morning, when we reaped one consolation—the dust was all gone, except that which had formed layers on our faces.

The morning was grey, gusty, and nipping; it might have been a summer morning at home.

General Hunter left this morning at daybreak, with the 1st and 3rd Egyptian Brigades, for Hajir, a two days' march for them.

The 2nd and 4th Brigades followed this afternoon.

If the rain had soaked their kits, at least it afforded cool, clean going.

The baggage of the Egyptian Infantry started in gyassas up the Sixth Cataract early this morning.

The second half of the Rifles and the Irish Fusiliers' Maxim detachment arrived during the night, completing the British division.

The cavalry and guns will leave to-morrow, the forty-pounders and the howitzers going by water.

The staff will follow, and then, as the Sirdar says, "We shall be in the straight."

Wad Hamed, Aug. 25 (2 p.m.)—Rumours from Omdurman continue to add vastly to the eager curiosity wherewith we advance to lift the veil from Khartum.

A trustworthy report asserts that Ali Wad Helu, the Mahdi's second Khalifa and titular heir to the present ruler, has fallen from his horse while drilling the dervish cavalry, and suffered severe injuries.

This, if true, presumably delights the Khalifa, who is jealous of Helu, but will tend to discourage the superstitious Sudanese, who hold that a fall from a horse when entering on an enterprise is the worst of omens.

Yesterday morning this camp was the most populous centre in the Sudan after Omdurman. This afternoon it is all but raw scrub again.

Out of the tangle of yellow halfa-grass the Sirdar's tent rises like an island, and except for the headquarters and the artillery and cavalry in the extreme north, the camp is completely deserted.

The Egyptian infantry division, which left yesterday morning, should reach Hajir—officially called Gebel Royan—to-day.

The 2nd British Brigade left here at daybreak this morning, and the 1st follows this afternoon.

The Rifles are remaining with detachments of other

battalions delayed on the journey up; they will probably proceed to Gebel Royan by boat, doing the distance in one day instead of two.

Perhaps even more striking than the disappearance
of the troops is the diminution of the vast accumula-
tion of supplies and stores.

The little town of cases and sacks has had street
after street lifted away and sent up to Shabluka.

Seeing the process thus in miniature, we can ap-
proach an adequate idea of the labour, promptness, and
system which brought all the necessaries for 25,000
men from Atbara, Merawi, Halfa, Egypt, and England
without a break or hitch.

Last night the whole upward course of the river
was fringed with the taper spars of the gyassas, and
festooned with the smoke from the camp-fires of the
towing-parties.

Everything has gone on in proper time and proper
order, and the weight of the material shifted is
enormous.

Multiply all this a hundredfold, and you appreciate
the standing miracle of Egyptian transport.

Wad Hamed, Aug. 25 (6 p.m.)—The march out of
the 1st British Brigade this afternoon was a most
imposing spectacle.

The four battalions had all their baggage packed to
the minute, and at the sound of the bugle moved off
and took the road in four parallel columns.

The Warwicks were on the left; next to them the Seaforths, then the Camerons, and on the right the Lincolns — the three last carrying battalion flags, a new element of colour since the Atbara campaign.

The ground just outside the camp was broken, but the men struck along with an easy swing from the loins, ignoring the weight of their kits.

Many of the men were bearded, and all were tanned by the sun, acclimatised by a summer in the country, hardened by perpetual labours, and confident from the recollection of victory—a magnificent force, which any man might be proud to accompany into the field.

Wad Hamed, Aug. 26 (11.45 a.m.) — The camp this morning shows even an emptier desolation than yesterday.

At the north end the Lancers are disembarking their last horses, preparatory to the march to Hajir to-morrow, the gunners are readying the 40-pounders and howitzers for the steam-up to-day, the rest of the artillery marches.

The medical staff is just leaving, having sent the sick down to Nasri yesterday.

The rest of the camp is a wilderness of broken biscuit-boxes and battered jam-tins, dotted with the half-naked Jaalin scallywags, male and female, once the richest slave-dealers in the Sudan, now glad to collect empty bottles and winnow the dust for broken biscuit.

With the departure of headquarters to - morrow the whole force will have shifted camp to Hajir.

Thence it is under forty miles to Omdurman.

For the first half of the distance the bank is flat with cultivation.

On nearing Kerreri, the ground becomes broken with thick low thorn scrub.

Thence to Omdurman rises a cluster of sandstone hills inland, 300 feet to 500 feet high.

In the present state of the Nile the river forms numerous khors, or small tributaries, flowing out instead of into the river, and many such on approaching Omdurman will perhaps necessitate detours on the line of march.

To the north-west of the town there is rising ground which is said to offer a favourable artillery position.

Wad Hamed, Aug. 26 (2.40 p.m.)—Major Stuart-Wortley, who went up to Khartum two days after Gordon's death, leaves to-night by the right bank with the friendlies, Jaalin and other tribes.

They will advance parallel with the Sirdar.

It is reported that a dervish force is on the right bank, under the Emirs Zeki and Wad Bishara.

A few dervish scouts are reported on this bank, near Gebel Royan, opposite our new camp and depot, also patrols on the left bank.

The Khalifa blundered heavily when he abandoned the Shabluka rapids, as even a small force among the rocks might have been troublesome, whereas now the Sirdar has been able to convey all his transport to the open water above without pause.

Gebel Royan, Aug. 28 (8.5 a.m.)—We are now within four marches of Khartum. From the brown shoulder of Royan mountain, which overlooks and gives its name to the camp, you can see long stretches of green-lipped desert, blinking in the sun, and cutting the blue ribbon of open water to Omdurman.

In the distance hangs a white speck of haze, which may be the Mahdi's tomb.

Yesterday I came up with the main force.

This morning it has gone forward again, and the four marches are becoming three.

General Hunter, with the Egyptian Division, began to move out before sunrise, and as I write — eight o'clock—their last drums are throbbing faintly in the distance.

The Egyptian cavalry, horse battery, camel corps, and galloping Maxims had preceded them before dawn.

Cavalry contact with the dervishes has been possible at any moment since Friday.

The patrols saw a few dervish horse, who, however, fell back rapidly, lighting alarm beacons.

Spies and deserters report that the advanced dervish force is near Kerreri, but it is impossible to tell at present if this be so.

Hitherto the Dervishes have made no attempt to raid convoys or to alarm the camp by night; they are simply falling back on the main positions.

Everybody observes that the farther you advance into their country, the more desirable, or rather the less undesirable, it becomes.

I marched here from Wad Hamed, so I cannot depict fully the beauties of the Shabluka cataract, but I have seen enough from above and below and from various points of the road to understand how grateful it is to eyes seared with burning plains.

The rapids are gemmed with green wooded islands and waist-high bush grass, and the rocky heights on either side are bathed in violet by the morning and evening lights.

At the gorge the cliffs close in, and the river narrows from 2000 to 200 yards.

Here are dervish forts, three on the left bank and one on the right.

They are now flush with the water, which is actually running into the embrasures.

Having had to march with the artillery, I had to content myself with the beauties of the Maxim-Nordenfeldt gun.

The Egyptian field artillery you can either draw with two mules or take the pieces and carry them on four—a vast advantage, as shown on yesterday's march, which was an alternation of stones and wallowing sand.

On entering the camp I came on the tail of the British Division, which had made four marches of twenty miles.

The Egyptians took two, but the going is exceptionally bad; natives and British alike fell out somewhat freely.

The massed black bands welcomed the British, thundering out the march past of each of the regiments.

The Rifles, though soft, were commended for smartness in marching, as were the Northumberland Fusiliers.

The flood has formed a khor across the original camp, and the British are in detached zariba to the southward, which is lined nightly with a living rampart of soldiers, alert, eager, and tingling in anticipation of a fight.

Gebel Royan, Aug. 28 (12.20 p.m.)—The "Zafir," the flagship of the gunboat flotilla, Captain Keppel, with General Rundle, chief of the staff, on board, sprang a leak the day before yesterday off Shendi.

The boat was headed for the shore, but sank within a few yards of the bank.

Only her funnel and mast are above water.

The barges in tow were cut adrift, and everybody behaved with the greatest coolness

Captain Keppel was the last man to leave.

All lives were saved, but a quantity of kit was lost.

Considering that the navy has been two years at work, that the steamers are of light draught, and that there is a tremendous head of water in the river, it is wonderful that this is the first serious mishap.

Everybody sympathises with Captain Keppel, and deplores this stroke of bad luck at the end of months of splendid work.

He transfers his flag to the Sultan.

The whole force advances this afternoon about eight miles.

Wady Abid, Aug. 29 (8.40 a.m.)—The whole army is camped here, the British division having left Royan in the cool of the evening and marching in by moonlight.

The camp is estimated to be twenty-eight miles from Omdurman and eighteen from Kerreri, where there is every reason to believe that the Dervishes are collecting.

The army will halt here at least till evening.

Meanwhile a reconnaissance, consisting of the Egyptian cavalry, with the Maxims and camel corps, is patrolling ten miles to the southward, and a gunboat has been despatched to patrol the stream.

A dervish patrol of ten men was seen yesterday evening. It fell back.

Deserters are now beginning to arrive in swarms, and a sifting of their reports shows that it may be considered certain that the Dervishes mean to fight.

The weather till now has been magnificent, and beyond the most optimistic expectations.

The heat is now extreme in the daytime, but the nights are cool and dry.

This morning was overcast, and there were furious gusts of wind from the north-east, which are supposed to be precursors of rain.

So far we have had only three rainstorms.

Violent and tempestuous weather at this stage might breed discomfort but not delay.

The correspondents would find the chief disadvantage of rain in the possible interruption of the field telegraph, which has been brought here, and will probably advance farther, though it is only poled as far as Nasri Island, and wet ground might cause a breakdown of communications.

10.15 a.m.—The reconnaissance has returned, having seen only a few fresh tracks of dervish horsemen, owing to the dust blown off the alluvial land into the desert having covered up their traces.

The fewness of the tracks confirms the conjecture that the Dervishes have resolved to retire to ground of their own choosing.

The cloudy morning turned to the opaquest dust-storm of recent experience.

The rushing south wind swishes through the camp,
whirling the dust of the old cultivation in yellow
clouds before it, and the desert outside the zariba
forms a half-solid curtain of flying earth.

Riding round the camp to-day, the dust of which
clung to my eyelashes and formed dangling screens
of accumulated Sudan before my eyes, I was much
struck by the advantage which experience in campaigning here gives the Egyptian over the British
troops.

All alike are under blanket shelters, but the
Egyptians rig up all the blankets of one company
into a continuous shed on high poles, which gives an
airy shelter, leaves the camping-ground clearer, and
economises blankets, so that enough are left to hap
round the rifles.

The British, contrariwise, fix one or two blankets
on low sticks, and their ground is less thoroughly
cleared of scrub to begin with.

Dotted promiscuously over the ground are tiny
booths, beneath which the men swelter, with the
back flaps of their helmets turned over their faces
to screen off the sun. Even through the veil of
dust he presses on to the blanket so close that the
men cannot uncover their heads.

This is not a white man's country.

1.15 p.m.—There is abundant evidence that the spot
where we are now camped was in the recent occupa-

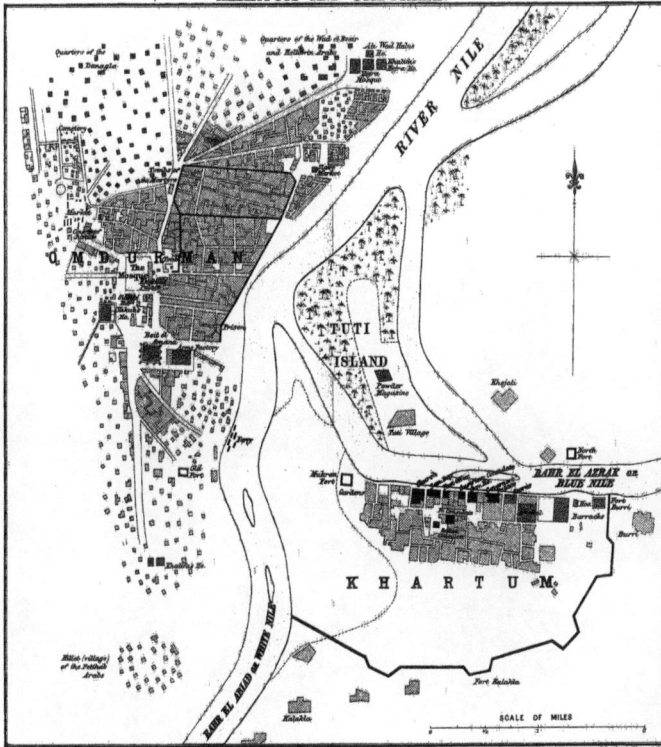

KHARTUM AND OMDURMAN

tion of the enemy—angarebs and women's trinket-
boxes being littered all over the place.

The Dervishes are almost certainly falling back before us on to positions determined beforehand, where
they expect advantage from scrub, and it would be no
surprise here if a decisive battle were fought some
distance north of Omdurman.

The Intelligence Department naturally keeps its own
counsel, since a daily interchange of spies between the
hostile headquarters is now easy.

It is safe to say that all the advantage of information is on our side, all the stories of the deserters being
carefully sifted by men accustomed to thread the tor-
tuous mazes of the Arab mind.

The Intelligence Department camp is to-day strewn
with plum-coloured, thin-cheeked dervishes squatting
in groups on the ground munching biscuit, the first
earnest of the renewed blessings of civilised rule.

It must not, however, be inferred from this that
the Khalifa's trusted fighting men are deserting.

These are so detested on account of half a generation of barbarities that they know there is no
asylum left them in all Africa : they will die
resolutely.

Wady Abid, Aug. 30 (9.40 a.m.)—We are again on
the march, the army advancing ten miles to Sayal—
another stride towards Omdurman.

Major Stuart - Wortley's friendlies have captured

five prisoners, together with a barge laden with grain, after a brush with some dervishes on the right bank of the Nile.

During the storm which continues to rage here the British outposts last night heard the patter of hoofs, and suddenly a dervish horseman rode up, shouting "Allah!" and hurled his spear over their heads; then, wheeling round, he galloped away unhurt.

XXXI.

THE RECONNAISSANCES.

REVEILLE at four had forestalled daybreak; at five we were between dawn and sunrise. Inside the swarming zariba of camp Sayal impatient bugles were hurrying whites and blacks under arms. Outside it the desert dust threw up a sooty film before the yellow east; the cavalry and camel-corps were forming up for the day's reconnaissance. Four squadrons of British 21st Lancers on the left, nine squadrons of Egyptian horsemen on the right with the horse guns, they trotted jangling into broad columns of troops, and spread fan-wise over the desert.

The camel-corps stayed a moment to practise a bit of drill of their own. One moment they were a huge oblong phalanx of waving necks and riders silhouetted against the sunrise; a couple of words in Turkish from their Bey and the necks were waving alone with the riders in a square round them; an instant more and camels and men had all knelt down. The camel-corps was a flat field of heads and humps hedged with a shining quickset of bayonets. That rehearsed, they loped away to the extreme right: they can wait longer for their water than the horses, so that their portion is always the outer desert.

One instant we were with the main army by the zariba. The next—so it seemed after a few days of marching with the infantry—we were off and clear away. The screen was spread far out before the toiling infantry, and the enemy who would harass or even look at them must slip through us or break us if he could. It looked little enough like either. As soon as our scouts were off the country was full of them.

It was the last day of August—above a month since the first battalions had left the Atbara, two days before we were to take Omdurman, and the first shot of the campaign was yet unfired. But before us rose cliff-like from the river, and sloped gently down to the plain, the outline of Seg-el-Taib hill; from that were only a dozen miles to Kerreri; from Kerreri were only ten to Omdurman. From the hill we should surely see.

So hoofs pattered, and curb-chains jingled, and stirrups rang, and behold we were round the inland base of Seg-el-Taib and scrambling up its shaly rise. From the top we looked out at the ten-mile reach of river and the hundred-mile stretch of plain, rejoicing in the young sunlight. On our left, four gunboats—two white of the new class, two black of the old—trudged deviously, slowly, surely up under the right bank. Across the shining steel ribbon of Nile lay a vast tangle of green—only a fifth funnel and Maxim-platforms crawling along its horizon revealed it an island. On our right, the brilliant mimosa-scrub—in this rainy country mimosa grows real leaves and the leaves are green —stretched forward to a dim double hill, a saddle in the middle, gentle ridges dipping down at each end to river and desert. At our feet, round a sandy creek, clustered white and brown cavalry like bees, lances planted in the sand, men bent over bits, horses down on their knees for the water. In the desert a slowly advancing lozenge under a cloud of dust stood for the camel corps. Over our shoulders a black tide licked yet more slowly southward; that was infantry and guns. Sun, river, birds, green; grim, stealthy gunboats and that awfully advancing host; it combined into the most heart-winning, most heart-quaking picture of all the war.

But we were looking for somebody to kill. Mudwalled villages, as everywhere, fringed the river-bank; by one the cavalry were watering; another further on focussed the landscape with the conical-pointed tomb of some sheikh or holy man. And—what ?—the glasses, quick !—yes, by George it is ! One, two, three, four, five—our scouts ? impossible ; there are our scouts a mile this side of them. No : Dervishes—

dervish horse ; the first sight of them, for me, in the campaign. Dervish horse three miles this side of Kerreri.

Stand to your horses ! Prepare to mount ! Mount ! This time the plain was fuller, the jingling merrier, the bobbing lance-points more alert than ever. On and on—a troop through the dense bush, a couple of squadrons in line over the open gravel, scrambling through a rocky rent in the ground, halting to breathe the horses and signal the scouts—but always on again. Always, by comparison with infantry, we seemed to fly, to spread out by magic, to leave the miles behind us in a flash.

But the Dervishes seemed to have vanished, as their wont is, swallowed up by dervish-land. We had already passed the spot chosen for the night's camp ; we were to go on a mile or two beyond " to make it good," as they say. At last we halted. " We shall water here," said the Colonel, " and then go home." Then suddenly somebody looked forward through his glasses. " By Gad, the Gippy cavalry are charging ! "

" That's not the Gippy cavalry," sings out somebody else ; " that's our advanced squadron." Mount and clatter off again. I didn't see them, but it was good enough to gallop for ; and now, sure enough, we plunge through the mimosa and find the advanced squadron pressing on furiously, and the best gentleman rider in the army with a dervish lance in his hand. The squadron found them in the bush, and galloped at them, but they were too quick away. We scrambled on, round that bush, down and up that gully, and presently came out again into a rising swell of gravel. And there were the lines of Kerreri.

Behind another stretch of thicker bush, perhaps a mile through, under the twin hills, was a flutter of something white—white splashed with crimson. Kerreri lines beyond a doubt; only what was the white? Loose garments of horsemen riding through the bush? Tents? Flags? Yes; it must be flags. Already a subaltern was picking his way through the bush with an officer's patrol. Immediately another strolled away to the left; already one white gunboat had almost outflanked the lines. The whole regiment was now up, and dismounted in columns of squadrons in the open. When the saddle alone weighs eight stone it is always useful to relieve a horse of the man. Colonel and majors, captains and adjutants and subalterns, sergeant-major and privates to hold the horses, grouped on a little knoll. Popular the man who had a good field-glass.

Tap, tap, tap, floated down the wind. They were beating their war-drum. "Where's Montmorency?" "Gone into the bush, sir." Pop! Very faint and muffled, but all hearts leaped: it was the first shot of the campaign. And then through the bushes galloped a bay horse riderless. Tap, tap, tap: they were still beating the war-drum. "What's that to right of the flags?" "Men, sir," says the sergeant-major, taking his pipe out of his mouth. " I can see them with the naked eye." Tap, tap, tap. " Where's Montmorency ? " " In the—— there he is, sir, coming back." " Very well ; send a man to recall that patrol on the left. We've seen where they are : we'll go home now, quietly."

Then in came the smiling subaltern. One man had thrown a spear at him and one had loosed off an elephant gun ; but he had dropped one man off the bay horse. There were thirty flags or so : it might mean perhaps 3000 men. The patrol from the left reported some 200 horsemen striking away to their right rear. It might mean retreat : it might mean a flank attack. It did not matter which. We had seen ; the reconnaissance had succeeded : we walked home quietly.

The next day,—the army had marched eight miles to Wady Suetne—it was the Egyptian cavalry,—nearly twice as many of them, and the camel-corps and horse-battery besides. This time we started only five miles or so from Kerreri, and before we had gone an hour the 21st were in the lines. It had been a retreat we had seen the day before ; anyhow, it had become so later, when the gunboats shelled the position ; the place was empty. We crossed over to the left and cantered up expectant, but there was nothing to see. Only a few miserable tukls twisted out of bushes : Jonah had a better house under his gourd. Kerreri had been a fable—a post of observation never meant to be held.

But the lines mattered little: it was to the hill behind it that eyes turned. Now we were on the very brink, and could look over it to forecast the great day. Should we see dervishes coming on, or should we see dervishes streaming away? We must see something, and we scrambled up, and at last, and at last, we saw Omdurman. We saw a broad plain, half sand, half pale grass; on the rim by the Nile rose a pale yellow dome, clear above everything. That was the Mahdi's tomb, divined from Gebel Royan, now seen. It was the centre of a purple stain on the yellow sand, going out for miles and miles on every side—the mud-houses of Omdurman. A great city—an enormous city—a city worth conquering indeed!

A while we looked; but this was a reconnaissance. The thing was to look nearer and see if there were any enemy. The Lancers had gone on towards some villages along the river, between our hill and another three or four miles on. The Egyptian mounted troops turned south-westward, inland. We did not altogether know what we were going to do or see: perhaps it was that dark patch halfway between our line of advance and the British, which might be trees or might be men. But Broadwood Bey knew very well where we were going, and what we were going to see. We began to march towards a clump of hills that drew in north-westward within three miles of the outskirts of Omdurman; the map calls it Gebel Feried. We came into swamps deepened by the last night's rain; we crossed soft-bottomed streams; it would have been desperate ground to be attacked in, but still the leader rode on and the heavy columns rode behind him. At last we came behind the south-easternmost hill, and the squadrons halted and the guns wheeled into line and the camels barracked. We went up the hill and again we saw.

Omdurman was nearer, more enormous, more worth conquering than ever. A gigantic tract of mud-houses; the Mahdi's tomb rising above them like a protecting genius; many other roofs rising tall above the wont of the Sudan, one or two with galvanised iron roofs to mirror the sunlight. With its huge extent, its obvious principal buildings, its fostering cathedral, the distant view of Omdurman would have disgraced no European capital: you might almost expect that the hotel omnibus would meet you at the railway station.

But once more we were on reconnaissance; we were there to look for men. In front of the city stretched a long white line—banners, it might be; more likely tents; most likely both. In front of that was a longer, thicker black line—no doubt a zariba or trench. Then they did mean to fight after all. Only as we sat and ate a biscuit and looked—the entrench-ment moved. The solid wall moved forward, and it was a wall of men.

Whew! What an army! Five huge brigades of it

—a three-mile front, and parts of it eight or ten men
deep. It was beginning to move directly for our hill,
and—tum, tum, tum—we heard the boom of a war-
drum of higher calibre than yesterday's. Now they
seemed to halt; now they came on. The five corps
never broke or shifted, the rigid front never bent;
their discipline must be perfect. And they covered
the ground. The three miles melted before them;
our scouts and the Lancers' and theirs were chasing
each other to and fro over the interval; we saw a
picket of the Lancers fire. "We'll go back now,"
said the serene voice of the leader. The force formed
up, and we started on the eight-mile walk between
ourselves and support.

The sun had hardened the swamp underfoot, but
the guns and camels still made heavy going of it.
We had not been moving twenty minutes before we
saw a black mass of the enemy watching us from the
hill whence we had watched them. And their line
was still coming on, black over a ridge not a mile
behind us. Tum, tum, tum — they were getting
nearer; now we heard their shouts, and saw their
swords brandishing in the sun. Tum, tum, tum—roar
—brandish — how slowly the camels moved! The
troopers in the long column of our outside flank were
beginning to look over their shoulders. Then the doctor came galloping like mad from behind. "Where's
Broadwood?"—and we saw the rear-guard squadron
faced about and galloping towards the enemy. The

R

bugle snapped out and the troops of the flanking regiment whipped round and walked towards the enemy too.   They were within a thousand yards. Now—

It was only a dismounted trooper they were fetching back.   The troops turned again, and we walked into camp.   It was a perfect reconnaissance,—not a man lost, not a shot fired, and everything seen.

XXXII.

THE BATTLE OF OMDURMAN.

OUR camp, for the night of September 1, was in the village of Agaiga, a mile south of Kerreri Hill. On our left front was another hill, higher, but single-peaked and rounder—Gebel Surgham. In front the ground was open for five miles or so—sand and grass broken by only a few folds—with a group of hills beyond.

The force had formed up in position in the afternoon, when the Dervishes followed the cavalry home, and had remained under arms all night; at half-past five in the morning, when the first howitzer-shell from opposite Omdurman opened the day's work, every man was in his place. The line formed an obtuse angle; the order of brigades and battalions, counting from the left, was the following: Lyttelton's 2nd British (Rifle Brigade, Lancashire Fusiliers, Northumberland Fusiliers, Grenadier Guards); Wauchope's 1st British (Warwicks, Seaforths, Camerons, Lincolns); Maxwell's 2nd Egyptian (14th, 12th, 13th Sudanese,

and 8th Egyptian in support).   Here came the point
of the angle; to the right of it were: Macdonald's
1st Egyptian (11th, 10th, 9th Sudanese, 2nd Egyptian
supporting); Lewis's 3rd Egyptian (4th, 15th, and
3rd and 7th Egyptian, in column on the right flank).
Collinson's 4th Egyptian Brigade (1st, 5th, 17th, and
18th Egyptian) was in reserve in the village.   All
the Egyptian battalions in the front were in their
usual formation, with four companies in line and two
in support.   The British had six in line and two in
support.

On the extreme left was the 32nd Field Battery;
the Maxims and Egyptian field-guns were mounted at
intervals in the infantry line.   The cavalry had gone
out at the first streak of grey, British on the left,
as usual, Egyptian with camel-corps and horse-battery
from the right moving across our front.   The gunboats
lay with steam up off the village.

Light stole quietly into the sky behind us; there
was no sound from the plain or the hills before us;
there was hardly a sound from our own line.   Everybody was very silent, but very curious.   Would they
be so mad as to come out and run their heads into our
fire?   It seemed beyond hoping for; yet certainly
they had been full of war the day before.   But most
of us were expecting instantly the order to advance
on Omdurman.

A trooper rose out of the dimness from behind the
shoulder of Gebel Surgham, grew larger and plainer,

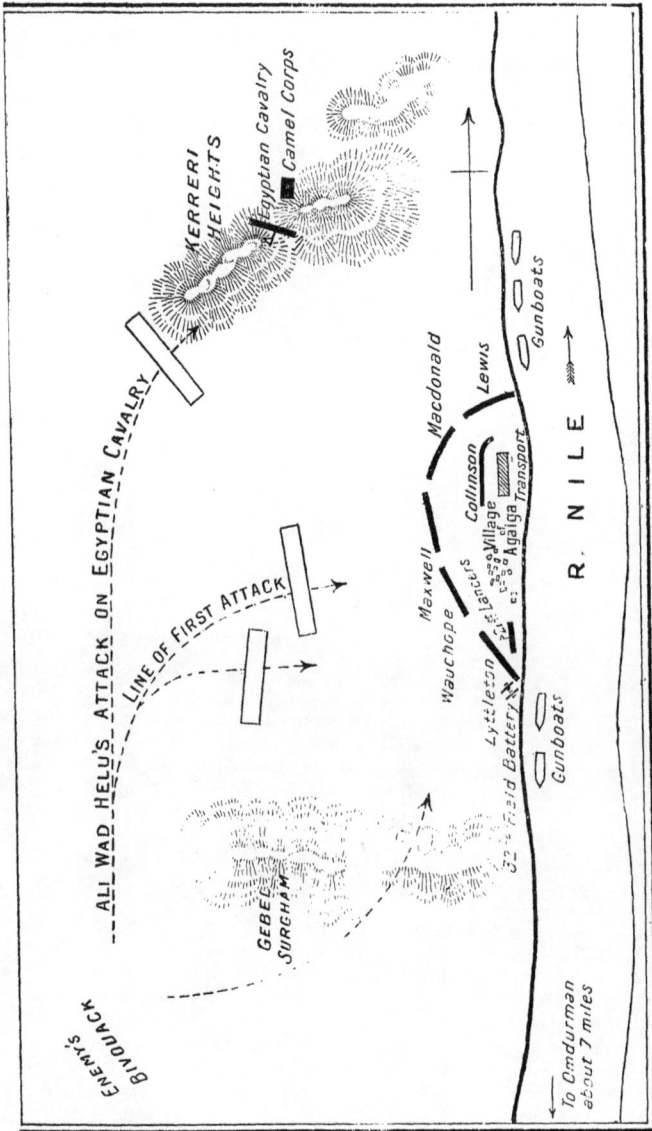

BATTLE OF OMDURMAN, Phase One, 7 A.M.

spurred violently up to the line and inside. A couple
more were silhouetted across our front. Then the
electric whisper came racing down the line; they
were coming. The Lancers came in on the left; the
Egyptian mounted troops drew like a curtain across
us from left to right. As they passed a flicker of
white flags began to extend and fill the front in their
place. The noise of something began to creep in upon
us; it cleared and divided into the tap of drums and
the far - away surf of raucous war-cries. A shiver
of expectancy thrilled along our army, and then a
sigh of content. They were coming on. Allah help
them! they were coming on.

It was now half-past six. The flags seemed still very
distant, the roar very faint, and the thud of our first
gun was almost startling. It may have startled them
too, but it startled them into life. The line of flags
swung forward, and a mass of white flying linen swung
forward with it too. They came very fast, and they
came very straight; and then presently they came no
farther. With a crash the bullets leaped out of the
British rifles. It began with the Guards and Warwicks
—section volleys at 2000 yards; then, as the Dervishes
edged rightward, it ran along to the Highlanders, the
Lincolns, and to Maxwell's Brigade. The British stood
up in double rank behind their zariba; the blacks lay
down in their shelter-trench; both poured out death
as fast as they could load and press trigger. Shrapnel
whistled and Maxims growled savagely. From all the

line came perpetual fire, fire, fire, and shrieked forth
in great gusts of destruction.

And the enemy? No white troops would have
faced that torrent of death for five minutes, but the
Baggara and the blacks came on. The torrent swept
into them and hurled them down in whole companies.
You saw a rigid line gather itself up and rush on
evenly; then before a shrapnel shell or a Maxim the
line suddenly quivered and stopped. The line was
yet unbroken, but it was quite still. But other lines
gathered up again, again, and yet again; they went
down, and yet others rushed on. Sometimes they
came near enough to see single figures quite plainly.
One old man with a white flag started with five
comrades; all dropped, but he alone came bounding
forward to within 200 yards of the 14th Sudanese.
Then he folded his arms across his face, and his limbs
loosened, and he dropped sprawling to earth beside
his flag.

It was the last day of Mahdism, and the greatest.
They could never get near, and they refused to hold
back. By now the ground before us was all white
with dead men's drapery. Rifles grew red-hot; the
soldiers seized them by the slings and dragged them
back to the reserve to change for cool ones. It was
not a battle, but an execution.

In the middle of it all you were surprised to find
that we were losing men. The crash of our own fire
was so prodigious that we could not hear their bullets

whistle; yet they came and swooped down and found victims. The Dervishes were firing at their extreme range, and their bullets were many of them almost spent; but as they always fire high they often hit. So that while you might have thought you were at a shoot of rabbits, you suddenly heard the sharp cry, "Bearer party there, quick," and a man was being borne rearward. Few went down, but there was a steady trickle to hospital. Bullets may have been spent, and Captain Caldecott, of the Warwicks, was one of the strongest men in the army; but that helped him nothing when the dropping ball took him in the temple and came out through the jugular. He lay an hour unconscious, then opened his eyes with "For God's sake, give me water!" and died as he drank. All mourned him for a smart officer and a winning comrade. Most of all the two Highland battalions dropped men. The zariba behind which they were unwisely posted obliged them to stand, besides hampering them both in fire and when it came to movement; a little clump of enemy gathered in a hole in front of them, and by the time guns came up to shell them out, the Camerons had lost some twenty-five and the Seaforths above a dozen.

But loss on this scale was not to be considered beside the awful slaughter of the Dervishes. If they still came on our men needed only time and ammunition and strength to point a rifle to kill them off to the very last man. Only by now—small wonder—

they were not coming on. They were not driven
back; they were all killed in coming on. One section
of fire after another hushed, and at eight o'clock the
village and the plain were still again. The last shell
had burst over the last visible group of Dervishes;
now there was nothing but the unbending, grimly
expectant line before Agaiga and the still carpet of
white in front.

We waited half an hour or so, and then the sudden
bugle called us to our feet. "Advance," it cried; "to
Omdurman!" added we. Slowly the force broke up,
and expanded. The evident intention was to march
in echelon of brigades—the Second British leading
along the river, the First British on their right rear,
then Maxwell's, Lewis's, and Macdonald's, with
Collinson's still supporting. Lewis and Macdonald
had changed places, the latter being now outermost
and rearmost; at the time few noticed that. The
moment the dervish attack had died down the 21st
Lancers had slipped out, and pushed straight for the
Khalifa's capital.

Movement was slow, since the leading brigades had
to wait till the others had gone far enough inland to
take their positions. We passed over a corner of the
field of fire, and saw for certain what awful slaughter
we had done. The bodies were not in heaps—bodies
hardly ever are; but they spread evenly over acres
and acres. And it was very remarkable, if you
remembered the Atbara, that you saw hardly a black;

BATTLE OF OMDURMAN, PHASE TWO, 9.40 A.M.

nearly all the dead had the high forehead and taper cheeks of the Arab. The Baggara had been met at last, and he was worth meeting. Some lay very composedly, with their slippers placed under their heads for a last pillow; some knelt, cut short in the middle of a last prayer. Others were torn to pieces, vermilion blood already drying on brown skin, killed instantly beyond doubt. Others, again, seemingly as dead as these, sprang up as we approached, and rushed savagely, hurling spears at the nearest enemy. They were bayoneted or shot. Once again the plain seemed empty, but for the advancing masses and the carpet of reddened white and broken bodies underfoot.

It was now twenty minutes to ten. The British had crested a low ridge between Gebel Surgham and the Nile; Maxwell's brigade was just ascending it, Lewis's just coming up under the hill. Men who could go where they liked were up with the British, staring hungrily at Omdurman. Suddenly from rearward broke out a heavy crackle of fire. We thought perhaps a dozen men or so had been shamming dead; we went on staring at Omdurman. But next instant we had to turn and gallop hot-heeled back again. For the crackle became a crashing, and the crashing waxed to a roar. Dervishes were firing at us from the top of Gebel Surgham, dervishes were firing behind and to the right of it. The 13th Sudanese were bounding up the hill; Lewis's brigade had hastily faced to its right westward, and was volleying for life; Mac-

donald's beyond, still facing northward, was a sheet of
flashes and a roll of smoke. What was it? Had they
come to life again? No time to ask; reinforcements
or ghosts, they were on us, and the battle was begun
all again.

To understand, you must hear now what we only
heard afterwards. The dervish army, it appeared,
had not returned to Omdurman on the night of the
1st, but had bivouacked—40,000 to 50,000 of them—
behind Gebel Surgham, south-westward from Agaiga.
The Khalifa had doubtless expected a sudden attack
at daybreak, as at Firket, at Abu Hamed, on the
Atbara; as we marched by night to our positions
before Omdurman he must have designed to spring
upon our right flank. When day broke and no
enemy appeared he divided his army into three
corps. The first, under Osman Azrak, attacked the
village; the second, with the green banner of Ali
Wad Helu—with him Abdullahi's eldest son, the
Sheik-ed-Din — moved towards Kerreri Heights to
envelop our right; the third, under Abdullahi himself
and his brother Yakub, remained behind Surgham,
ready, as need might be, to envelop our left, or to act
as reserve and bar our road to Omdurman.

What befell the first you know; Osman Azrak died
with them. The second spread out towards our right,
and there it fell in with the Egyptian cavalry, horse-
battery, and camel-corps. When Broadwood Bey fell
back before the attack, he sent word of its coming to

the Sirdar, and received orders to remain outside the
trench and keep the enemy in front, instead of letting
them get round the right. Accordingly he occupied
the Heights of Kerreri. But the moment he got to the
top he found himself in face of Wad Helu's unsuspected
army-corps—12,000 to 15,000 men against less than
2000 — and the moment he saw them they began
swarming up the hill. There was just a moment for
decision, but one moment is all that a born cavalry
general needs. The next his galloper was flying with
the news to the Sirdar, and the mounted troops were
retreating northward. The choice lay between isola-
tion, annihilation, or retreat on Agaiga and envelop-
ment of the right. Broadwood chose the first, but
even for that the time was short enough. The camels
floundered on the rocky hillside; the guns dragged;
the whole mass of dervishes pursued them with a
pelting fire. Two guns lost all their horses and were
abandoned; the camel-corps alone had over sixty men
hit. As for the cavalry, they went back very hard
pressed, covering their comrades' retreat and their own
by carbine fire. If the Egyptian army but gave
Victoria Crosses, there were many earned that day.
Man after man rode back to bring in dismounted
officers, and would hardly be dissuaded from their
endeavour when it was seen the rescued were plainly
dead. It was the great day of trial—the day the pick
of our cavalry officers have worked for through a weary
decade and more—and the Fayum fellah fought like a

hero and died like a man.   One or two short of forty
killed and wounded was the day's loss; but they came
off handsomely.   The army of the green flag was now
on Kerreri Heights, between them and the camp; but
with Broadwood's force unbroken behind it, it paused
from the meditated attack on the Egyptian right.   In
the pause three of the five gunboats caught it, and
pepper-castored it over with shell and Maxim fire.   It
withdrew from the river towards the centre again: the
instant a way was cleared the out-paced camel-corps
was passed back to Agaiga.   The cavalry hung upon
the green flag's left, till they withdrew clean westward and inland; then it moved placidly back to the
infantry again.

Thus much for the right; on the left the British
cavalry were in the stress of an engagement, less perfectly conducted, even more hardily fought out.   They
left the zariba, as you heard, the moment the attack
burned out, and pricked eagerly off to Omdurman.
Verging somewhat westward, to the rear of Gebel
Surgham, they came on 300 Dervishes.   Their scouts
had been over the ground a thousand yards ahead of
them, and it was clear for a charge.   Only to cut them
off it was thought better to get a little west of them,
then left wheel, and thus gallop down on them and
drive them away from their supports.   The trumpets
sang out the order, the troops glided into squadrons,
and, four squadrons in line, the 21st Lancers swung
into their first charge.

Knee to knee they swept on till they were but 200 yards from the enemy. Then suddenly — then in a flash—they saw the trap. Between them and the 300 there yawned suddenly a deep ravine; out of the ravine there sprang instantly a cloud of dark heads and a brandished lightning of swords, and a thunder of savage voices. Mahmud smiled when he heard the tale in prison at Halfa, and said it was their favourite stratagem. It had succeeded. Three thousand, if there was one, to a short four hundred; but it was too late to check now. Must go through with it now! The blunders of British cavalry are the fertile seed of British glory: knee to knee the Lancers whirled on. One hundred yards—fifty—knee to knee——

Slap! "It was just like that," said a captain, bringing his fist hard into his open palm. Through the swordsmen they shore without checking—and then came the khor. The colonel at their head, riding straight through everything without sword or revolver drawn, found his horse on its head, and the swords swooping about his own. He got the charger up again, and rode on straight, unarmed, through everything. The squadrons followed him down the fall. Horses plunged, blundered, recovered, fell; dervishes on the ground lay for the hamstringing cut; officers pistolled them in passing over, as one drops a stone into a bucket; troopers thrust till lances broke, then cut; everybody went on straight, through everything.

And through everything clean out the other side

s

they came — those that kept up or got up in time. The others were on the ground—in pieces by now, for the cruel swords shore through shoulder and thigh, and carved the dead into fillets. Twenty-four of these, and of those that came out over fifty had felt sword or bullet or spear. Few horses stayed behind among the swords, but nearly 130 were wounded. Lieutenant Robert Grenfell's troop came on a place with a jump out as well as a jump in; it lost officer, centre guide, and both flank guides, ten killed, and eleven wounded. Yet, when they burst straggling out, their only thought was to rally and go in again. "Rally, No. 2!" yelled a sergeant, so mangled across the face that his body was a cascade of blood, and nose and cheeks flapped hideously as he yelled. "Fall out, sergeant, you're wounded," said the subaltern of his troop. "No, no, sir; fall in!" came the hoarse answer; and the man reeled in his saddle. "Fall in, No. 2; fall in. Where are the devils? Show me the devils!" And No. 2 fell in—four whole men out of twenty.

They chafed and stamped and blasphemed to go through them again, though the colonel wisely forbade them to face the pit anew. There were gnashings of teeth and howls of speechless rage—things half theatrical, half brutal to tell of when blood has cooled, yet things to rejoice over, in that they show the fighting devil has not, after all, been civilised out of Britons.

Also there are many and many deeds of self-abandon-
ing heroism; of which tale the half will never be
told. Take only one. Lieutenant de Montmorency
missed his troop-sergeant, and rode back among the
slashes to look for him. There he found the hacked
body of Lieutenant Grenfell. He dismounted, and
put it up on his horse, not seeing, in his heat, that
life had drained out long since by a dozen chan-
nels. The horse bolted under the slackened muscles,
and De Montmorency was left alone with his revolver
and 3000 screaming fiends. Captain Kenna and
Corporal Swarbrick rode out, caught his horse, and
brought it back; the three answered the fire of the
3000 at fifty yards, and got quietly back to their
own line untouched.

Forbearing a second charge, the Lancers dismounted
and opened fire; the carbines at short range took an
opulent vengeance for the lost. Back, back, back they
drove them, till they came into the fire of the 32nd
Battery. The shrapnel flew shrieking over them;
the 3000 fell all ways, and died.

All this from hearsay; now to go back to what
we saw. When the Sirdar moved his brigades
southward he knew what he was doing. He was
giving his right to an unbeaten enemy; with his
usual daring he made it so. His game now was to
get between the dervishes and Omdurman. Perhaps
he did not guess what a bellyful of beating the un-

beaten enemy would take; but he trusted to his
generals and his star, and, as always, they bore him
to victory.

The blacks of the 13th Battalion were storming
Gebel Surgham.   Lewis and Macdonald, facing west
and south, had formed a right angle.   They were
receiving the fire of the Khalifa's division, and the
charge of the Khalifa's horsemen; behind these the
Khalifa's huge black standard was flapping raven-
like.   The Baggara horsemen were few and ill-
mounted—perhaps 200 altogether—but they rode to
get home or die.   They died.   There was a time
when one galloping Baggara would have chased a
thousand Egyptians, but that time is very long past.
The fellaheen stood like a wall, and aimed steadily at
the word; the chargers swerved towards Macdonald.
The blacks, as cool as any Scotsmen, stood and
aimed likewise; the last Baggara fell at the muzzles
of the rifles.   Our fire went on, steady, remorseless.
The Remington bullets piped more and more rarely
overhead, and the black heads thinned out in front.
A second time the attack guttered and flickered out.
It was just past ten.   Once more to Omdurman!

Two minutes' silence.   Then once more the howling
storm rushed down upon us; once more crashed forth
the answering tempest.   This time it burst upon Macdonald alone—from the north-westward upon his right
flank, spreading and gathering to his right rear.   For
all their sudden swiftness of movement the Dervishes

throughout this day never lost their formation; their lines drove on as rigidly as ours, regiment alongside regiment in lines of six and eight and a dozen ranks, till you might have fancied the Macedonian phalanx was alive again. Left and front and right and rear the masses ate up the desert—12,000 unbroken fast and fearless warriors leaping round 3000.

Now began the fiercest fight of that fierce day. The Khalifa brought up his own black banner again; his staunchest die-hards drove it into the earth and locked their ranks about it. The green flag danced encouragement to the Allah-intoxicated battalions of Wad Helu and the Sheikh-ed-Din. It was victory or Paradise now.

For us it was victory or shredded flesh and bones unburied, crackling under the red slippers of Baggara victors. It was the very crux and crisis of the fight. If Macdonald went, Lewis on his left and Collinson and the supporting camel-corps and the newly returned cavalry, all on his right or rear, must all go too. The Second British and Second Egyptian Brigades were far off by now, advancing by the left of Surgham hill; if they had to be recalled the Khalifa could walk back into his stronghold, and then all our fighting was to begin anew. But Hunter Pasha was there and Macdonald Bey was there, born fighting men both, whom no danger can flurry and no sudden shift in the kaleidoscope of battle disconcert. Hunter sent for Wauchope's first British Brigade to fill the

gap between Macdonald and Lewis. The order went
to General Gatacre first instead of to the Sirdar : with
the soldier's instinct he set the brigade moving on the
instant. The khaki columns faced round and edged
rightward, rightward till the fighting line was backed
with 3000 Lee-Metfords, which no man on earth
could face and live. Later the Lincolns were moved
farther still on to Macdonald's right. They dispute
with the Warwicks the title of the best shooting
regiment in the British army ; the men they shot at
will dispute no claim of the Lincolns for ever.

But the cockpit of the fight was Macdonald's. The
British might avenge his brigade ; it was his to keep
it and to kill off the attack. To meet it he turned his
front through a complete half-circle, facing succes-
sively south, west, and north. Every tactician in
the army was delirious in his praise : the ignorant
correspondent was content to watch the man and his
blacks. "Cool as on parade," is an old phrase ; Macdonald Bey was very much cooler. Beneath the
strong, square-hewn face you could tell that the
brain was working as if packed in ice. He sat
solid on his horse, and bent his black brows towards
the green flag and the Remingtons. Then he turned
to a galloper with an order, and cantered easily up to
a battalion-commander. Magically the rifles hushed,
the stinging powder smoke wisped away, and the
companies were rapidly threading back and forward,
round and round, in and out, as if it were a figure

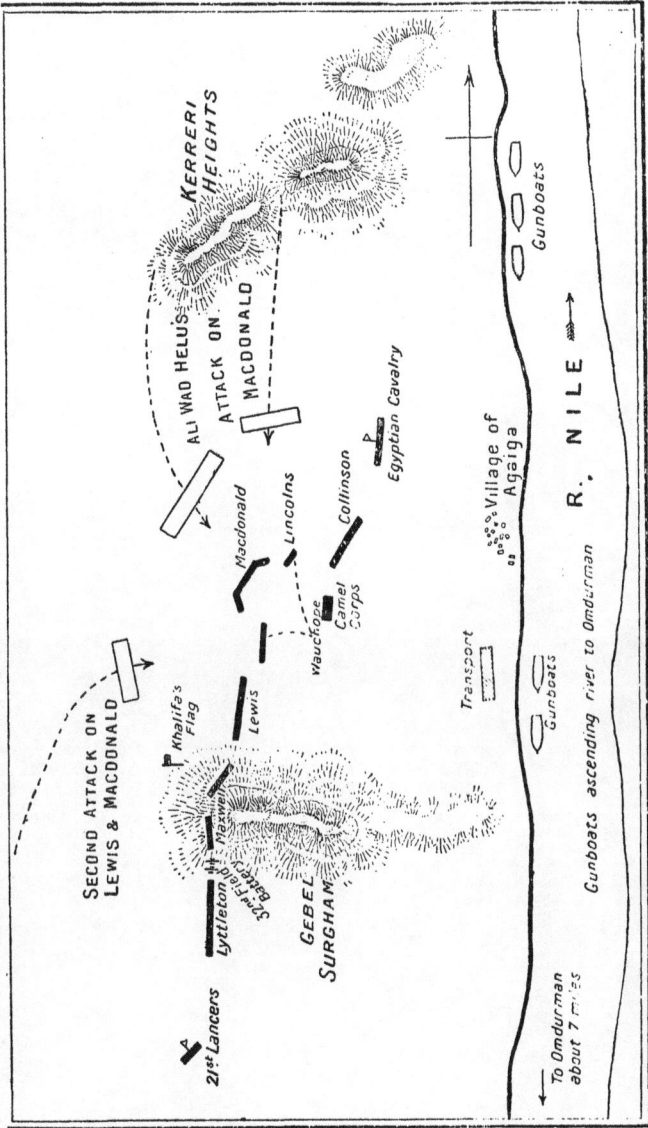

BATTLE OF OMDURMAN, PHASE THREE, 10.10 A.M.

of a dance. In two minutes the brigade was together again in a new place. The field in front
was hastening towards us in a whitey-brown cloud
of dervishes. An order. Macdonald's jaws gripped
and hardened as the flame spurted out again, and
the whitey-brown cloud quivered and stood still.
He saw everything; knew what to do; knew how
to do it; did it. At the fire he was ever brooding
watchfully behind his firing-line; at the cease fire
he was instantly in front of it: all saw him, and
knew that they were being nursed to triumph.

His blacks of the 9th, 10th, and 11th, the historic
fighting regiments of the Egyptian army, were worthy
of their chief. The 2nd Egyptian, brigaded with them
and fighting in the line, were worthy of their comrades, and of their own reputation as the best disciplined battalion in the world. A few had feared
that the blacks would be too forward, the yellows
too backward: except that the blacks, as always,
looked happier, there was no difference at all between
them. The Egyptians sprang to the advance at the
bugle; the Sudanese ceased fire in an instant silence
at the whistle. They were losing men, too, for though
eyes were clamped on the dervish charges, the dervish
fire was brisk. Man after man dropped out behind
the firing-line. Here was a white officer with a red-
lathered charger; there a black stretched straight,
bare-headed in the sun, dry-lipped, uncomplaining,
a bullet through his liver; two yards away a dead

driver by a dead battery mule, his whip still glued in his hand. The table of loss topped 100—150—neared 200. Still they stood, fired, advanced, fired, changed front, fired—firing, firing always, deaf in the din, blind in the smarting smoke, hot, dry, bleeding, bloodthirsty, enduring the devilish fight to the end.

And the Dervishes? The honour of the fight must still go with the men who died. Our men were perfect, but the Dervishes were superb—beyond perfection. It was their largest, best, and bravest army that ever fought against us for Mahdism, and it died worthily of the huge empire that Mahdism won and kept so long. Their riflemen, mangled by every kind of death and torment that man can devise, clung round the black flag and the green, emptying their poor, rotten, home-made cartridges dauntlessly. Their spearmen charged death at every minute hopelessly. Their horsemen led each attack, riding into the bullets till nothing was left but three horses trotting up to our line, heads down, saying, "For goodness' sake, let us in out of this." Not one rush, or two, or ten—but rush on rush, company on company, never stopping, though all their view that was not unshaken enemy was the bodies of the men who had rushed before them. A dusky line got up and stormed forward: it bent, broke up, fell apart, and disappeared. Before the smoke had cleared, another line was bending and storming forward in the same track.

It was over. The avenging squadrons of the Egyp-

tian cavalry swept over the field. The Khalifa and
the Sheikh-ed-Din had galloped back to Omdurman.
Ali Wad Helu was borne away on an angareb with
a bullet through his thigh-bone. Yakub lay dead
under his brother's banner. From the green army
there now came only death-enamoured desperadoes,
strolling one by one towards the rifles, pausing to
shake a spear, turning aside to recognise a corpse,
then, caught by a sudden jet of fury, bounding forward, checking, sinking limply to the ground. Now
under the black flag in a ring of bodies stood only
three men, facing the three thousand of the Third
Brigade. They folded their arms about the staff and
gazed steadily forward. Two fell. The last dervish
stood up and filled his chest; he shouted the name
of his God and hurled his spear. Then he stood quite
still, waiting. It took him full; he quivered, gave
at the knees, and toppled with his head on his arms
and his face towards the legions of his conquerors.

XXXIII.

ANALYSIS AND CRITICISM.

OVER 11,000 killed, 16,000 wounded, 4000 prisoners,
—that was the astounding bill of dervish casualties
officially presented after the battle of Omdurman.
Some people had estimated the whole dervish army
at 1000 less than this total: few had put it above
50,000. The Anglo-Egyptian army on the day of
battle numbered, perhaps, 22,000 men: if the Allies
had done the same proportional execution at Waterloo,
not one Frenchman would have escaped.

How the figures of wounded were arrived at I
do not know. The wounded of a dervish army ought
not really to be counted at all, since the badly
wounded die and the slightly wounded are just as
dangerous as if they were whole. It is conceivable
that some of the wounded may have been counted
twice over—either as dead, when they were certain
to perish of their wounds or of thirst, or else as
prisoners when they gave themselves up. Yet, with
all the deductions that moderation can suggest, it was

a most appalling slaughter. The dervish army was killed out as hardly an army has been killed out in the history of war.

It will shock you, but it was simply unavoidable. Not a man was killed except resisting — very few except attacking. Many wounded were killed, it is true, but that again was absolutely unavoidable. At the very end of the battle, when Macdonald's brigade was advancing after its long fight, the leading files of the 9th Sudanese passed by a young Baggara who was not quite dead. In a second he was up and at the nearest mounted white officer. The first spear flew like a streak, but just missed. The officer assailed put a man-stopping revolver bullet into him, but it did not stop him. He whipped up another spear, and only a swerve in the saddle saved the Englishman's body at the expense of a wounded right hand. This happened not once but a hundred times, and all over the field. It was impossible not to kill the dervishes: they refused to go back alive. At the very finish — the 11,000 killed, the Khalifa fled, the army hopelessly smashed to pieces —a band of some 3000 men stood firm against the pursuing Egyptian cavalry. "They were very sticky," said an officer simply, "and we couldn't take 'em on." Later they admitted they were beaten, and came in. But except for sheer weariness of our troops, that 3000 would have been added to the eleven. As it was, they outmarched our advance, slipped into Omdurman before us, changed their gibbas, and looted the Khalifa's dhurra.

Nor was that the end of the sullen resistance of the Baggara. Even after they realised that they were hopelessly beaten in the field, they relaxed but little of their sullen hostility. Probably they were encouraged by the Sirdar's moderation in sparing indiscriminately all the inhabitants of Omdurman : whether that or no, it is certain that from the day of the fight to the 8th, the day I came down, it was not safe for any white man to go into the city unarmed. I do not think any white man was actually attacked,— certainly none was killed. But wandering Egyptian soldiers were, and it was not until a batch or two of francs - tirailleurs had been taken out and shot that decent order could be maintained in the town. That was natural enough. Omdurman's only idea of maintaining order was massacre : how could it appreciate mercy ?

By the side of the immense slaughter of dervishes, the tale of our casualties is so small as to be almost ridiculous. The first official list was this. British troops: 2 officers (Captain Caldecott and Lieut. Grenfell) killed, 7 wounded; 23 non-commissioned officers and men killed, 99 wounded. Egyptian army: 5 British officers and 1 non - commissioned officer wounded; 1 native officer killed, 8 wounded; 20 non-commissioned officers and men killed, 221 wounded. Total casualties: 131 British, 256 native—387.

But this estimate, like all early estimates, was under the mark. Some of the wounded died—among them a private of the Lincolns not previously reported; others were late in reporting themselves. The Egyptian casualties among non-commissioned officers and men rose to 30 killed and 279 wounded. Among the British many slight wounds were never reported at all. The 21st Lancers, especially, according to the testimony of their own officers, lost 24 killed or died of wounds, and 74 wounded. Of the latter, hardly more than half came under surgical treatment at all. Such wounds, of course, were very slight, and were properly omitted from the official list. Still, if you count every scratch, the British casualties go up to nearly 200, and the Egyptian to over 300. Of the British infantry, the Camerons, with a total of 2 killed and 25 wounded, lost most severely, as they did at Atbara; and they were again followed by the Seaforths with 2 killed and 16 wounded.

Putting it at its highest, however, the victory was even more incredibly cheap than the Atbara. But for the rash handling of the 21st Lancers, the mistake of putting the British infantry behind a zariba instead of a trench, and the curious perversity which sent the slow camel-corps out into the open with the Egyptian cavalry, the losses would have been more insignificant still. The enemy's fire, as always, was too high, and the Egyptians in their shelter-trench hardly suffered from it at all. Perhaps the heaviest fire of the first

part of the action was borne by Collinson's supporting
brigade and by the hospitals.   In the second action,
Macdonald's four battalions suffered most severely of
any in the field—again, as at the Atbara.

Among correspondents, the Hon. Hubert Howard,
acting for the 'Times' and the 'New York Herald' in
conjunction, was killed by a chance shot at the gate
of the Mahdi's tomb at the very end of the day.   From
Oxford onward his one end in life had been the woo-
ing of adventures.   He had found them with the Cuban
insurgents and in the Matabele rebellion, where he
was wounded in leading a charge of Cape boys.   He
was foredoomed from the cradle to die in his boots,
and asked no better.   Earlier in the day he had ridden
with the Lancers through their charge ; earlier still he
had been out with the pickets and jumped his horse
over the zariba as the dervishes came on to attack it.
No man ever born was more insensible to fear.   Ten
minutes before he was killed he said, " This is the best
day of my life."

Colonel Frank Rhodes, the formally accredited correspondent of the 'Times,' was shot through the flesh
of the right shoulder very early in the fight.   From
the very beginning no Sudan campaign has been complete without Colonel Rhodes, and it must have been
a keen disappointment to him to miss Omdurman ;
but he bore that and the wound with his usual hum-
orous fortitude.   Mr Williams, of the 'Daily Chron-
icle,' had his cheek abraded by a bullet or a chip

of masonry from a ricochet : it was nothing, and he
made of it even less than it was. Mr Cross, of the
'Manchester Guardian,' died afterwards of enteric
fever at Abeidieh. Years ago he had rowed in the
Oxford Eight, but enteric delights in seizing the most
powerful frames. Quiet, gentle, patient, brave, sincere—Mr Cross was the type of an English gentleman.

However, the battle of Omdurman was almost a
miracle of success. For that thanks are due, first,
to the Khalifa, whose generalship throughout was a
masterpiece of imbecility. Had he attacked us at
night with the force and impetuous courage he showed
by day, it was not at all impossible that he might have
got inside our position. Nothing could have come
alive up to the Lee-Metfords ; but the Martinis might
have proved less irresistible—and once inside in the
dark his death-scorning fanatics would have punished
us fearfully. At close fighting they would have been
as good as we, and far more numerous : if they had
been met with rifle-fire, we must have inevitably
shot hundreds of our own men.

If he had stood in Omdurman and fought as well as
he fought in the open, our loss must needs have been
reckoned in thousands instead of hundreds. Instead,
he chose the one form of fight which gave him no
possibility of even a partial success. We heard he
boasted that his men always had broken our squares,
and he would see if they could not do it again. They
would have broken us if valour could have done it ;

T

but he forgot that the squares were bigger than before, were better armed, so far as the British went, and especially that men like the Sirdar and Hunter and Macdonald knew every turn and twist of dervish tactics, and are not in the habit of giving points away to the enemy.

The Khalifa, therefore, came to utter grief as a general. As a ruler he fought harder than many had expected of him; even when the mass of his army was dead or yielded, he was ready for one throw more. When that failed, he rode for it: suicide would have been more dignified, as well as simpler for us, but besides suicide there was only flight open to him. Perhaps suicide would have been simpler for him too in the end. As a ruler he finished when he rode out of Omdurman. His own pampered Baggara killed his herdsmen and looted the cattle that were to feed him. Somebody betrayed the position of the reserve camels that were to carry his reserve wives: the camel-corps brought them in, and with them Fatima—the Sheikh-ed-Din's mother—an enormous lady, his faithful and candid chief partner from the days when he could carry all his property on a donkey. Other wives, less staunch, voluntarily deserted him; his followers took to killing one another.

He is no more Khalifa. He evaded the pursuit of the cavalry, however, joined the Sheikh-ed-Din, who had fled by a different route, and struck south-westward. He may reach his own country, and if, from

an Emperor, he likes to pass into a petty bandit, he
may possibly have a few months yet before him. But
his following is too small even for successful brigan-
dage; and he has earned too general detestation.
Any day his head may be brought into Omdurman.
Last month he was the arbitrary master of one of
the greatest dominions—looking only to extent of
country—in the whole world. To-day he is merely
a criminal at large.

The remainder of his forces took little reduction.
Major Stuart Wortley had cleared the right bank up
to the Blue Nile. Luckily for him, the opposition was
not severe, for most of the friendlies bolted at sight
of a Baggara, as everybody knew they would. The
Jaalin, however, behaved well.

There now remained only one dervish force in the
field—the garrison of Gedaref, up the Blue Nile and
on the Abyssinian border. It numbered 3000 men,
under Ahmed Fadil, the Khalifa's cousin. The reduction of this body was left to Parsons Pasha, Governor
of Kassala, and he executed his task brilliantly. The
details of the action are not yet known; perhaps
nobody will ever take the trouble to ask them. The
main fact is, that Parsons, with the 16th Egyptian
battalion, the Arab Kassala Regulars (under two
British Bimbashis), some camel-corps and irregulars
—in all 1300 men—attacked Ahmed Fadil's 3000, and
after three hours' fighting dispersed them. They lost
700 killed; Parsons's casualties were 37 men killed,

4 native officers and 53 men wounded.   Osman Digna
was believed to have fled in this direction, but no
word has yet come in about him.   We are not likely
to hear much more about Osman Digna.

For a point or two of criticism—if the unprofes-
sional observer may allow himself the liberty—the
battle of Omdurman was a less brilliant affair than
the Atbara: on the other hand, it was more com-
plex, more like a modern battle.   The Atbara took
more fighting, Omdurman more generalship.   Success
in each was complete and crushing.   Omdurman was
final; but it occurred to a good many of us between
10 and 11 that morning that it was just as well we
had put Mahmud's 16,000 out of harm's way at the
Atbara.   That these were not at the Khalifa's dis-
posal on September 2nd was one more of his blunders,
one piece more of the Sirdar's luck.

The Sirdar would have won in any case: that he
won so crushingly and so cheaply was the gift of luck
and the Khalifa.   Three distinct mistakes—as has, perhaps impertinently, been hinted above—were made on
our side.   Of these the charge of the 21st Lancers was
the most flagrant.   It is perhaps an unfortunate consequence of the modern development of war-correspon-
dence, and the general influence of popular feeling on
every branch of our Government, that what the street
applauds the War Office is compelled at least to con-
done.   The populace has glorified the charge of the

21st for its indisputable heroism; the War Office will
hardly be able to condemn it for its equally indisputable folly.   That being so, it is the less invidious to
say that the charge was a gross blunder.   For cavalry
to charge unbroken infantry, of unknown strength,
over unknown ground, within a mile of their own
advancing infantry, was as grave a tactical crime as
cavalry could possibly commit.   Their orders, it is
believed, were to find out the strength of the enemy
south of Gebel Surgham, report to the British infantry
behind them, and, if possible, to prevent the enemy
from re-entering Omdurman.   The charge implied dis-
regard, or at least inversion, of these orders.   Had the
cavalry merely reconnoitred the body of dervishes they
attacked, and kept them occupied till Lyttelton's
brigade came up, the enemy would have been
annihilated, probably without the loss of a man to our
side.   As it was, the British cavalry in the charge
itself suffered far heavier loss than it inflicted.   And
by its loss in horses it practically put itself out of
action for the rest of the day, when it ought to have
saved itself for the pursuit.   Thereby it contributed
as much as any one cause to the escape of the Khalifa.

For the other two points, General Gatacre, being new
to zaribas, appears to have throughout attached undue
importance to them.   At the Atbara he squandered
much of the force of his attack through an over-
estimation of the difficulty of Mahmud's zariba; here

he crippled both defence and readiness of offence through overestimating the difficulty of his own. A zariba looks far more formidable than a light shelter-trench such as General Hunter's division employed: in truth it is as easy to shoot through as a sheet of paper, and, for Sudanis, almost as easy to charge through. As for sending out the camel-corps with the Egyptian cavalry, it is exceedingly difficult to understand why this was done the very day after Broadwood's reconnaissance to Gebel Feried had demonstrated their immobility. The truth appears to be that it is very difficult to find a place for such a force in a general action. When the frontier was Halfa, and the war was mostly desert raids and counter-raids, nothing could have replaced this corps; for other than desert work it has become something of an anomaly.

These amateur criticisms are put forward with diffidence, and will, I hope, be tentatively received. Turning to what is indisputable, it is impossible to overpraise the conduct of every branch of the force. Those of the longest and widest experience said over and over again that they had never seen a battle in which everybody was so completely cool and set on his business. Two features were especially prominent. The first was the shooting of the British. It was perfect. Some thought that the Dervishes were mown down principally by artillery and Maxim fire; but if

the gun did more execution than the rifle, it was probably for the first time in the history of war. An
examination of the dead — cursory and partial, but
probably fairly representative—tends to the opinion
that most of the killing, as usual, was done by rifles.
From the British you heard not one ragged volley :
every section fired with a single report. The individ-
ual firing was lively and evenly maintained. The
satisfactory conclusion is that the British soldier will
keep absolutely steady in action, and knows how to
use his weapon : given these two conditions, no force
existing will ever get within half a mile of him on
open ground, and hardly any will try.

The native troops vindicated their courage, discipline, and endurance most nobly. The sudden, unforeseen charges might well have shaken the nerve of
the Egyptians and over-excited the blacks ; both were
absolutely cool. Their only fault was in shooting.
At almost every volley you saw a bullet kick the
sand within fifty yards of the firing - line. Others
flew almost perpendicular into the air. Still, given
steadiness, the mechanical art of shooting can be
taught with time and patience. When you consider
that less than six months ago the equivalent of one
company in each black battalion were raw dervishes,
utterly untrained in the use of fire-arms, the wonder
is they shot as well as they did. Anyhow they shot
well enough, and in trying circumstances they shot

as well as they knew how. That is the root of the matter.

As for the leading — happy the country which possessed a Hunter, a Macdonald, a Broadwood, and had hardly heard of any one of them. It has heard of them now, and it will be strange if it does not presently hear further.

XXXIV.

OMDURMAN.

IT was eleven o'clock. Four brigades were passing slowly to right and left of Gebel Surgham : the Second British and Second Egyptian were far ahead, filmy shadows on the eye-searing sand. The dervish dead and dying were strewn already over some thirty square miles—killed by bullets, killed by shrapnel, killed by shell from the gunboats, dying of wounds by the water, dying of thirst in the desert. But most lay dead in the fighting line. Mahdism had died well. If it had earned its death by its iniquities, it had condoned its iniquities by its death.

Now on to overtake the Sirdar, to see the city of the Khalifa. Even now, after our triple fight, none was quite assured of final victory. We had killed a prodigious number of men, but where there were so many there might yet be more. Probably the same thought ran through many minds. If only they fought as well inside Omdurman! That would have spelt days of fighting and thousands of dead.

One thing, indeed, we knew by now : the defences of
Omdurman on the river side existed no longer. On
the 1st, from Gebel Feried, we had seen the gun-boats
begin the bombardment, backed by the 37th Battery,
with its howitzers, on the opposite bank. We had
heard since of the effects.   " It was the funniest thing
you ever saw," said a captain of marines.   " The boats
went up one after another ; when we got opposite the
first fort, ' pop' went their guns. ' Bang, bang, bang,'
went three boats and stopped up the embrasure.
Came to the next fort : ' pop' ; ' bang, bang, bang' :
stopped up that embrasure. So on all the way up. A
little fort on Tuti Island had the cheek to loose off its
pop-gun ; stopped that up.   Then we went on to
Khartum.   Forts there thought perhaps the boats
couldn't shoot from behind, so they lay doggo till we
had gone past. They found we could shoot from
behind."

So far so good. But what should we find on the
land side ? Above all, should we find the Khalifa ?
The only answer was to go and see. Four miles or so
south of Agaiga the yellow streak of Khor Shamba
marks roughly the northern limit of Omdurman ;
thence to the Mahdi's tomb, the great mosque, and the
Khalifa's house is a short three miles. The Second
British Brigade was watering at the Khor—men and
horses lapping up the half solid stuff till they must
have been as thick with mud inside as they were out.
Beyond it a sprinkling of tumble-down huts refracted

and heated sevenfold the furnace of the sunlight; from among them beckoned the Sirdar's flag.

It was about two o'clock when the red flag moved onward towards the Mahdi's tomb, heaving its torn dome above the sea of mud walls. The red and white looked light and gay beside the huge, cumbrous raven-banner of the Khalifa, which flew sullenly at its side. Before the twin emblems of victory and defeat rode the straight-backed Sirdar, General Hunter a head behind him, behind them the staff. Behind came the trampling 2nd Egyptian Brigade and the deadly smooth-gliding guns of the 32nd Battery. Through the sparse hovels they moved on; presently they began to densen into streets. We were on the threshold of the capital of Mahdism.

And on the threshold came out an old man on a donkey with a white flag. The Khalifa — so we believed — had fled to Omdurman, and was at this very moment within his wall in the centre of the town; but the inhabitants had come out to surrender. Only one point the old gentleman wished to be assured of: were we likely to massacre everybody if we let them in without resistance? The Sirdar thought not. The old man beamed at the answer, and conveyed it to his fellow-townsmen; on the top of which ceremony we marched into Omdurman.

It began just like any other town or village of the mean Sudan. Half the huts seemed left unfinished, the other half to have been deserted and fallen to pieces. There were no streets, no doors or windows except holes, usually no roofs. As for a garden, a tree, a steading for a beast—any evidence of thrift or intelligence, any attempt at comfort or amenity or common cleanliness,—not a single trace of any of it. Omdurman was just planless confusion of blind walls and gaping holes, shiftless stupidity, contented filth and beastliness.

But that, we said, was only the outskirts: when we come farther in we shall surely find this mass of population manifesting some small symbols of a great dominion. And presently we came indeed into a broader way than the rest—something with the rude semblance of a street. Only it was paved with dead donkeys, and here and there it disappeared in a cullender of deep holes where green water festered. Beside it stood a few houses, such as you see in Metemmeh or Berber—two large, naked rooms standing in a naked walled courtyard. Even these were rare: for the rest, in this main street, Omdurman was a rabbit-warren—a threadless labyrinth of tiny huts or shelters, too flimsy for the name of sheds. Oppression, stagnation, degradation, were stamped deep on every yard of miserable Omdurman.

But the people! We could hardly see the place for the people. We could hardly hear our own voices for their shrieks of welcome. We could hardly move for their importunate greetings. They tumbled over each other like ants from every mud heap, from behind every dunghill, from under every mat. Most of the men still wore their gibbas turned inside out; you could see the shadows of the patches through the sackcloth. They had been trying to kill us three hours before. But they salaamed, none the less, and volleyed " Peace be with you " in our track. All the miscellaneous tribes of Arabs whom Abdullahi's fears or suspicions had congregated in his capital, all the blacks his captains had gathered together into franker slavery— indiscriminate, half-naked, grinning the grin of the sycophant, they held out their hands and asked for backsheesh.

Yet more wonderful were the women. The multitude of women whom concupiscence had harried from every recess of Africa and mewed up in Baggara harems came out to salute their new masters. There were at least three of them to every man. Black women from Equatoria and almost white women from Egypt, plum-skinned Arabs and a strange yellow type with square, bony faces and tightly-ringleted black hair; old women and little girls and mothers with babies at the breast; women who could hardly walk for dyed cotton swattings, muffled in close veils, and women with only a rag between themselves and nakedness —the whole city was a huge harem, a museum of African races, a monstrosity of African lust.

The steady columns drove through the surge of people: then halted in lines of ebony statues, the open-mouthed guns crawling between them to the

front. We had come opposite the corner of a high
wall of faced stones, a high twenty feet solid without
a chip or chink. Now! This was the great wall of
Omdurman, the Khalifa's citadel. And listen! Boom
—boom—a heavy melancholy note, half bellow, half
wail. It was the great ombeya, the war-horn. The
Khalifa was inside, and he was rallying the malazemin
of his bodyguard to fight their last fight in their last
stronghold.

Less than 3000 men were standing, surrounded by
ten times their number, within ten feet of this gigantic
wall. But for the moment they were safe enough.
The Khalifa, demented in all he did through these last
days of his perdition, had made no banquette inside
his rampart; and if it was hard to scale, it was impossible to defend. The pinch would come when we
went inside.

One column moved off along the street; another—
the 13th Sudanese with four guns of the battery—
away to the left under the wall towards the Nile. The
road was what you already felt to be typical of Mahdism—pools of rank stagnation, hills and chasms of
rubble. The guns fell behind to cut their road a bit;
the infantry went on till they came down to the brim-
ming blue river. Here were the forts and the loop-
holed walls, and here, steaming serene and masterful
to and fro, were the inevitable gunboats. Cr-r-rack!
Three crisp Maxim rounds: the place was tenanted
yet.

At the corner we come upon a breach—500 cubic feet or so of fissure—torn by a lyddite shell. Over the rubble we scrambled, then through a stout double-leafed gate, pulses leaping: we were inside. But as yet only half inside—only in a broad road between another high stone wall on our right and the river on our left. We saw the choked embrasures and a maimed gun or two, and walls so clownishly loop-holed that a man could only get one oblique shot at a gun-boat, and then wait till the next came up to have one shot at that. We saw worse things—horrors such as do not sicken in the mass on the battle-field—a scarlet man sitting with his chin on his knees, hit by a shell, clothed from head to foot in his own blood,—a woman, young and beautifully formed, stark naked, rolling from side to side, moaning. As yet we saw not one fighting man, and still we could feel that the place was alive. We pushed on between walls, we knew not whither, through breathing emptiness, through pulsing silence.

Round a corner we came suddenly on a bundle of dirty patched cloth and dirty, lean, black limbs — a typical dervish. He was alive and unarmed, and threw up his hands: he was taken for a guide. Next at our feet, cutting the road, we found a broad khor, flowing in from the Nile, washing up above the base of the wall. Four dervishes popped out, seemingly from dead walls beyond. They came towards us and pro-bably wished to surrender; but the blacks fired, and they dived into their dead walls again. The guide

said the water was not deep, and a crowd of men and
women suddenly shooting up from the rear bore him
out by fording it.   Most of these new - reconciled
foes had baskets to take away their late master's loot.
We plashed through the water—and here at last, in
the face of the high wall on our right, was a great
wooden gate.   Six blacks stood by with the bayonet,
while another beat it open with his rifle-butt.   We
stepped inside and gasped with wonder and disappointment.

For the inside of the Kalifa's own enclosure was
even more squalid, an even more wonderful teeming
beehive than the outer town itself.   Like all tyrants,
he was constantly increasing his body-guard, till the
fortified enclosure was bursting with them.   From the
height of a saddle you could see that this was only
part of the citadel, an enclosure within an enclosure.
Past a little guard-house at the gate a narrow path
ran up the centre of it ; all the rest was a chaos of
piggish dwelling-holes.   Tiny round straw tukls, mats
propped up a foot from earth with crooked sticks,
dome-topped mud kennels that a man could just crawl
into, exaggerated bird's nests falling to pieces of stick
and straw—lucky was the man of the Khalifa's guard
who could house himself and his family in a mud
cabin the size of an omnibus.   On every side, of every
type, they jumbled and jostled and crushed ; and they
sweated and stank with people.   For one or two old
men in new gibbas came out, and one or two younger

men naked and wounded. When we offered them
no harm the Khalifa's body-guard broke cover. One
second the place might have been an uncouth
cemetery; the next it was a gibbering monkey-house.
From naked hovels, presto! it turned to naked bodies.
Climbing, squeezing, burrowing, they came out like
vermin from a burning coat.

They were just as skinny and shabby as any other
dervishes; as the Omdurman Guards they were a
failure. They were all very friendly, the men anxious
to tell what they knew of the Khalifa's movements—
which was nothing—the women overjoyed to fetch
drinks of water. But when they were told to bring
out their arms and ammunition they became a bit
sticky, as soldiers say. They looked like refusing,
and a snap-shot round a corner which killed a black
soldier began to look nasty. There must have been
thousands of them all about us, all under cover, all
knowing every twist and turn of their warren. But a
confident front imposed on them, as it will on all
savages. A raised voice, a hand on the shoulder—and
they were slipping away to their dens and slouching
back with Remingtons and bandoliers. The first
came very, very slowly; as the pile grew they came
quicker and quicker. From crawling they changed
in five minutes to a trot; they smiled all over, and
informed zealously against anybody who hung back.
Why not? Three masterless hours will hardly wipe
out the rest of a lifetime of slavery.

U

Maxwell Bey left a guard over the arms, and went back: it was not in this compartment that we should find the Khalifa. We went on through the walled street along the river-front; the gunboats were still Maximing now and again a cable or two ahead. So on, until we came to the southern river corner of the hold, and here was a winding, ascending path between two higher, stouter walls than ever. Here was a stouter wooden gate; it must be here. In this enclosure, too, was a multitude of dwellings, but larger and more amply spaced. The Sirdar overtook us now, and the guns: the gunners had cut their road and levelled the breach, and tugged the first gate off its hinges. On; we must be coming to it now. We were quite close upon the towering, shell - torn skeleton of the Mahdi's tomb. The way broadened to a square. But the sun had some time struck level into our eyes. He went down; in ten minutes it would be dark. Now or never! Here we were opposite the tomb; to our left front was the Khalifa's own palace. We were there, if only he was. A section of blacks filed away to the left through the walled passage that led to the door. Another filed to the right, behind the tomb, towards his private iron mosque. We waited. We waited. And then, on left and right, they reappeared, rather draggingly.

Gone! None could know it for certain till the place had been searched through as well as the darkness would let it. Next morning some of the

smaller Emirs avowed that they knew it. He had
been supposed to be surrounded, but who could stop
every earth in such a spinny? He had bolted out
of one door as we went in at another.

We filed back. For the present we had missed
the crowning capture. But going back under the
wall we found a very good assurance that Abudullahi
was no more a ruler. The street under the wall was
now a breathless stream of men and women, all carrying baskets—the whole population of the Khalifa's
capital racing to pilfer the Khalifa's grain. There
was no doubt about their good disposition now. They
salaamed with enthusiasm, and "lued" most genuinely;
one flat-nosed black lady forgot propriety so far as to
kiss my hand. Wonderful workings of the savage
mind! Six hours before they were dying in regiments
for their master; now they were looting his corn.
Six hours before they were slashing our wounded
to pieces; now they were asking us for coppers.

By this time the darkling streets were choked
with the men and horses and guns and camels of
the inpouring army. You dragged along a mile an
hour, clamped immovably into a mass of troops.
A hundred good spearmen now—but the Dervishes
were true savages to the end: they had decided
that they were beaten, and beaten they remained.
Soon it was pitchy night; where the bulk of the
army bivouacked, I know not, neither do they. I
stumbled on the Second British Brigade, which had

had a relatively easy day, and there, by a solitary candle, the Sirdar, flat on his back, was dictating his despatch to Colonel Wingate, flat on his belly. I scraped a short hieroglyphic scrawl on a telegraph form, and fell asleep on the gravel with a half-eaten biscuit in my mouth.

Next morning the army awoke refreshed, and was able to appreciate to the full the beauties of Omdurman. When you saw it close, and by the light of day, the last suggestion of stateliness vanished. It had nothing left but size—mere stupid multiplication of rubbish. One or two relics of civilisation were found. Taps in the Khalifa's bath; a ship's chronometer; a small pair of compasses in a boy's writing-desk, and a larger pair modelled clumsily upon them; the drooping telegraph wire and cable to Khartum; Gordon's old "Bordein," a shell-torn husk of broken wood round engines that still worked marvellously; a few half-naked Egyptians, once Government servants; Charles Neufeld, the captive German merchant, quoting Schiller over his ankle-chains; Sister Teresa, the captive nun, forcibly married to a Greek, presenting a green orange to Colonel Wingate, the tried friend she had never seen before,—such was the pathetic flotsam overtaken by the advancing wave of Mahdism, now stranded by its ebb.

The Mahdi's tomb was shoddy brick, and you dared not talk in it lest the rest of the dome should come on your head. The inside was tawdry panels and

railings round a gaudy pall. The Khalifa's house was
the house of a well-to-do-fellah, and a dead donkey
putrified under its window-holes. The arsenal was
the reduplication of all the loot that has gone for half
a dollar apiece these three years. The great mosque
was a wall round a biggish square with a few stick-
and-thatch booths at one end of it. The iron mosque
was a galvanised shed, and would have repulsed
the customers of a third-rate country photographer.
Everything was wretched.

And foul. They dropped their dung where they
listed; they drew their water from beside green
sewers; they had filled the streets and khors with
dead donkeys; they left their brothers to rot and puff
up hideously in the sun. The stench of the place was
in your nostrils, in your throat, in your stomach. You
could not eat; you dared not drink. Well you could
believe that this was the city where they crucified a
man to steal a handful of base dollars, and sold
mother and daughter together to be divided five
hundred miles apart, to live and die in the same
bestial concubinage.

The army moved out to Khor Shamba during the
3rd. The accursed place was left to fester and fry in
its own filth and lust and blood. The reek of its
abominations steamed up to heaven to justify us of
our vengeance.

XXXV.

THE FUNERAL OF GORDON.

THE steamers—screws, paddles, stern-wheelers—plug-plugged their steady way up the full Nile. Past the northern fringe of Omdurman where the sheikh came out with the white flag, past the breach where we went in to the Khalifa's stronghold, past the choked embrasures and the lacerated Mahdi's tomb, past the swamp-rooted palms of Tuti Island. We looked at it all with a dispassionate, impersonal curiosity. It was Sunday morning, and that furious Friday seemed already half a lifetime behind us. The volleys had dwindled out of our ears, and the smoke out of our nostrils; and to-day we were going to the funeral of Gordon. After nearly fourteen years the Christian soldier was to have Christian burial.

On the steamers there was a detachment of every corps, white or black or yellow, that had taken part in the vengeance. Every white officer that could be spared from duty was there, fifty men picked from each British battalion, one or two from each unit of the Egyptian army. That we were going up to Khartum at all was evidence of our triumph; yet, if you looked about you, triumph was not the note. The most reckless subaltern, the most barbarous black, was touched with gravity. We were going to perform a necessary duty, which had been put off far, far too long.

Fourteen years next January—yet even through that humiliating thought there ran a whisper of triumph. We may be slow; but in that very slowness we show that we do not forget. Soon or late, we give our own their due. Here were men that fought for Gordon's life while he lived,—Kitchener, who went disguised and alone among furious enemies to get news of him; Wauchope, who poured out his blood like water at Tamai and Kirbekan; Stuart-Wortley, who missed by but two days the chance of dying at Gordon's side. And here, too, were boys who could hardly lisp when their mothers told them that Gordon was dead, grown up now and appearing in the fulness of time to exact eleven thousand lives for one. Gordon may die—other Gordons may die in the future—but the same clean-limbed brood will grow up and avenge them.

The boats stopped plugging and there was silence. We were tying up opposite a grove of tall palms; on the bank was a crowd of natives curiously like the backsheesh - hunters who gather to greet the Nile steamers. They stared at us; but we looked beyond

them to a large building rising from a crumbling quay.
You could see that it had once been a handsome edi-
fice of the type you know in Cairo or Alexandria—all
stone and stucco, two-storied, faced with tall regular
windows. Now the upper storey was clean gone; the
blind windows were filled up with bricks; the stucco
was all scars, and you could walk up to the roof on
rubble. In front was an acacia, such as grow in
Ismailia or the Gezireh at Cairo, only unpruned—
deep luscious green, only drooping like a weeping
willow. At that most ordinary sight everybody grew
very solemn. For it was a piece of a new world, or
rather of an old world, utterly different from the
squalid mud, the baking barrenness of Omdurman. A
façade with tall windows, a tree with green leaves—
the façade battered and blind, the tree drooping to
earth—there was no need to tell us we were at a grave.
In that forlorn ruin, and that disconsolate acacia, the
bones of murdered civilisation lay before us.

The troops formed up before the palace in three
sides of a rectangle—Egyptians to our left as we looked
from the river, British to the right. The Sirdar, the
generals of division and brigade, and the staff stood in
the open space facing the palace. Then on the roof
—almost on the very spot where Gordon fell, though
the steps by which the butchers mounted have long
since vanished—we were aware of two flagstaves. By
the right - hand halliards stood Lieutenant Staveley,
R.N., and Captain Watson, K.R.R.; by the left hand

Bimbashi Mitford and his Excellency's Egyptian A.D.C.

The Sirdar raised his hand. A pull on the halliards: up ran, out flew, the Union Jack, tugging eagerly at his reins, dazzling gloriously in the sun, rejoicing in his strength and his freedom. "Bang!" went the "Melik's" 12½-pounder, and the boat quivered to her backbone. "God Save our Gracious Queen" hymned the Guards' band—"bang!" from the "Melik"—and Sirdar and private stood stiff—"bang!"—to attention, every hand at the helmet peak in—"bang!"—salute. The Egyptian flag had gone up at the same instant; and now, the same ear-smashing, soul-uplifting bangs marking time, the band of the 11th Sudanese was playing the Khedivial hymn. "Three cheers for the Queen!" cried the Sirdar: helmets leaped in the air, and the melancholy ruins woke to the first wholesome shout of all these years. Then the same for the Khedive. The comrade flags stretched themselves lustily, enjoying their own again; the bands pealed forth the pride of country; the twenty-one guns banged forth the strength of war. Thus, white men and black, Christian and Moslem, Anglo-Egypt set her seal once more, for ever, on Khartum.

Before we had time to think such thoughts over to ourselves, the Guards were playing the Dead March in "Saul." Then the black band was playing the march from Handel's "Scipio," which in England generally goes with "Toll for the Brave"; this was in memory

of those loyal men among the Khedive's subjects who
could have saved themselves by treachery, but preferred to die with Gordon.   Next fell a deeper hush
than ever, except for the solemn minute guns that
had followed the fierce salute.   Four chaplains—
Catholic, Anglican, Presbyterian, and Methodist—
came slowly forward and ranged themselves, with
their backs to the palace, just before the Sirdar.   The
Presbyterian read the Fifteenth Psalm.   The Anglican
led the rustling whisper of the Lord's Prayer.   Snow-
haired Father Brindle, best beloved of priests, laid his
helmet at his feet, and read a memorial prayer bare-
headed in the sun.   Then came forward the pipers
and wailed a dirge, and the Sudanese played "Abide
with me."   Perhaps lips did twitch just a little to see
the ebony heathens fervently blowing out Gordon's
favourite hymn; but the most irrestible incongruity
would hardly have made us laugh at that moment.
And there were those who said the cold Sirdar himself
could hardly speak or see, as General Hunter and the
rest stepped out according to their rank and shook his
hand.   What wonder ?   He has trodden this road to
Khartum for fourteen years, and he stood at the goal
at last.

Thus with Maxim-Nordenfeldt and Bible we buried
Gordon after the manner of his race.   The parade
was over, the troops were dismissed, and for a short
space we walked in Gordon's garden.   Gordon has
become a legend with his countrymen, and they all

but deify him dead who would never have heard of
him had he lived. But in this garden you somehow
came to know Gordon the man, not the myth, and to
feel near to him. Here was an Englishman doing his
duty, alone and at the instant peril of his life; yet
still he loved his garden. The garden was a yet more
pathetic ruin than the palace. The palace accepted
its doom mutely; the garden strove against it. Un-
trimmed, unwatered, the oranges and citrons still
struggled to bear their little, hard, green knobs, as if
they had been full ripe fruit. The pomegranates put
out their vermilion star-flowers, but the fruit was
small and woody and juiceless. The figs bore better,
but they, too, were small and without vigour. Rankly
overgrown with dhurra, a vine still trailed over a low
roof its pale leaves and limp tendrils, but yielded
not a sign of grapes. It was all green, and so far
vivid and refreshing after Omdurman. But it was
the green of nature, not of cultivation: leaves grew
large and fruit grew small, and dwindled away. Re-
luctantly, despairingly, Gordon's garden was dropping
back to wilderness. And in the middle of the defeated
fruit-trees grew rankly the hateful Sodom apple, the
poisonous herald of desolation.

The bugle broke in upon us; we went back to the
boats. We were quicker steaming back than steaming
up. We were not a whit less chastened, but every
man felt lighter. We came with a sigh of shame: we
went away with a sigh of relief. The long-delayed

duty was done. The bones of our countrymen were shattered and scattered abroad, and no man knows their place; none the less Gordon had his due burial at last. So we steamed away to the roaring camp and left him alone again. Yet not one nor two looked back at the mouldering palace and the tangled garden with a new and a great contentment. We left Gordon alone again—but alone in majesty under the conquering ensign of his own people.

XXXVI.

AFTER THE CONQUEST.

THE curtain comes down; the tragedy of the Sudan is played out. Sixteen years of toilsome failure, of toilsome, slow success, and at the end we have fought our way triumphantly to the point where we began.

It has cost us much, and it has profited us—how little? It would be hard to count the money, impossible to measure the blood. Blood goes by quality as well as quantity; who can tell what future deeds we lost when we lost Gordon and Stewart and Earle, Burnaby who rode to Khiva, and Owen who rode Father O'Flynn? By shot and steel, by sunstroke and pestilence, by sheer wear of work, the Sudan has eaten up our best by hundreds. Of the men who escaped with their lives, hundreds more will bear the mark of its fangs till they die; hardly one of them but will die the sooner for the Sudan. And what have we to show in return?

At first you think we have nothing; then you think again, and see we have very much. We have gained precious national self-respect. We wished to keep our hands clear of the Sudan; we were drawn unwillingly to meddle with it; we blundered when we suffered Gordon to go out; we fiddled and failed when we tried to bring him back. We were humiliated and we were out of pocket; we had embarked in a foolish venture, and it had turned out even worse than anybody had foreseen. Now this was surely the very point where a nation of shopkeepers should have cut its losses and turned to better business elsewhere. If we were the sordid counter-jumpers that Frenchmen try to think us, we should have ruled a red line, and thought no more of a worthless land, bottomless for our gold, thirsty for our blood. We did nothing such. We tried to; but our dogged fighting dander would not let us. We could not sit down till the defeat was redeemed. We gave more money; we gave the lives of men we loved—and we conquered the Sudan again. Now we can permit ourselves to think of it in peace.

The vindication of our self-respect was the great treasure we won at Khartum, and it was worth the price we paid for it. Most people will hardly persuade themselves there is not something else thrown in. The trade of the Sudan? For now and for many years you may leave that out of the account. The Sudan is a desert, and a depopulated desert. Northward of Khartum it is a wilderness; southward it is a devastation. It was always a poor country, and it always must be. Slaves and ivory were its wealth in the old time, but now ivory is all but exterminated, and slaves must be sold no more. Gum-arabic and ostrich feathers and Dongola dates will hardly buy cotton stuffs enough for Lancashire to feel the difference.

From Halfa to above Berber, where rain never falls, the Nile only licks the lip of the desert. The father of Egypt is the stepfather of the Sudan. With the help of water-wheels and water-hoists a few patches of corn and fodder can be grown, enough for a dotted population on the bank. But hardly anywhere does the area of vegetation push out more than a mile from the stream; oftener it is a matter of yards. Such a country can never be rich. But why not irrigate? Simply because every pint of water you take out of the Nile for the Sudan means a pint less for Egypt. And it so happens that at this very moment the new barrages at Assuan and Assiut are making the distribution of water to Egypt more precise and scientific than ever. Lower Egypt is to be enlarged; Upper Egypt is, in part at least, to secure permanent irrigation, independent of the Nile flood, and therewith two crops a-year. This means a more rigid economy of water than ever, and who will give a thought to the lean Sudan? What it can dip up in buckets fat Egypt will never miss, and that it may take—no more.

As for the southward lands, they get rain, to be sure, and so far they are cultivable; only there is nobody left to cultivate them. For three years now the Egyptian army has been marching past broken mud hovels by the river - side. Dust has blown over their foundations, Dead Sea fruit grows rankly within their walls. Sometimes, as in old Berber, you come on a city with streets and shops— quite ruined and empty. Here lived the Sudanese whom the Khalifa has killed out. And in the more fertile parts of the Sudan it is the same. Worse still—in that the very fertility woke up the cupidity of the Baggara, and the owner was driven out, sold in the slave-market, shipped up Nile to die of Fashoda fever, cut to pieces, crucified, impaled—anything you like, so long as the Khalifa's fellow-tribesmen got his land. In Kordofan, even of old days, lions in bad years would attack villages in bands : to - day they openly dispute the mastery of creation with men. From Abyssinia to Wadai swelters the miserable Sudan—beggarly, empty, weed-grown, rank with blood.

It will recover,—with time, no doubt, but it will recover. Only, meanwhile, it will want some tending. There is not likely to be much trouble in the way of fighting : in the present weariness of slaughter the people will be but too glad to sit down under any decent Government. There is no reason—unless it be complications with outside Powers, like France or Abyssinia—why the old Egyptian empire should not be reoccupied up to the Albert Nyanza and Western

Darfur. But if this is done—and done it surely should
be—two things must be remembered. First, it must
be militarily administered for many years to come,
and that by British men. Take the native Egyptian
official even to-day. No words can express his ineptitude, his laziness, his helplessness, his dread of
responsibility, his maddening red-tape formalism. His
panacea in every unexpected case is the same. "It
must be put in writing; I must ask for instructions."
He is no longer corrupt—at least, no longer so corrupt as he was—but he would be if he dared. The
native officer is better than the civilian official; but
even with him it is the exception to find a man both
capable and incorruptible. To put Egyptians, corrupt, lazy, timid, often rank cowards, to rule the
Sudan, would be to invite another Mahdi as soon
as the country had grown up enough to make him
formidable.

The Sudan must be ruled by military law strong
enough to be feared, administered by British officers
just enough to be respected. For the second point, it
must not be expected that it will pay until many years
have passed. The cost of a military administration
would not be very great, but it must be considered
money out of pocket. The experience of Dongola,
whence the army has been drawing large stores of
dhurra, where the number of water-wheels has multi-
plied itself enormously in less than a couple of years,
shows well enough that only patience is wanted. The

Sudan will improve : it will never be an Egypt, but
it will pay its way. But, before all things, you must
give it time to repopulate itself.

Well, then, if Egypt is not to get good places for
her people, and is to be out of pocket for administration—how much does Egypt profit by the fall of Abdullahi and the reconquest of the Sudan ? Much.
Inestimably. For as the master-gain of England is
the vindication of her self-respect, so the master-gain
of Egypt is the assurance of her security. As long as
dervish raiders loomed on the horizon of her frontier,
Egypt was only half a State. She lived on a perpetual
war-footing. Her finances are pinched enough at the
best; every little economy had to go to the Sirdar.
Never was general so jealous—even miserly—of public
money as the Sirdar; but even so he was spending
Egypt's all. That strain will henceforth be loosened.
Egypt will have enough work for five years in the new
barrages, which are a public work directly transliter-
able in pounds and piastres. Egypt will be able to
give a little attention to her taxes, which are anomal-
ous ; to her education, which is backward; to her railways, which are vile.

Whether she will be able to reduce her army is
doubtful. The occupation of the banks of the Blue and
White Nile, to say nothing of the peaceful reabsorp-
tion of Kordofan and Darfur, would open up some of
the finest raw fighting material in the world. Frankly,
it is very raw indeed—the rawest savagery you can

well imagine,—but British officers and sergeants have made fairly drilled troops, fairly good shots, superb marchers and bayonet-fighters out of the same material, and they could do it again. To put the matter brutally, having this field for recruiting, we have too many enemies in the world to afford to lose it. We have made the Egyptian army, and we have saved Egypt with it and with our own : we should now make of it an African second to our Indian army, and use it, when the time comes, to repay the debt to ourselves.

We have saved Egypt, and thereby we have paid another debt. The Khedive is but half a monarch at the best: while a hostile force sat on his borders to destroy him, and every couple of years actually came down to do it, he was not more than a quarter. There was plenty of sneaking sympathy with Mahdism in Egypt — even in Cairo, and not very far from the Khedive's own palace. But for British help the sympathisers would long ago, but yet too late, have recognised their foolishness in the obliteration of Egypt. Egypt alone could by no miracle have saved herself from utter destruction by Mahdist invasion. We have saved her—and therewith we have paid off the purblind, sincere undertakings of Mr Gladstone. We undertook to leave Egypt ; we have redeemed the promise in an unforeseen manner, but we have redeemed it amply. If we undertook to evacuate the old Egypt, we have fathered a new one, saved from imminent extinction by our gold and our sword.

Without us there would have been no Egypt to-day; what we made we shall keep.

That is our double gain—the vindication of our own honour and the vindication of our right to go on making Egypt a country fit to live in. Egypt's gain is her existence to-day. The world's gain is the downfall of the worst tyranny in the world, and the acquisition of a limited opportunity for open trade. The Sudan's gain is immunity from rape and torture and every extreme of misery.

The poor Sudan! The wretched, dry Sudan! Count up all the gains you will, yet what a hideous irony it remains, this fight of half a generation for such an emptiness. People talk of the Sudan as the East; it is not the East. The East has age and colour; the Sudan has no colour and no age—just a monotone of squalid barbarism. It is not a country; it has nothing that makes a country. Some brutish institutions it has, and some bloodthirsty chivalry. But it is not a country: it has neither nationality, nor history, nor arts, nor even natural features. Just the Nile—the niggard Nile refusing himself to the desert—and for the rest there is absolutely nothing to look at in the Sudan. Nothing grows green. Only yellow halfa-grass to make you stumble, and sapless mimosa to tear your eyes; dom-palms that mock with wooden fruit, and Sodom apples that lure with flatulent poison. For beasts it has tarantulas and scorpions and serpents, devouring white ants, and every kind

of loathsome bug that flies or crawls. Its people are
naked and dirty, ignorant and besotted. It is a
quarter of a continent of sheer squalor. Overhead
the pitiless furnace of the sun, under foot the never-
easing treadmill of the sand, dust in the throat, tune-
less singing in the ears, searing flame in the eye,—the
Sudan is a God-accursed wilderness, an empty limbo
of torment for ever and ever.

Surely enough, "When Allah made the Sudan,"
say the Arabs, "he laughed." You can almost hear
the fiendish echo of it crackling over the fiery sand.
And yet—and yet there never was an Englishman
who had been there, but was ready and eager to go
again. "Drink of Nile water," say the same Arabs,
"and you will return to drink it again." Nile water
is either very brown or very green, according to the
season; yet you do go back and drink it again. Perhaps to Englishmen—half-savage still on the pinnacle
of their civilisation—the very charm of the land lies
in its empty barbarism. There is space in the Sudan.
There is the fine, purified desert air, and the long
stretching gallops over its sand. There are the things
at the very back of life, and no other to posture in
front of them,—hunger and thirst to assuage, distance
to win through, pain to bear, life to defend, and death
to face. You have gone back to the spring water of
your infancy. You are a savage again—a savage with
Rosbach water, if there is any left, and a Mauser
repeating pistol-carbine, if the sand has not jammed

it, but still at the last word a savage. You are un-
prejudiced, simple, free. You are a naked man, facing
naked nature.

I do not believe that any of us who come home
whole will think, from our easy-chairs, unkindly of
the Sudan.

THE END.